WORKING FOR YOURSELF

Working for Yourself

The *Daily Telegraph* Guide to Self-Employment

Godfrey Golzen

Kogan Page

First published 1975. This sixth edition
published 1983 by Kogan Page Ltd,
120 Pentonville Road,
London N1 9JN

Copyright © 1975, 1978, 1980, 1981, 1982, 1983 Godfrey Golzen,
contributors and Kogan Page Ltd.

British Library Cataloguing in Publication Data
Golzen, Godfrey
   Working for yourself. — 6th ed.
   1. Self-employed
   I. Title
   658'.041   HD62.7

   ISBN 0-85038-692-6
   ISBN 0-85038-693-4 Pbk

Printed and bound by
Redwood Burn Ltd, Trowbridge

We are looking for small businesses looking for money.

In a time of recession, you may well be thinking the prospects of obtaining a business loan are wilting fast. Nothing could be further from the truth.

Because we at NatWest are convinced that financial assistance for the many up-and-coming businesses in this country is exactly what our economy needs. That's why we pay out some £35 million in Business Development Loans

each and every month to over 3,000 customers.

And why we're looking to talk to more small businesses in need of finance for sound and promising business ventures.

NatWest Business Development Loans range from £2,000 to £250,000 and can be granted for periods between 1 and 20 years. The rates of interest are highly competitive.

Rates are fixed in advance, and repayments are worked out in equal monthly instalments.

So everything's planned in advance and cash flow's kept well under control.

Now we've made our postion clear, all that may stand between you and a flourishing business is a phone call to the Manager at a NatWest branch near you.

Fixed sum • Fixed interest • Fixed repayments • Fixed term now up to 20 years…for easier cash flow.

♻ **NatWest** *Ready to do business.*

Contents

Acknowledgements   11

Preface   13

PART 1: RUNNING YOUR OWN BUSINESS   15

1.1: Going it Alone   17
1.2: Starting a Business   26
1.3: Raising Capital   41
1.4: Professional and Other Outside Advisers   81
1.5: Simple Accounting Systems and Their Uses   89
1.6: Invoicing and Credit Control   99
1.7: Budgeting and Cash Flow Forecasting   104
1.8: Costing, Pricing and Estimating   109
1.9: Marketing Your Work   117
1.10: Employing People   128
1.11: Taxation   137
1.12: Introducing Microcomputers   153
1.13: Legal Basics   160
1.14: Pensions and the Self-employed   165
1.15: Retirement and the Self-employed Person   171

PART 2: BUSINESSES REQUIRING CAPITAL   185

2.1: Starting Your Business   187
2.2: Farming and Market Gardening   190
2.3: Retailing   194
2.4: Franchising   207
2.5: Hotels, Catering and Entertainment   226
2.6: Construction, Building and Maintenance Services   235
2.7: Transport   238

PART 3: DIRECTORY OF LOW INVESTMENT, PART-TIME
          OPPORTUNITIES FOR THE SELF-EMPLOYED   241

3.1: Part-time Work   243
3.2: Crafts and Domestic Skills   252
3.3: Driving   260
3.4: Entertainment   262
3.5: Media and Communications   264
3.6: Office Skills   272
3.7: Playgroups   275
3.8: Selling   277

PART 4: FREELANCE WORK   281

4.1: Introduction   283
4.2: Management Consultancy   286
4.3: Media and Communications   287
4.4: Repairs and Servicing of Vehicles   293

APPENDICES   295

1: Further Information   297
2: Select Bibliography   305
3: Glossary of Key Business Terms   307

Index   313

Index of Advertisers   319

Acknowledgements

We should like to thank John Slade, R W Leff and R Lobatto for their advice on accountancy and taxation; H F Armstrong of Development Capital Ltd for assistance with the chapter on raising capital; Dryden Gilling-Smith of Employee Benefit Services (Management) Ltd for his help on the financial advantages enjoyed by limited companies; John Blundell who read the whole book in manuscript; and the freelance and self-employed people who have contributed to Parts 2 and 3, particularly those who have answered questionnaires and allowed us to reproduce their comments. We would also like to thank Simon Williamson of Anderson Sinclair and Company for reading the chapter on pensions and making various suggestions on it.

We would be grateful for readers' comments and suggestions. There are as many ways of running small businesses as there are proprietors, and any advice on methods other than those we have indicated will be considered for inclusion in future editions of the book.

Preface

The scope of the book

The self-employed are a very diverse group, providing every conceivable type of product or service. In this book we have excluded one major group — members of the professions — because although there are certain sections of it that they would find helpful, there are nevertheless crucial differences between running a professional practice like that of an architect, doctor or lawyer and an ordinary business. Otherwise we have identified the self-employed as falling into the following broad categories.

- ☐ People working part-time, often from home, in addition to a main job, perhaps as an interim stage to setting up a full-time business of their own.
- ☐ Freelances who provide a service and work full-time for several different principals.
- ☐ Those who provide goods and services as sole traders or partners, usually from premises other than their own home.
- ☐ Shareholders in small private companies who are also working directors. They are not strictly speaking self-employed, being employees of the companies they control, but in every practical sense the lessons of this book apply to them.

For any enterprise Part 1, which covers the problems of raising capital, making financial projections and understanding commercial and employment law, will be useful. But it is particularly valuable as a crash course in basic business principles for those starting a small business. Yet the person (designer, typist, teacher, etc) who is simply supplementing his income by some freelance work will also find something of value in Part 1: how to assess himself for tax purposes, the importance of proper invoicing, the part played by professional advisers, the need to plan workload and meet schedules.

Though the reader should be aware of the several 'audiences' at which the book is aimed and should pay closest attention to the section which concerns him most directly, he may also profit from the other sections. And, who knows, today's freelance book designer may tomorrow have his own art studio, with staff to manage, creditors to satisfy and clients to cultivate. The section on business management will at least make you aware of the problems and pressures of expanding the scope of any business, and of the pleasures that come with success.

The second part of this book looks at some specific self-employment opportunities which are divided broadly between those that require capital investment — if on a small scale — and those where the level of investment is minimal or even non-existent. The range of activities described is obviously not comprehensive, but it covers, if briefly, some of the areas in which people thinking of self-employment have been found to be most interested. Certainly the principles that emerge are those that can be applied to any type of enterprise one cares to look at.

- ☐ Consider the drawbacks
- ☐ Be realistic about the risk you are taking
- ☐ Be aware of the competition to what you offer
- ☐ Be certain that your enterprise is financially sound
- ☐ Know and act within the law as it applies to you
- ☐ Use professional advice where necessary
- ☐ Fulfil commissions accurately and on time
- ☐ Commit yourself totally to a project.

These principles apply to the man with a medium-sized business as much as to the retailer or restaurateur, the part-time editor, typist or translator. If a service is required and completion is guaranteed to a satisfactory standard, people are prepared to pay for it. A reputation is established and customers return. An established group of clients provides a basis on which to expand and perhaps diversify, and, if this is achieved without standards falling, the process will be repeated. Whatever your area of interest and size of operation, we hope that our advice aids that process and enables you to avoid the pitfalls and enjoy the profits of self-employment.

The text of this book was correct at the time of going to press. It incorporates the 1983 Budget changes which may not all be implemented because of the general election.

Part 1:
Running Your Own
Business

A unique Business Opportunity!

The Big Orange is a franchise system comprising an eye-catching 7 ft. diameter orange kiosk, with a unique visual juicing system which produces 100% Freshly Squeezed Orange Juice. This is a 'one-product' operation - simplicity is its secret. It attracts attention - and Business!

For an investment of around £12,000, you could be in business, making Big Profits with the Big Orange.

We'll give you all the help you need, including training, assistance with finance and help with choosing the most profitable site.

16

1.1: Going it Alone

Since the first edition of this book was published in 1975, there has been a shift of attitudes towards the self-employed in general and small businesses in particular that could almost be called revolutionary. Even under the last Labour Government some important changes were enacted to make life easier for this section of the business community and the process has continued in subsequent Finance and other Acts of Parliament to such an extent that annual revisions of *Working for Yourself* have become necessary. In the 1983 Budget, for instance, although no substantial new concessions were made, there was a general tendency to lift the financial thresholds that would benefit small business, either by bringing these in line with inflation or broadening them in such a way as to extend the definition of small business. The trend is likely to continue, because both political parties seem to agree that the encouragement of small businesses may provide the answer to one of our most worrying problems: chronic unemployment. It was demonstrated throughout the 1970s that creating jobs in the public sector — the solution favoured by the left — is vastly expensive and, in draining workers from potentially productive areas of the economy, carries the seeds of its own bankruptcy. From an ideological point of view there is also an increasing feeling that a highly bureaucratic corporate state, limiting people's choice about how they spend their money, or even ultimately where and at what they want to work, is a road down which we have travelled far enough. As for the belief that encouraging public and discouraging private ownership would lead to better industrial relations, that pious myth has been destroyed by the countless public sector strikes in the last 30 years.

Yet there is no doubt that unemployment is unacceptably high and that it is here to stay unless we do something about it. In fact it is here to increase, because automation of all kinds of processes, from controlling production lines to checking tins of groceries on supermarket shelves, will soon be within the financial reach of even the small firms. More automation may mean fewer jobs for people in the short term, and some readers of this book may already have fallen victim of this process. But it also means more uniformity, less flexibility and less choice and this is where the self-employed come into their own as a new kind of labour force, operating at every level from providing specialist consultancy to making goods and selling services which are still needed, but which the big firms with their colossal overheads no longer find it worthwhile to supply. Ironically, among the customers of many small independent companies are some of the big firms themselves, which find some service or part is unobtainable because of strikes, production hold-ups or because some other big firm has given up producing it. Not infrequently, they have to turn to some former employee who has gone into business for himself, having anticipated or had prior knowledge of exactly such a problem.

Often such a man or woman might have been made redundant as a result of technological change. Here the person affected may find two kinds of opportunities for self-employment. The first arises because skills which are obsolete in one context may be greatly in demand in another; a case in point would be middle-level accounting experience, desperately needed by many small firms in the form of a consultancy service. The second because not everyone wants machine-made products off the assembly line. Indeed, all the indications are that as people become more affluent they want more, not less, individuality. The insatiable appetite for antiques does not arise simply because they are a good investment. They are also more individual and more human than mass-produced consumer items.

It is this human element in self-employment that is increasingly attracting the sort of thinkers who, a decade or so ago, might have been more interested in socialist solutions. As people become less and less involved in what they produce and are consigned to the role of button-pushers on machines, they become alienated from their labour or in simpler terms, fed up — a situation of perpetual boredom which finds expression in strikes, absenteeism, general bloody-mindedness on the factory floor or total lack of interest in the office. There is no way, of course, that we can go back to a society of individual craftsmen without an unacceptable drop in our standards of living. But maybe, so the argument runs, we should leave to machines what machines do best and get human beings to cater to the individual taste, the quirky needs, the one-off problems and the sudden

QUITE SIMPLY, BRITAIN'S TOP PERFORMING PERSONAL PENSION PLAN

PENSION SCHEME (fund link)	Accumulated fund for 10 annual premiums of £500 effected in 1972 by male aged 55
Save & Prosper (Property Pension Fund)	£**15,140**
Save & Prosper (Equity Pension Fund)	£**12,112**
Third placed scheme	£**12,045**
Fourth placed scheme	£**11,250**

Source: Planned Savings, November 1982

Planned Savings' most recent survey of personal pension plans showed that the Save & Prosper Self-Employed Pension Scheme outperformed every other plan on the market over a 10-year period.

It also demonstrates the all-round investment expertise of Save & Prosper in taking first and second place with the Property and Equity Pension Funds.

For full details of the Save & Prosper Self-Employed Pension Scheme please phone Romford (0708) 66966 or write to Save & Prosper Group, 4 Great St. Helens, London EC3P 3EP.

SAVE & PROSPER PENSIONS

emergencies and breakdowns that machines cannot handle.

This is certainly where the opportunities for the self-employed lie, and one of the objects of this preamble is to make an important practical point. The game the giants play has its limitations, but do not take them on direct. If, for instance, you are a skilled cabinetmaker, do not get into mass-produced furniture: you simply will not be able to get your prices down far enough to make a living, nor will you be able to handle distribution on the scale that mass production implies. Do something the giants do not do, such as making things to individual specifications. If you have always wanted to own a grocery shop, do not do the same thing as the supermarket round the corner. Bake your own bread or make your delicatessen or stay open round the clock — do something you can do better or differently.

How well prepared are you?

Having a sound idea is only part of the story. How prepared you are to take it further depends on the extent of your experience; not that it is absolutely essential at the 'thinking about it' stage to have all-round direct experience of the sort of self-employment opportunity you want to exploit. But you have to be aware of what you know and do not know about it. You may be a manager who is also a keen gardener and you want to set up a market gardening business. In that case you probably have a rather better knowledge of management essentials than that of a hypothetical competitor who is currently employed by a market gardener and wants to set up on his own. But on the finer points of growing techniques and hazards, and where to sell the products, your competitor is going to be much better equipped than you.

The first step, therefore, is to make a list of all the aspects you can think of about running the business: show it to someone who is already in the field to make sure nothing of importance has been missed out, and tick off the ones you think you can handle and consider how you are going to deal with the areas where your experience is limited. The best way may well be to gain practical first-hand experience. If you are thinking of buying a shop, for instance, working in one for a few weeks will teach you an amazing amount about the public's tastes — what sells and what does not — and you may save yourself hundreds of pounds in making the right buying decisions later on. As far as management principles are concerned, your library will provide you with lists for further reading.

You should also take advice from your regional Small Firms Centre. These provide consultancy services and a wide range of useful publications. Information is free and counselling incurs only a modest charge. The addresses of the regional centres are given in Appendix 1. In Scotland the service is operated through the Scottish Development Agency. In Wales the information service is provided by the Welsh Office and the counselling service is operated by the Welsh Development Agency. In Northern Ireland, the Department of Commerce provides an information service.

Such national services are now being increasingly augmented by business advice given at local level and related to local conditions. An extremely useful directory of such bodies is a publication called *Local Initiatives in Great Britain* published by New Foundations for Local Initiative Support, The Rookery, Adderbury, Banbury, Oxon OX17 3NA. They tend to be funded by a mixture of local authority grants and finance from businesses in the area and are often very knowledgeable about local business opportunities. The larger ones run courses, provide guidance on grant and loan schemes, operate professional advice panels and even issue registers of suitable vacant properties. They are run in many cases by experienced businessmen who have been seconded by their firms to help neighbouring industries − a recognition of the fact, perhaps, that no business is an island and the health of larger firms depends also on the prosperity of smaller ones.

Another invaluable source of information on the various kinds of advice available to small businesses is *The Small Business Guide* by Colin Barrow, published by BBC Publications, PO Box 234, London SE1 3TH. It contains details of some 1200 helping agencies of various kinds, ranging from the local enterprise initiatives referred to above to sources of legal advice and possible finance. There is also a gazetteer at the back which lists advice centres throughout the UK on a town-by-town basis.

Both of these books should be available at your local library; though neither of them is expensive, the small business boom is attracting publishers in droves and it is already possible to spend quite a lot of money on books of advice of varying quality. It is worth mentioning, therefore, that several of the clearing banks have got into the act and are producing free books and pamphlets, some of which are very good. Ask your bank manager for any such material.

The importance of planning

If you are going to borrow money to get your firm off the ground, the lender (if he has any sense!) will want to know how you plan to use his money and if the operation you have in mind is going to give him an adequate return on his investment. This means that you must have a clear idea of how your business is going to develop, at least for the next year, where you see work coming from and whether you are going to have the future resources, human and financial, to handle it (see Chapter 1.7 on the importance of cash flow and financial forecasting).

Even if you do not need to borrow money, planning is vital. Landing a big contract or assignment for a new business is a heartening beginning, but well before work on it is completed you should be looking around for the next job. The completion dates you have given should take this into account, unless the amount of money you are going to get from it is so much that you will have plenty of time to look around for more work after this first job is done. But that, too, is a matter of planning.

Is self-employment right for you?

Let us leave aside Samuel Smiles-like homilies about having to be your own hardest taskmaster. We will take it for granted that you are not considering working for yourself as a soft option. But apart from the question of whether your health can stand the fairly demanding regime that full-time self-employment implies, there are also other questions you have to ask yourself about your aptitude — as opposed to a mere hankering — for going it alone. First of all, there are severely practical considerations: whether you have enough money or the means of raising it. And remember you will need money not only to finance your business or practice, but also for your own personal needs, including sickness and holiday periods.

Self-employment may mean a drop in your standard of living, possibly a permanent one, if things do not go as planned. Are you prepared for that? Is your family going to like it? Have you seriously considered the full price to be paid for independence? Is your wife (or husband) able and willing to lend a hand?

Insecurity, a necessary condition of self-employment, is not everyone's cup of tea. Neither are some of the implications of being your own master. One of the most important of them is the ability to make decisions and if you very much dislike doing this, self-employment is probably not the right channel for your abilities. You are constantly going to be called on to make decisions, some of them rather trivial, where it does not matter greatly what you do decide, so long as you decide *something*; but some of them will be fundamental policy decisions that could make or break your business.

You are also going to be called on to make decisions about people, and these are often the hardest of all. It is terribly difficult to sack someone with whom you have worked in the intimacy of a small office, but sooner or later that kind of situation will land in your lap. So another quality that is called for is toughness. This does not mean overbearing nastiness, but it does mean the readiness, for instance, to part company with a supplier, even if he is a personal friend, if his service starts to fall consistently below standard.

We have touched on the question of your aptitude for self-employment as such, but there remains the matter of your aptitude for the sphere of activity you have chosen. A management consultant friend of the writer's uses a basic precept in advising companies on personnel problems: staff are best employed doing what they are best at. The same applies to self-employment and most people go into it with that in mind. The problem with self-employment, however, is that at least at the outset you cannot absolutely avoid all the aspects of the work, such as bookkeeping, that in a bigger organisation you might have delegated or passed on to another department because you yourself do not much enjoy doing them. What you have to do is to maximise the number of tasks you are good at and minimise the others. This may mean taking a partner to complement your skills or employing an outside agency to handle some things for you: selling, for instance, if you are good at making things but not so good at negotiating or dealing with people. That means less money for you, but at the risk of sounding moralistic, you are unlikely to succeed if making money is the only thing you have in mind and overrides considerations like job satisfaction.

At the same time, the costs of doing anything in business must always be taken into account. For example, if you take a partner, is there going to be enough money coming in to make a living for both of you? Unless you constantly quantify your business decisions in this way, you are unlikely to stay in business very long. In fact, you should not even start on your career as a self-employed person without investigating very carefully whether there is a big and lasting enough demand for the product or service you are proposing to offer, and whether it can be sold at a competitive price that will enable you to earn a living after meeting all the expenses of running a business.

It is, of course, said that business is a gamble and that there comes the point where you must take the plunge. However, there are certain times when the odds are better than at others. At the moment, in the middle of a recession, the failure rate for new businesses is said to be as high as 70 per cent, which indicates that one's chances of success ought to be better than 50:50. Unless you are reasonably sure you can beat those odds with whatever it is you are setting out to do, you ought to think again or get further advice on how you can either improve your chances or minimise your financial risk.

In conclusion

If you have faced the issues we have touched on in the last paragraphs and feel confident about dealing with them, your chances of success in self-employment, whether full-time or part-time, are good. As for the opportunities, they are legion and later we examine what is involved in some areas. The list obviously cannot be comprehensive (though it should serve as a stimulus to looking in other directions as well) and neither can the coverage of basic management techniques in Part 1. But one of the essentials of effective management is to pick out no more from any topic than you need to know to accomplish the task in hand. We hope that these chapters give you the kind of technical information that you will be concerned with at this early stage of your career as a self-employed person.

Checklist: going it alone

1. Can you measure the demand for your product or service in terms of money?
2. Who are your competitors and what can you offer that they cannot?
3. Is the market local or national and how can you reach it? Can you measure the cost of doing so in financial terms?

4. How much capital have you got and how easy is it to realise?
5. How much money do you need for start-up costs and if it is more than your capital, how can you make up the difference?
6. How long is it likely to be before your income meets your outgoings and how do you propose to manage until then?
7. Do you have any established contacts who can give you business?
8. Is your proposed activity a one-off opportunity or a line for which there is a continuing demand?
9. What aspects of your proposed activity do you have first-hand experience in and how do you propose to fill in the gaps?
10. How good is your health?
11. What are you best at/worst at in your present job and how does this relate to your area of self-employment?
12. Is there any way you can combine your present job with self-employment for an experimental period while you see how it goes?
13. Have you made a realistic appraisal of your aptitude for going it alone, both generally and in the context of the line of work you have chosen?
14. Should you join up with someone else and, if so, is the net income you anticipate going to provide a livelihood for all the people involved?

1.2: Starting a Business

Before you start talking to bank managers, solicitors, accountants or tax inspectors you will have to start thinking about what sort of legal entity the business you are going to operate is to be. The kind of advice you seek from them will depend on this decision, and you have three choices. You can operate as a sole trader (ie a one-man business — it does not necessarily have to be a 'trade'), a partnership, or as a private limited company. Let us see what each of these options implies.

Sole trader

There is nothing — or at least very little — to stop you from starting a business under your own name, operating from a back room of your own house.* But if the place you live in is owned by someone else, you should get the landlord's permission. If the business you are starting in your home is one that involves a change of use of the premises, you will have to get planning permission from the local authority's planning officer. In that case you may also find that you are re-rated on a commercial basis. If you own your house, you should also check that there are no restrictive covenants in the deeds governing its use. On the whole, a business conducted unobtrusively from a private residence is unlikely to attract attention from the local authority but, to be perfectly safe, it is as well to have a word with the authority's planning department since any change of use, even of part of your residence, requires planning permission.

The next step is to inform your local tax inspector or to get your accountant to do so (see Chapter 1.4 on choosing professional advisers). This is always advisable if the nature of your earnings is changing and imperative if you are moving from employee to full-time self-employed status, because it changes

*If your business is likely to disturb neighbours or cause a nuisance (noise, smells, clients taking up parking space) or if it necessitates your building an extension, converting an attic, etc, you must apply for planning permission. Your property may then be given a higher, commercial rateable value.

the basis on which you pay tax. The inspector will give you some indication of allowable business expenses to be set off against your earnings for tax purposes. These will not include entertainment of potential customers (unless they are overseas buyers) but will cover items 'wholly and exclusively incurred for the purposes of business'. These are spelt out in more detail in Chapter 1.11. Some things, of course, are used partly for private and partly for business purposes — your car or your telephone, for instance. In these cases only that proportion of expenditure that can definitely be attributed to business use is chargeable against tax. Careful records of such use must, therefore, be kept, and its extent must also be credible. If you are not exporting anything in the way of a product or service, you may be unable to convince the inspector that a weekend in Paris was in the course of business! But if you are, he is unlikely to quibble about a modest hotel bill, even if the business part of your visit only took a couple of hours.

The principal cautionary point to bear in mind about operating as a sole trader is that you are personally liable for the debts of your business. If you go bankrupt your creditors are entitled to seize and sell your *personal* possessions, not just equipment, cars and other items directly related to your business.

Partnerships

Most of the above points are also true if you are setting up in partnership with other people. Once again, there are very few restrictions against setting up in partnership with someone to carry on a business, but because all the members of a partnership are personally liable for its debts, even if these are incurred by a piece of mismanagement by one partner which was not known to his colleagues, the choice of partners is a step that requires very careful thought. So should you have a partner at all? Certainly it is not advisable to do so just for the sake of having company, because unless the partner can really contribute something to the business, you are giving away a part of what could in time be a very valuable asset to little purpose. A partner should be able to make an important contribution to running the business in an area which you are unable to take care of. He may have some range of specialised expertise that is vital to the business; or he may have a range of contacts to bring in work; or the work may be of such a nature that the executive

27

tasks and decisions cannot be handled by one person. He may even be a 'sleeping partner' who is doing little else apart from putting up some money in return for a share of the eventual profits.

But whatever the reason for establishing a partnership as opposed to going it alone and owning the whole business may be, you should be sure that your partner (of course, there may be more than one, but for the sake of simplicity we will assume that only one person is involved) is someone you know well in a business, not just a social, capacity. Because of this, before formally establishing a partnership, it may be advisable to tackle, as an informal joint venture, one or two jobs with the person you are thinking of setting up with, carrying at the end of the day an agreed share of the costs and profits. That way you will learn about each other's strengths and weaknesses, and indeed whether you can work together harmoniously at all. It may turn out, for instance, that your prospective partner's expertise or contacts, while useful, do not justify giving him a share of the business and that in fact a consultancy fee is the right way of remunerating him.

Even if all goes well and you find that you can cooperate, it is vital that a formal partnership agreement should be drawn up by a solicitor. This is true even of husband-and-wife partnerships. The agreement should cover such points as the following:

1. Who is responsible for what aspects of the operation (eg production, marketing, etc)?
2. What constitutes a policy decision (eg whether or not to take on a contract) and how is it taken? By a majority vote, if there is an uneven number of partners? By the partner concerned with that aspect of things? Only if all partners agree?
3. How are the profits to be divided? According to the amount of capital put in? According to the amount of work done by each partner? Over the whole business done by the partnership over a year? On a job-by-job basis? How much money can be drawn, on what basis, and how often in the way of remuneration?
4. What items, like cars, not exclusively used for business can be charged to the partnership? And is there any limitation to the amount of money involved?
5. If one of the partners retires or withdraws how is his share of the business to be valued?

6. If work is done in office hours, outside the framework of the partnership, to whom does the income accrue?
7. What arbitration arrangements are there, in case of irreconcilable differences?
8. If one of the partners dies, what provisions should the others make for his dependants?

There are obviously many kinds of eventualities that have to be provided for, depending on the kind of business that is going to be carried on. Some professional partnerships, for instance, may consist of little more than an agreement to pool office expenses like the services of typists and telephonists, with each partner drawing his own fees quite independently of the rest. The best way to prepare the ground for a solicitor to draw up an agreement is for each partner to make a list of possible points of dispute and to leave it to the legal adviser to produce a form of words to cover these and any other points he may come up with himself.

Private limited companies

Except when your business or freelance occupation is on a very small scale — something that brings in only a few extra pounds a week — it is generally advisable to set up as a private limited company, unless you are prevented from doing so for professional reasons or if you are under a legal disability such as applies to undischarged bankrupts. The advantage of a limited company is that, in law, it has an identity distinct from that of the shareholders who are its owners. Consequently, if a limited company goes bankrupt, the claims of the creditors are limited to the assets of the company. This includes any capital issued to shareholders which they have either paid for in full or in part. We shall return to the question of share capital in a moment, but the principle at work here is that when shares are issued the shareholders need not necessarily pay for them in full, though they have a legal obligation to do so if the company goes bankrupt. Shareholders are not, however, liable as individuals and their private assets outside the company may not be touched, unless their company has been trading fraudulently. On the other hand, if creditors ask for personal guarantees directors of limited companies are not protected and *personal* assets to the amount of the guarantee as well as business assets are at risk in the event of bankruptcy.

A limited company can be formed by two shareholders (who

can be husband and wife), one of whom must be a director. It must also have a company secretary, who can be an outside person, such as your solicitor or accountant. Apart from this, the main requirements relate to documentation. Like sole traders or partnerships, a limited company must prepare a set of accounts annually for the inspector of taxes, but it has the further obligation that these have to be audited, normally by an accountant, who has to certify that they present 'a true and fair view' of the company's finances; and it must make an annual return to the Registrar of Companies, showing all the shareholders and directors, any changes of ownership that have taken place, a profit and loss account over the year and a balance sheet.

Apart from the more exacting requirements regarding documentation, a significant disadvantage of setting up a limited company as compared to a partnership or sole trader has emerged with some of the tax changes of recent years. In Chapter 1.11 we show that losses incurred by partnerships and sole traders in the first four years' trading can be set off retrospectively against the owners' income tax on earnings in the three years before they set up in business. This concession does not apply, however, to investment in your own limited company, or to investments made in such a company by those closely connected with the shareholders. If it makes losses, those losses can only be set off against the *company's* corporation tax in other years when it makes a profit. If it fails altogether, then the loss of your investment is a *capital* loss which can only be set off against other capital gains you make — not against other earned income. Therefore, if the nature of your business is a service which does not involve exposure to liabilities that you need to protect — for instance, if you are a consultant, rather than a shopkeeper or a manufacturer incurring liabilities to suppliers — there may be a distinct advantage in opting for partnership or sole trader status rather than establishing a limited company; but see the recommendation to seek professional advice below. There may, for instance, be factors other than trading risks which need to be protected by limited liability.

The cost of forming a company, including the capital duty which is based on the issued capital (we shall come to the distinction between this and nominal capital shortly), is likely to be around £100, depending on what method you use to go about it. The cheapest way is to buy a ready-made ('off the

shelf') company from one of the registration agents who
advertise their services in specialist financial journals. Such a
company will not actually have been trading, but will be
properly registered by the agents. All that has to be done is for
the existing 'shareholders' (who are probably the agent's
nominees) to resign and for the purchasers to become the new
shareholders and to appoint directors.

Alternatively you can start your own company from scratch,
but whichever course you choose professional advice is vital at
this stage. The technicalities are trickier than they sound,
though simple enough to those versed in such transactions.

Registration of business names

One problem you may encounter with an 'off the shelf' company
is when it has a name that does not relate meaningfully to the
activity you are proposing to carry on. In that case you can
apply to the Registrar of Companies (Companies Registration
Office, Crown Way, Maindy, Cardiff CF4 3UZ) to change the
name. A fee of £10 will be charged for this.

The other option is to trade under a name which is different

31

from the company's official one; for instance your company may be called 'Period Investments Ltd', but you trade as 'Regency Antiques'. Until recently you had to register your business name with the Registrar of Business Names but that office has now been abolished. Instead, if you trade under any name other than your own — in the case of a sole trader or partnership — or that of the name of the company carrying on the business, in the case of a company, you have to disclose the name of the owner or owners and, for each owner, a business or other address within the UK.

The rules of disclosure are quite far reaching and failure to comply with them is a criminal offence. You must show the information about owners and their addresses on all business letters, written orders for the supply of goods or services, invoices and receipts issued in the course of business and written demands for payment of business debts. Furthermore you have to display this information prominently and readably in any premises where the business is carried on and to which customers and suppliers have access.

It is worth giving a good deal of thought to the choice of a business name. Clever names are all very well, but if they do not clearly establish the nature of the business you are in, prospective customers leafing through a telephone or business directory may have trouble in finding you; or, if they do find you, they may not readily match your name to their needs. For instance, if you are a furniture repairer, it is far better to describe yourself as such in your business name than to call yourself something like 'Chippendale Restorations'. On the other hand if you already have a big reputation in some specialised sector, stick with it. Arguably, some of the Beatles' business ventures might have been more successful if they had traded on that name, instead of using the label 'Apple' for their other activities.

The rules governing the use of business names are like those for company names, except that the Registrar is less concerned about the fact that a similar trading name may already be in existence. Obviously, however, it is advisable in both cases to wait until the name you have put forward is accepted before having any stationery printed. There are, it should be said, certain words that the Registrar of Companies has proved likely to object to: those that could mislead the public by suggesting that an enterprise is larger or has a more prestigious status than circumstances indicate. Cases in point are the use of words like

Trust, University, Group. National adjectives ('British') are also unpopular. When you get to this stage the names of the proprietors (or, in the case of a limited company, the directors) have to be shown not only on letterheads, but also on catalogues and trade literature. Limited companies, in addition, have to show their registration number and the address of their registered office on such stationery.

This address may not necessarily be the same as the one at which business is normally transacted. Some firms use their accountant's or solicitor's premises as their registered office. You will probably see quite a number of registration certificates hanging in their office (they are required by law to be so displayed) when you go there. This is because it is to that address that all legal and official documents are sent. If you have placed complete responsibility for dealing with such matters in the hands of professional advisers, it is obviously convenient that the related correspondence should also be directed there. Bear in mind, though, that this does involve a certain loss of control on your part. Unless you at least first see these documents yourself, you will have no idea, for instance, whether the important ones are being handled with due dispatch.

33

Limited company documents

When you set up a limited company, your solicitor or accountant will be involved in drafting certain papers and documents which govern its structure and the way it is to be run. When this process has been completed you will receive copies of the company's Memorandum and Articles of Association, some share transfer forms, a Minute Book, the Company Seal and the Certificate of Incorporation. Let us explain briefly what these mean.

The Memorandum

This document sets out the main objects for which the company is formed and what it is allowed to do. There are standard clauses for this and your professional adviser will use these in drafting the document. The main thing to watch out for is that he should not be too specific in setting out the limits of the proposed operation, because if you change tack somewhere along the line — for instance if you move from mail order to making goods for the customers you have built up — you may lose the protection of your limited liability unless the Memorandum provides for this. There are, however, catch-all clauses which allow you to trade in pretty much anything or in any manner you like. Furthermore, the 'objects' clauses can be changed by a special resolution, passed by 75 per cent of the shareholders.

The Memorandum also sets out the company's nominal or authorised share capital and the par value per share. This is a point about which many newcomers to this aspect of business get very confused. The thing to remember is that in this context the value of share capital is a purely *nominal* value. You can have a company operating with thousands of pounds' worth of nominal share capital. This sounds very impressive, but what counts is the *issued* share capital, because this represents what the shareholders have actually put into the business or pledged themselves so to do. It is quite possible to have a company with a nominal capital of £1000, but with only two issued shares of £1 each to the two shareholders that are required by law.

The issued share capital also determines the ownership of a company. In the case we have just quoted, the two shareholders would own the company jointly. But if they then issue a third £1 share to another person without issuing any more to themselves they would now only own two-thirds of the company. This is a vital point to remember when raising capital by means of selling shares.

Apart from determining proportions of ownership, issued share capital also signifies how much of their own money the shareholders have put into the company or are prepared to accept liability for. Therefore in raising money from a bank or finance house, the manager there will look closely at the issued share capital. To the extent that he is not satisfied that the liability for the amount he is being asked to put up is adequately backed by issued share capital, he is likely to ask the shareholders to guarantee a loan or overdraft with their own personal assets — for instance by depositing shares they privately hold in a public quoted company or unit trust as security. In the case of a new company without a track record this would, in fact, be the usual procedure.

The nominal share capital of a new small-scale business is usually £100. It can be increased later on, as business grows, on application to the Registrar of Companies. The point of such a move would be to increase the *issued* share capital, for instance, if a new shareholder were to put money into the company. But, once again, it should be borne in mind that if the issued share capital was increased from £100 to £1000, and a backer were to buy £900 worth of shares at par value, the original shareholders would only own one-tenth of the business; the fact that they got the whole thing going is quite beside the point.

One last question about issued share capital which sometimes puzzles people. Must you actually hand over money for the shares when you start your own company, as is the case when you buy shares on the stock market, and what happens to it? The answer is yes. You pay it into the company's bank account because, remember, it has a separate legal identity from the shareholders who own it. However, you need not pay for your shares in full. You can, for instance, pay 50p per share for a hundred £1 shares. The balance of £50 represents your liability if the company goes bankrupt and you only actually have to hand over the money if that happens or if a majority at a shareholders' meeting requires you to do so. The fact that you have not paid in full for shares issued to you does not, however, diminish your entitlement to share in the profits, these being distributed as dividends according to the proportion of share capital issued. The same applies to outside shareholders, so if you are raising money by selling shares to people outside the

firm, you should normally ensure that they pay in full for any
capital that is issued to them.

The Articles of Association

These are coupled together with the Memorandum, and set out
the rules under which the company is run. They govern matters
like issue of the share capital, the appointment and powers of
directors and the proceedings at general meetings. As in the case
of the Memorandum the clauses are largely standard ones, but
those relating to the issue of shares should be read carefully. It
is most important that there should be a proviso under which
any new shares that are issued should be offered first of all to
the existing shareholders in the proportion in which they
already hold shares. This is particularly so when three or more
shareholders are involved, or when you are buying into a
company; otherwise the other shareholders can vote to water
down your holding in the company whenever they see fit by
issuing further shares. For the same reason, there should be a
clause under which any shareholder who wants to transfer
shares should offer them first of all to the existing shareholders.
The Articles of Association also state how the value of the
shares is to be determined, the point here being that if the
company is successful and makes large profits, the true value of
the shares will be much greater than their 'par' value of £1,
50p or whatever. It should be noted, though, that the market
valuation of the shares does not increase the liability of shareholders accordingly. In other words, if your £1 'par' shares are
actually valued at, say, £50, your liability still remains at £1.

Table A of the Companies Act of 1948, which can be purchased at any HMSO branch, sets out a specimen Memorandum
and Articles.

The Minute Book

Company law requires that a record be kept of the proceedings
at both shareholders' and directors' meetings. These proceedings
are recorded in the minute book, which is held at the company's
registered office. Decisions made at company meetings are
signed by the chairman and are legally binding on the directors
if they are agreed by a majority. Therefore, any points of
procedure that are not covered by the Memorandum and
Articles of Association can be written into the minutes and have

the force of law, provided that they do not conflict with the former two documents. Thus, the various responsibilities of the directors can be defined and minuted at the first company meeting; so can important matters such as who signs the cheques. It is generally a good idea for these to carry two signatures to be valid.

The Company Seal

The company seal is a metal disc bearing the name of the company in raised letters. The disc is pressed into all official documents and its use on any occasion must be authorised by the directors.

The Certificate of Incorporation

When the wording of the Memorandum and Articles of Association has been agreed and the names of the directors and the size of the nominal capital have been settled, your professional adviser will send the documents concerned to the Registrar of

Companies. He will issue a Certificate of Incorporation which is, as it were, the birth certificate of your company.

Company directors

When your Certificate of Incorporation arrives you and your fellow shareholders are the owners of a fully fledged private limited company. You will almost certainly also be the directors. This title in fact means very little. A director is merely an employee of the company, who is entrusted by the shareholders with the running of it. He need not himself be a shareholder at all; and he can be removed by a vote of the shareholders which, since each share normally carries one vote, is a good reason for not losing control of your company by issuing a majority shareholding to outsiders.

Another good reason is that since the ownership of the company is in proportion to the issued share capital, so also is the allocation of profits, when you come to make them. If you let control pass to an outsider for the sake of raising a few hundred pounds now — there are other means of raising capital than the sale of shares, as we shall show in Chapter 1.3 — you will have had all the problems of getting things going, while only receiving a small part of the rewards. Remember, furthermore, that without control you are only an employee, even if you are called 'managing director'.

Checklist: setting up in business

Sole trader

1. Do you need planning permission to operate from your own home?
2. Does your lease allow you to carry on a trade from the premises you intend to use?
3. If you own the premises, whether or not they are your home as well, are there any restrictive covenants which might prevent you from using them for the purpose intended?
4. Have you notified your tax inspector that the nature of your earnings is changing?
5. Are you aware of the implications of being a sole trader if your business fails?
6. Have you taken steps to register a business name?

Partnerships

1. Points 1 to 6 above also apply to partnerships. Have you taken care of them?
2. How well do you know your partners — personally and as people to work with?
3. If you do not know them well what evidence do you have about their personal and business qualities?
4. What skills, contacts or other assets (like capital) can they bring into the business?
5. Have you asked your solicitor to draw up a deed of partnership and does it cover all the eventualities you can think of?
6. Have you talked to anybody who is in, or has tried, partnership in the same line of business, to see what the snags are?

Private limited companies

1. Do you have the requisite minimum number of shareholders (2)?
2. Do you have a competent company secretary, who can carry out the legal duties required under the Companies Acts?
3. Are you yourself reasonably conversant with those duties?
4. Have you registered, if this is required, a company name and a business name?
5. Has permission been granted to use the names chosen?
6. Have the necessary documents been deposited with the Registrar of Companies? (Memorandum and Articles of Agreement, a statutory declaration of compliance with registration requirements, a statement of nominal share capital.)
7. Have you read and understood the Memorandum and Articles? Do they enable you to carry out all present and any possible future objects for which the company is formed?
8. Do your stationery, catalogues, letterheads, etc show all the details required by the Companies Acts?
9. Is the Registration Certificate displayed in the company's registered office, as required by law?
10. Do you understand the wide range of benefits — company cars, other business expenses, limited liability, self-administered pension schemes, etc — enjoyed by limited companies?
11. Clauses 1 to 3 of the 'Sole Trader' checklist may also apply to you. If so, have you taken care of them?

1.3: Raising Capital

There are many methods of raising money. Some of these are direct forms of borrowing or obtaining loans, others are ways in which you can spin out your cash resources. But for most small businesses, and many large ones, bank borrowing is the one most widely used.

Approaching your bank

Banks make money by using the funds deposited with them to lend out at rates of interest which vary according to government policy. During periods of economic expansion that rate will be lower — and money easier to get — than during the 'stop' parts of the 'stop and go cycle' which has characterised the British economy since the war. But banks, like everybody else, have to continue to trade even through less prosperous times. You will find, therefore, that the bank manager will be willing to discuss making money available to you, because potentially you are a source of income to him. How much that will be depends somewhat on the size of the branch you are approaching. This is an argument in favour of going to a large branch if you need a sizeable sum; on the other hand in a smaller community, where personal contacts still matter, your professional adviser may well have a shrewd idea of what the bank manager's lending limits are.

Whether you can convince him that your business is a good risk depends on how well you have thought out your approach. To some extent he will go on personal impressions and on what he can gather of your previous business experience. If you have already been running your own firm for a year or two he will have some hard evidence to go on in the shape of your profit and loss account and your balance sheet. He will look at the financial position of your firm, particularly the relationship of current assets to current liabilities and of debtors to creditors (see Chapter 1.5). He will want to be satisfied that you are valuing your stock realistically and he will want to know how much money you (and your partners, if you have any) have put into the business from your own resources. In the case of a limited company he will want to know what the issued share capital is. Proposals for lending to a new business will need to be fully worked out and have realistic and thorough cash flow protection.

The bank will be looking to see whether your business satisfies three criteria. First, that its money is secure, and in the case of new business will probably ask for security to be in the shape of tangible items like fixed assets within the business or shares and other assets belonging to the owners in their private capacity in a ratio which may be as high as 1:1. Second, that your firm is likely to have an inflow of enough liquid assets to enable it to recall its money, if necessary. Third, that you will be able to make profitable use of it and pay the interest without difficulty.

There is a saying that banks will only lend you money if you do not need it and reading these requirements you may be coming to the conclusion that there is an element of truth in it. But what it really means is that it is no use going to a bank to bail you out of trouble. A business in trouble generally requires assistance on the management side at the very least and banks are just not in a position to provide such assistance, no matter how glowing the prospects might be if the firm could be brought back on track. So the bank manager is only going to be looking at present and quantifiable situations. He will not be very interested in often vague assets like goodwill and even less in your hopes for the future.

If you have only just set up in business you may not have much more than hopes for the future to offer, and the bank manager will obviously be cautious in such cases. But can these hopes can be quantified, and have you outlined a thorough cash flow budget? If you are opening, say, a new restaurant facts such as that you and your wife are excellent cooks, have attended courses in catering and have established that there would be a demand for a good place to eat in a particular locality are relevant. But what the bank also wants to know is what your start-up costs are going to be, whether you have fully worked out what your overheads and direct costs are (ie items like rent, rates, gas and electricity, depreciation on equipment, staff wages and the cost of food), what relation these are going to bear to your charges for meals, and what levels of seat occupancy you need to achieve to make a profit. This may take

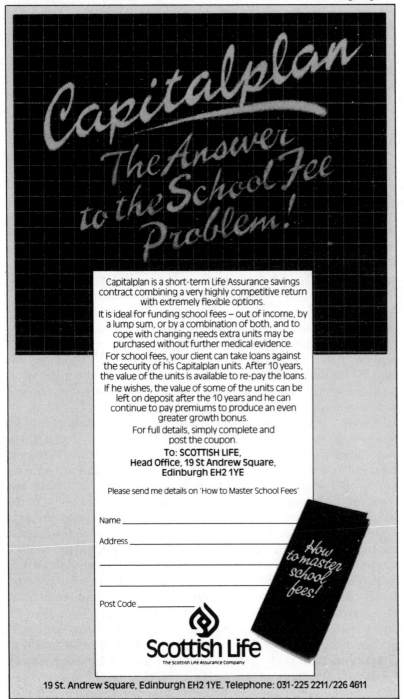

quite a lot of working out and it is advisable that you consult closely with your accountant in preparing your case for the bank. Indeed it may be a good idea to take your accountant along with you when you are approaching the bank for financial help.

The commonest form of help, as far as the small business is concerned, is an overdraft, rather than a bank loan. You will be given facilities to overdraw up to a certain amount, but the advantage of an overdraft, as opposed to a loan, is that interest (usually 2 to 3 per cent above base lending rate) is paid only on the actual amount by which you are overdrawn. Overdrafts are particularly useful, therefore, for the firm whose pattern of business fluctuates, such as the market gardener whose income is higher in spring than in winter, or a business which needs money to finance a large contract until the first progress payments are received. The disadvantage of an overdraft is that it can be called in. Though in practice this rarely happens, it is unwise to use money raised in this way to finance medium- and long-term requirements, particularly those which make no immediate contribution to profits, like having your office done up! A more likely peril than the overdraft being called in, however, is the fluctuation of interest rates. If these go up sharply because of some economic crisis, you want to be in a position where you are keeping the facility you are using down to a minimum.

If you do need to finance the cost of purchasing plant or equipment, however, you might sleep more easily if you have negotiated a bank loan. This would normally run for between two and five years, would have repayment periods built into it and would carry a somewhat higher rate of interest than an overdraft. Alternatively, you may need a mixed package — both overdraft facilities and a term loan. Your bank manager and your accountant should be able to advise you on your requirements, provided you have worked out a clear plan for the course of your business over the period during which you need financial help. For larger sums you might consider, with the help of your trusty financial adviser, an approach to the Industrial and Commercial Finance Corporation (ICFC). Its London office is at 91 Waterloo Road, London SE1 8XP, but it also has local offices in other cities. The advantage of ICFC is that although it is a commercial body (it was in fact founded by the clearing banks and the Bank of England), it is rather less aggressive than some of its competitors in its approach to participation in the equity and management of the companies to which it lends money; but it is not, on the whole, interested in getting involved in businesses that are not yet established, especially small ones.

In the case of a limited company, the bank is likely to call on individual directors to guarantee any overdrafts or loans against their personal resources. There are certain pitfalls about some forms of guarantee and it is vital that you check with your solicitor when entering into such an arrangement. The most common cause of problems comes when you form a business with partners or shareholders outside your family. The bank will ask that your guarantee will be on a 'joint and several' basis. This harmless-sounding phrase means that if things go wrong and the bank calls in its guarantee, they will collect the money not from the individual guarantors but from the one or ones whom they have identified as being most able to pay. Those who have met their obligations are then left to make their own arrangements to collect from those who have not — the banks will not take action to pursue the defaulter. The enormous costs of litigation then mean that unless the sums involved are very large it is not worthwhile taking legal action. For instance one group of 'joint and several' guarantors among whom such a problem arose were told by their bank manager that it would probably not be worth taking action over a default of over £3000. Legal costs would swallow up such a sum and even if they won their case they might not get costs.

If you find the terms under which your bank is offering finance unacceptable, it is worth shopping around to see if you can get a better deal elsewhere.

Alternatively you might try one of the growing number of foreign banks now located in London. The American ones are reported to combine the highest degree of reputability with adventurousness in advancing risk capital.

Private loans

You may have friends or relatives who are prepared to lend you money, but private loans are a rich source of misunderstanding, so you should be clear about all the implications of such an arrangement. The best plan is to get a solicitor to draw up the terms of the loan, covering the rate of interest, the period over which the loan is repayable and the circumstances under which it can be withdrawn. It must also be made clear to what extent, if any, the lender has any say in the running of the business and what the nature of this control is. Normally, however, the lender should not be entitled to participation in management matters; nor does the existence of his loan entitle him to a share of the profits, no matter how strong a moral claim he thinks he might have once your business starts making real money. In the case of a limited company, you must explain to the lender that a loan is not the same thing as a shareholding, though of course the offer of a loan might be conditional on acquiring shares or the option to acquire them. You should be clear about the implications of this: it entitles the shareholder to a percentage of profits in proportion to his holdings; and though loans can be repaid it is virtually impossible to dismantle issued share capital in this way.

Often private loans are not offered directly; but in the form of guaranteeing an overdraft on the basis that, if the recipient of the overdraft is unable to repay it, then the guarantor is liable for that amount. In the 1978 Budget an important concession was made in relation to such arrangements. Losses incurred by the guarantor of a business loan can now be treated as a capital loss, which can be offset against capital gains. This principle was extended in the 1980 Budget, and tax relief can now be claimed by private investors on investment losses.

The 1981 Budget took matters even further and after a good deal of criticism of the initial proposals, which were so full of restrictions as to be unworkable, a scheme was set out which could be a useful source of finance for small businesses and which was extended in 1983.

The business expansion scheme. Formerly called the business start-up scheme, this provides, at least in theory, a powerful tax incentive to investors in small companies. Initially it covered only start-ups, but it has now been extended to cover established, small unquoted companies as well.

Relief is available at the investor's top rate on up to £40,000 in any one year, provided he is not connected with the company in which he invests. This proviso, dictated no doubt by the Inland Revenue's preoccupation with tax loopholes, would seem to undo much of the potential good of the scheme, since it is largely from people with close relationships with the owners of such companies that investment would be most likely to come.

This same preoccupation was also reflected when the scheme was introduced, in all kinds of limitations as to the type of business investment which would qualify for relief. It was only when it was made clear by numerous critics that this would make the scheme almost worthless that it was extended to cover virtually any kind of commercial enterprise, other than that which could fairly be regarded as being in the nature of financial speculation rather than trading.

Apart from raising the limit that could be invested from £20,000 to £40,000 the 1983 Budget also dropped the limitation on the proportion of issued share capital that the investment should represent and extended the duration of the scheme until 1987. Just exactly what a 'small company' means in terms of the scheme currently awaits clarification.

The loan guarantee scheme. This scheme was introduced by the government in 1981 and under it they guarantee up to 80 per cent of loans to the lending bank in cases where the bank feels the idea is basically sound but the borrower does not have the resources or the collateral they require. The upper limit to the sum which can be lent is £75,000. The total sum allocated to the scheme was originally £50 million, but the demand for it has proved so strong — over 4000 loans have been made under the scheme — that this has since been raised to £600 million.

Notwithstanding the success of the scheme in terms of demand there have been a number of criticisms of it. First, there have been quite a few failures among the borrowers which some commentators say means that the banks have not been sufficiently discriminating about the degree of risk involved; or alternatively, that in a cold economic climate one blanket is not enough for survival. Second, it has been widely pointed out that the cost of such loans is very high, with a premium of 3 per cent above the normal bank lending rate. A further criticism of the scheme is that the upper limit of £75,000 is too low for small businesses in the high technology field where start-up costs can be far in excess of this.

It is possible in the case of a limited company for the shareholders to lend money to the company. This does not increase their liability in the same way as taking up issued share capital. However, outside lenders like banks do not take kindly to such arrangements because it indicates a certain reluctance by the shareholders to put their money where their mouth is!

The banks' own start-up schemes

Several of the clearing banks have produced start-up schemes of their own and you should ask your bank manager for details. They vary somewhat from bank to bank. To take a case in point, Barclays have a scheme, available to limited companies only, where for an initial period the bank takes a royalty on sales rather than making an interest charge. The attraction of this method of funding is that servicing the loan is related to the success of the venture rather than to a fixed percentage of the sum lent. On the other hand, it could work out very costly for the borrower — and very profitable for the bank — if the venture is unusually successful from the very start.

Money from the government

One of the problems of excessive government legislation is that it becomes increasingly difficult to sort out the useful bits from the others, so that there is a tendency to shove the whole lot to one side. This was certainly true of the Industry Act of 1972, which in fact included provision for financial help to businesses, large and small. The government has millions of pounds available for this purpose, the money being offered in the form of cash grants and special rate loans. In particular, they are trying to promote industrial development in the so-called special development areas, which in the main are those areas where traditional industries, like shipbuilding, are on the decline and where unemployment is therefore apt to be high. The minimum project values go as low as £10,000 to £50,000 and though the authorities tend to look more favourably at established businesses who are relocating in development areas, the prospects are certainly worth investigating if you are in or are thinking of moving to such an area. Development areas have the further advantage of usually having a large pool of local labour, and though the spectre of unemployment is no longer a guarantee for getting a cooperative labour force together, unions in such areas are often fairly realistic in their demands. Application forms for assistance in moving to a development area can be obtained from the Department of Industry, 1 Victoria Street, London SW1.

If your proposed enterprise is in a small town or a rural area in England or Wales, you should contact the Council for Small Industries in Rural Areas (CoSIRA). Its head office is Queen's House, Fish Row, Salisbury, Wiltshire SP1 1EX (tel: 0772-24411). As the name implies, it concentrates on industries, including tourism, and cannot offer assistance in the spheres of agriculture, horticulture or, except in priority areas, retail shops. CoSIRA provides finance up to a maximum of £75,000 though there is a joint scheme between it and Natwest providing for amounts of up to £250,000.

A number of similar regional bodies also exists. These include the Welsh Development Office, the Scottish Development Office, the Highlands and Islands Development Board, and the Northern Ireland Development Office. Your regional Small Firms Centre should be able to advise you whether you have a case for approaching them. Addresses are given in Appendix 1.

A good deal of encouragement is now being given to small firms setting up in run-down urban areas and this can take the form of actual risk-funding. Details are available from one of the Department of Industry's regional Small Firms Centres. You can get hold of the nearest one to you by dialling 100 and asking for Freephone number 2444.

But what about the marvellous invention that nobody will finance? Is the government prepared to sponsor British initiatives in new technology? The answer is a guarded yes. There is such a body, but it is reputed to take an extremely cautious view of approaches made to it. Perhaps for this reason and because it demands a 50:50 share of the action if the idea works, it has been financially very successful. The body in question is the National Research Development Corporation, 66 Victoria Street, London SW1. Yet another source of government finance was announced in the 1983 Budget. If you have been unemployed for 13 weeks, have a viable idea for starting your own business and are prepared to put £1000 of your own money into it, you can get a grant from the DHSS of £40 a week for 52 weeks.

Finance houses and merchant banks

Though many business success stories one reads about in the financial sections of the press begin with the owners getting a loan from a merchant bank, this is not usually a viable source of finance for the small business (ie one with an existing or rapidly foreseeable turnover of much under £100,000). These banks — and in this context we are using the term to include finance companies acting on behalf of institutional and other clients with risk capital to invest — are set up to fund medium- and large-scale enterprises and do not usually involve themselves with smaller firms, even if they are profitable and soundly run.

A typical example of such a finance house is Development

Capital Ltd. It looks for investment opportunities in businesses with a turnover of between £100,000 and £3 to £4 million which are funded largely from insurance companies and pension funds. They are interested in expansions, acquisitions, managers buying the equity of an established company back from a corporate holding body or promising new ventures, etc. They expect to be represented on the board in a non-executive capacity, to have a minority equity stake, to provide loan funds over a 10 to 15 year period and, of course, to receive a return on their investment. The sort of investment criteria they look for can be summarised as follows:

1. *Management*. Must have proven expertise in the field in which it is seeking to start up or to expand.
2. *Market*. Must be expanding and provide the opportunity for substantial growth over the next few years.
3. *Product or service*. Should possess advantages over other products in the same market and use the latest technology available in that field.
4. *Duration of investment*. Normally 5 to 15 years; but both shorter and longer periods are considered.
5. *Area of operation*. All UK companies including those with overseas subsidiaries or branches.
6. *Return on capital*. Must be attractive over the medium-term.

These are fairly characteristic funding prerequisites for finance companies, though there are considerable variations on such important details as the amount of the equity stake they require, the degree of involvement in management matters, the length of time over which they are prepared to lend and whether or not they are prepared to consider new and untried ventures.

If you feel that your firm offers prospects that are likely to interest a merchant bank or similar financial institution, it is certainly worth talking to them. The regional Chambers of Commerce or Small Firms Centre, or your accountant or bank manager may be able to advise you on suitable houses to approach. Before meeting them you should be careful to prepare your case for financial help. Development Capital Ltd, for instance, look for the following basic information from applicants.

1. *The business*. A short description of the company, its history, its products or services mentioning any 'bull

points' and patent protection if applicable. Trade brochures and catalogues are also useful if available.

2. *Management*. Brief details giving age, business experience and background of the full-time directors and senior executives.

3. *Market*. An outline of the opportunity for substantial growth accompanied by a forecast of sales and profits over the next two to three years, assuming the company is adequately financed.

4. *Finance*. An estimate of the total development capital required with an indication of how it is intended to be used and a copy of the company's audited accounts for the last two years (if applicable).

Hire purchase arrangements can also be made with the help of a finance company. This is a useful way of financing medium- to longer-term commitments, such as the purchase of machinery, equipment and vehicles. The arrangements are basically similar to a private hire purchase contract, in that the buyer asks the finance company to buy the asset. He then hires it for a specific period, paying hiring charges and interest as he goes along; and can then exercise an option to buy goods at the end of an agreed period. Until that point they remain the property of the finance company, and there is thus no need, as a rule, for the hirer to provide security as is the case with a loan. On the other hand, the finance company will require him to maintain the asset in good order, to insure it and possibly to fulfil other special conditions such as providing satisfactory evidence that the money earned from it will at least cover the high interest charges (around 20 per cent at present) involved.

The periods over which a hire purchase agreement may run vary with the nature of the asset, but in general terms the Finance Houses Association lays down that 'the goods should have a useful life greater than the period of the hire purchase agreement'.

It is worth calculating the true rate of interest reflected in leasing or hire purchase charges over the given period of time. As in every other form of business, there are sharks around who turn out to charge astronomical rates of interest. It is worth getting more than one quote if there are several possible sources from which to obtain equipment on lease or hire purchase.

Vehicle for capital	Backers	Capital earmarked	Type of client or situation	Min/Max funds injected	Start up capital
Abingworth Tel: (01) 839 6745	Leading UK and European institutions	Open	Usually established profitable companies	£100,000– £500,000 and occasionally larger amounts	Possibly, if management o proven calibre
Advent Eurofund Ltd Tel: Jersey (0534) 75151	Monsanto— 50% UK financial institutions universities and colleges —50%	£10m	New technology at all stages of development	£100,000 to £500,000	Yes, but not exclusively
Anglo-American Venture Fund Ltd Tel: (061) 236 7302	British Technology Group (BTG)	£2m initially	New technology, with emphasis on electronics	Up to £300,000 but will syndicate	Yes
APA Venture Capital Fund Tel: (01) 388 1811	Pension funds, Insurance companies and institutions primarily from the UK	£10m	Companies with high growth prospects, management buy-outs	£100,000– £1m.	Yes
Barclays Development Capital Tel: (01) 623 4321	Barclays Bank Group	Open	Established growth companies earning £100,000+ pre-tax	£150,000 minimum but may syndicate large investments	No
Biotechnology Investments Limited Tel: (01) 280 5000	NM Rothschild and leading UK institutions	$50m	Biotechnology companies worldwide at all stages of development	Flexible; generally $500,000– $2m; would syndicate larger investments	Yes
Birmingham Technology Ltd Tel: Birmingham (021) 359 0981	Lloyds Bank PLC; Birmingham City Council; University of Aston in Birmingham	£2m to be augmented as and when needed	Hi-tech research, development and/ or hi-tech manufacturing companies	Depending on requirements	Yes

Table 3.1 *Sources of Finance*
Where to go when the bank manger says 'no'.

Rescue capital	Equity stake	Seat on Board	Term of funding	Exit criteria	Special features	Portfolio
Occasionally	Always minority	Usually	Open	Flexible, but happy to take long term view	Extensive overseas contacts, particularly in the US, Europe and the Far East	£25m + in the UK and US
A possibility	Significant minority	Yes	Flexible	Flexible	"Hands on" management support Significant US contacts. Significant contacts in British universities	Founded July 1982
No	Yes	Yes	Equity and preference shares	Flexible	"Hands on" management support. US connections	Launched 1981—five investments
Yes	Minority equity investments	Yes	Approximately 5 years	Generally USM or other market listing	Int'l presence in New York and Paris. High and low-tech Active help to companies	£1·3m in 6 companies
Exceptionally	Yes, 10–40%	Yes	Open	Flexible	Able to formulate equity/loan packages in co-operation with Barclays branches	19 companies —£8m
Occasionally	Up to 20%, exceptionally higher	Normally	Flexible; usually equity	Flexible; flotation preferred but aim to be long-term investors	Active management support. Long experience of venture capital in USA. Team of high-level scientific consultants	$11m in 11 companies
Possibly	Possibly, but not exclusively	Possibly, but not exclusively	Flexible according to requirements	Flexible	Exclusively hi-tech related enterprise	

This table is reproduced by kind permission of *Investors Chronicle.*

Vehicle for capital	Backers	Capital earmarked	Type of client or situation	Min/Max funds injected	Start up capital
British Technology Group (BTG) *Tel:* *(01) 403 6666*	HM Government	Open	Companies of all sizes, engaged in advanced technology. Two special schemes for small companies. Regional finance available	As appropriate	Yes
Brown Shipley Developments *Tel:* *(01) 606 9833*	Brown, Shipley & Co.	Open	Quality of individuals of prime importance and above average growth sectors	£50,000 minimum equity preference shares, may syndicate larger investments and provide loans	Yes, if individuals have previous experience
Candover Investments *Tel:* *(01) 583 5090*	7 leading UK institutions	Open	Management buy-outs and conventional development capital situations	£2m+	No
Capital Partners International *Tel:* *(01) 351 4899*	Private European Investors	Open	Companies with overseas expansion potential, i.e. an internationally marketable know-how	£10,000–£350,000 Would form syndicate for larger investments	Yes, if management has relevant experience, a detailed business plan and exceptional growth potential
Capital Ventures Ltd *Tel: Glos* *(0242) 584380*	The Colgrave Fund supported by private investors	Open	New or recently established business ventures qualifying for inclusion under the 1981 Business Start-Up Scheme	£25,000–£600,000 ordinary capital. Complete package with loan/ preference gearing can be arranged	Yes
Castle Finance *Tel: Norwich* *(0603) 22200*	Norwich Union Insurance	Open	Profitable private companies requiring capital for expansion	Normally £30,000–£500,000	Exceptionally
Cayzer, Gartmore Investments Limited *Tel:* *(01) 623 1212*	Cayzer Gartmore, subsidiary of British & Commonwealth Shipping	£30m	Small and medium sized companies with growth potential requiring equity and/or loan capital	£0·2m–£2m Larger sums syndicated	Exceptionally

Rescue capital	Equity stake	Seat on Board	Term of funding	Exit criteria	Special features	Portfolio
Exceptionally	Yes	As appropriate	Finance provided in form of share capital or project finance. Equity, preference and loan capital offered on venture capital terms	Flexible	Availability of technical, patent, management expertise.	About 400 investments and projects with a total book value of £148m
Exceptionally	Yes, usually 10–30%	Frequently in active non-executive capacity	Equity: open Loans: up to 8 years	Flexible. Aim to capitalise by flotation or sale or require running yield if little prospect of realising capital gain at outset	Other merchant banking facilities available. Aim to establish a close relationship and provide continuing financial support	32 companies
No	Always minority	Yes	Open	Flexible	Investment arranged through syndicate of shareholders and possibly other investors. Non-executive director or Chairman appointed if required to provide continuing support	12 companies £75m invested in the UK and US
By backing and/or introducing new management	Yes	Yes	Flexible to suit each situation	Flexible to suit company and other share-holders but willing to stay involved long-term	Management support and overseas marketing development	15 companies —£1·6m
No	Yes, 10–49%	Yes	Equity to be held for a minimum of 5 years	Some kind of marketability to be sought	Managers specialising in finance for new businesses	New fund
No	Yes, up to 30%	No	Medium and long term loans—fixed or variable interest	Looking for dividends: sale of equity when convenient to all shareholders	Supplementary financial services of the Norwich Union Group	Group holdings 54 companies —£11·2m
Exceptionally	Yes. Minority	Normally	Medium	Flexible	Rapid response. Creative support. Other financial services available	6 investments

Vehicle for capital	Backers	Capital earmarked	Type of client or situation	Min/Max funds injected	Start up capital
Charterhouse Development *Tel: (01) 606 7070*	Charterhouse Group	Not disclosed	Companies of above average quality, i.e. with good growing earnings	£250,000	No
CIN Industrial Finance *Tel: (01) 353 1500*	National Coal Board Pension Funds	£45m–£50m per annum	Small and medium sized companies public or private with growth potential. Equity subscription loan and equity packages, development capital and project finance are undertaken	£500,000–£2m—smaller amounts are referred to our small companies investment fund	Yes, this is also referred to our small companies investment fund
Citicorp Development Capital *Tel: (01) 438 1280*	Citicorp/Citibank	Open	Expansion capital for technology growth companies. Management buy-outs. Acquisition etc, finance for mature companies	£200,000–£5m	Exceptionally; proven management team and high growth prospects required
Clydesdale Bank Industrial Finance *Tel: Glasgow (041) 248 7070*	Clydesdale Bank/Midland Bank	£5m	Profitable private companies with potential for growth	Normally £100,000+ but will consider proposals at lower level	Yes—highly selective
Commercial Bank of the Near East *Tel: (01) 283 4041*	Range of shareholders predominantly Greek	Open	Small and medium sized companies public & private	Up to £400,000	Yes
Commonwealth Development Finance Company Ltd *Tel: (01) 407 9711*	Several Commonwealth Central Banks and 140 major UK companies	£30m or equivalent in foreign exchange	Company with proven management and profit record, preferably seeking funds for expansion	£300,000 to £1·5m	No
Council for Small Industries in Rural Areas (CoSIRA) *Tel: Salisbury (0722) 6255*	HM Government plus financial institutions including ICFC under new scheme	£20m	Companies with no more than 20 skilled employees in countryside or in towns with less than 10,000 population	£250–£75,000 or maximum ½ or ⅓ of project cost, depending upon location	Loans are available for new starters

Rescue capital	Equity stake	Seat on Board	Term of funding	Exit criteria	Special features	Portfolio
No	Yes	Yes	Open	To suit company and shareholders	Non-executive director with financial skills and experience advising and helping the company but no interference with day-to-day management	Over 125 companies in UK, France, US and Canada—£100m in unlisted companies
Yes, viable subsidiaries or divisions sometimes in the form of management takeouts	Yes, 10–49%	Yes, when a significant stake is taken in a company; panel of experienced non-executive directors available	Medium and long term loans available only with some form of equity participation	Flexible to suit the company and the shareholders	Individual equity/loan packages formulated to match the needs of company. Support given for acquisitions and developments Close working relationship with senior management encouraged	£150m in 120 investments
Exceptionally	Yes. 10–40% desired	Often	Open. Structured to suit company requirements	Open, possible flotation preferred	Fast response. Will syndicate larger transactions. Close and extensive overseas contacts through Citibank and US venture capital contacts	£8m in 15 companies in UK. $100m + in over 100 companies in US
Exceptionally— would consider backing new management	Normally 20–40%	Yes	Open	Running yield with sale when convenient to majority shareholders	Flexibility	6 companies —£900,000
Exceptionally	No	Not under normal circumstances	Open	Flexible. Good performance would encourage continuing contact	Close working relationships with senior management to promote trust and without unnecessary involvement. No bank charges	Cannot be differentiated from total bank holdings
No	Yes, 10–45%	In most cases	Up to ten years	Through local flotation or sale to partners. Looks for dividends. Discussed fully at outset	Highly flexible as to form of equity financing	75 worldwide investments— £25m
No	No	No	Building loans— 20 yrs. Working capital—5 yrs. Equipment loans— 5 yrs.	Repayment of loan	Availability of long term building loans. Local representatives throughout the country.	2,500 "live" loans—£16m committed

Vehicle for capital	Backers	Capital earmarked	Type of client or situation	Min/Max funds injected	Start up capital
County Bank *Tel:* *(01) 638 6000*	National Westminster Bank	Open	Any growing company with proven management; fianance for the company, to enable shareholders to realise part of their investment or to assist management in buying an equity stake	£100,000+	Yes for sound projects
Development Capital Group *Tel:* *(01) 486 5021*	Insurance & Pension funds, industrial companies and a major clearing bank	Open	Proven management. Minimum £100,000 pretax profit potential	£150,000– £1·5m+	Yes, under certain circumstances
East of Scotland Industrial Investments *Tel: Edinburgh (031) 225 7515*	Leading UK Institutions	£3·6m	Established profitable companies	£20,000– £400,000	Occasionally, if proven management
East of Scotland Onshore *Tel: Edinburgh (031) 225 7515*	Leading UK institutions	£8m	Established companies—the oil service sector	£30,000–£1m	Occasionally if proven management
EDITH PLC *Tel:* *(01) 928 7822*	Listed authorised investment trust, (managed by ICFC)	£24m issued share capital	Established private and unlisted public companies and smaller listed companies	£5,000–£1m	No
Electra Risk Capital *Tel:* *(01) 836 7766*	Private individual investors	£8·7m	Investments qualifying for business start up relief. Start-ups and companies who have traded for less than five years	£100,000 to £750,000 over a period	Yes

Rescue capital	Equity stake	Seat on Board	Term of funding	Exit criteria	Special features	Portfolio
Exceptionally	If appropriate; often 10–15%; usually less than 25%	Usually ask for the right but rarely exercise it	Loans up to 20 years; equity open	No set criteria— whenever it suits the company and its shareholders	Full range of merchant banking services including advice on financial and other matters; further substantial funds available if company wishes to expand	Over £80m provided in equity linked funding to more than 160 companies
Yes	Yes, minority	Yes, in participating non-executive capacity	5 years upwards	As seems appropriate	Directors are all highly experienced ex-industry	30-40 companies— £20m
Exceptionally	Always minority	Yes	Equity and long term loan capital	Open	Able to formulate financial package to suit client. Supplementary financial advice available. Close working relationship with management	5 companies —£1·1m
Occasionally	Yes, always minority	Yes	Equity and long term capital	Open	Able to formulate financial package to suit client. Extensive contacts in the oil service industry. Supplementary financial advice available	14 companies —£8m
No	Yes, minority, enabling shareholders to realise investment	No	Provision of cash or exchange of shares for personal shareholders or family trusts	No time limit on duration of investment	Roll-over relief on CGT	200 companies —£20m (by cost)
Yes (for qualifying companies)	Yes to 50%	Yes	Only equity investment— no dividend	Flexible	Approved investment fund under Business Start Up Scheme. Rapid decisions and close co-operation with entrepreneur	Existing fund to include some 40 investments and expected to issue new fund in early 1983

Vehicle for capital	Backers	Capital earmarked	Type of client or situation	Min/Max funds injected	Start up capital
English & Caledonian PLC *Tel:* *(01) 626 7197* *(01) 283 3531*	Clients of Gartmore Investment, Scottish United Investors and other investors	Initially £5m	Private companies able and willing to obtain a USM placing or a full listing within 5 years	£200,000–£750,000. Larger sums can be syndicated among existing shareholders	Yes, if management has previous experience in similar markets
Equity Capital for Industry *Tel:* *(01) 606 8513*	City Institutions	Initially £42m	Industrial companies with capitalisation of £1m–£40m or similar unquoted	£200,000–£2m Smaller sums available from associate fund	Exceptionally
European Investment Bank (European Community's long term bank) *Tel:* *(01) 222 2933*	1) Scheme operated by DoI and Scottish, Welsh and Northern Ireland Offices 2) Schemes operated by ICFC, Midland Bank 3) Schemes operated by WDA, SDA and Clydesdale Bank 4) Scheme operated by ICFC (under Ortoli facility)	Total £36m in facilities in operation at end-1982; extra funding expected to be available in 1983	For small and medium sized ventures (in UK assisted areas for 1, 2 + 3)	In all cases maximum contribution is 50% of fixed asset cost of project 1) Loans between £15,000 and £4·25m 2) £15,000 and £2m 3) £15,000 and £250,000 4) £15,000–£250,000	Loans can be made for sound projects by new companies with adequate equity
Federation Pension Fund *Tel:* *(01) 636 3828*	The National Federation of Self Employed and Small Businesses, City of Westminster Assurance	Open	Established self employed/small business; 3 year record; must be a member of the Federation	£15,000–£250,000 now under review	No
First Welsh General Investment Trust Limited *Tel: Cardiff* *(0222) 396131*	Commercial Bank of Wales PLC	£100,000 initially	Management buy-out	Subject to negotiation	In certain circumstances
Fountain Development Capital Fund *Tel:* *(01) 628 8011*	Hill Samuel, pension funds and insurance companies	£7m	Any company with two years trading record	£50,000–£750,000	Yes in certain situations

escue pital	Equity stake	Seat on Board	Term of funding	Exit criteria	Special features	Portfolio
s, if new anagement roduced or uation is a anagement y-out"	Yes 10–49%	Yes	Preferably an equity stake. Loans can be arranged subject to an equity stake	Flexible. Aim to capitalise by flotation	Do not necessarily require dividend on equity stake. Wide industrial experience available to support management	5 companies —£2m. Its shareholders have in the last 4 years invested £15m in similar ventures
es	Yes, usually 5–25%	Depends on circumstances	Long term: equity/convertible/loan package; tailored to circumstances	Flexible	Long term relationship with undertaking not to deal in shares	27 companies —£29m invested
o	No	No	1) 7 years including 2 year capital repayment moratorium. Fixed rate in region of 10% (end 1982) 2, 3+4) Up to 8 years including 2 year capital repayment moratorium. Fixed rate in region of 11% (end-1982)	Not applicable	Priority to small and medium sized companies. EIB disburses in foreign currency but UK Government covers exchange risk for small premium (included in final lending rate)	Over £60m lent since 1978 to about 175 companies
lo	No	No	Up to 20 years	Repayment of loan	Available to Federation members only. Linked with competitive retirement benefit scheme. Available from Federation member brokers	The fund is being built up by pension contributions. Currently, no loans have been granted but the Assurer accepts applications for use of its own or other capital
lo	Yes and/or option— not essential	Possibly by nominee — not essential	Up to ten years	By negotiation	None	New fund
ccasionally	Always minority	Yes	Equity and/or loan	Open	Availability of merchant bank services and other specialist management assistance	UK only

61

Vehicle for capital	Backers	Capital earmarked	Type of client or situation	Min/Max funds injected	Start up capital
Greater London Enterprise Board *Tel: (01) 633 1487*	Greater London Council	£25m	Must be of 'benefit to London'	Up to £1m but higher in exceptional circumstances	Yes
Gresham Trust *Tel: (01) 606 6474*	Grovewood Securities Ltd (Ultimate holding company Eagle Star Holdings PLC)	Open	Profitable private companies looking for expansion, realisation of shareholders' interests, help in management buy-outs	£50,000–£500,000 Will syndicate larger amounts	Where experience and track record exists in previous business
Guidehouse Limited *Tel: (01) 606 6321*	Private	Open	Completely open and flexible Syndicated purchases, management buy-outs, USM venture or development capital	Up to £200,000 directly—syndicate or advise in larger situations	Yes
Hafren Investment Finance Ltd. *Tel: Treforest (044 385) 2666*	Welsh Development Agency	£1m	High growth operations	£10,000–£100,000	Yes
Hambro International Venture Fund	Various	$50·5m	Growth Companies	$250,000–$500,000	Yes
Hambros Advanced Technology Trust	Hambros Bank	£5m	Technology Industries. High Growth	£100,000–£500,000	Yes
Highlands and Islands Development Board *Tel: Inverness (0463) 34171*	HM Government (Scottish Office)	£15m per annum	Manufacturing tourist, agriculture, fisheries and other industries in the Scottish Highlands and Islands	Up to £400,000	Yes
Industrial and Commercial Finance Corporation (ICFC) *Tel: (01) 928 7822*	Finance for Industry (Bank of England and clearing banks)	Open	Small and medium sized companies public and private	£5,000–£2m	Yes
Innotech Investments Limited *Tel: (01) 834 2492*	Private Individuals	Open	Fast growing small to medium sized companies operating in higher technology areas	£100,000 to £500,000	Exceptionally

escue apital	Equity stake	Seat on Board	Term of funding	Exit criteria	Special features	Portfolio
s	As necessary	As necessary	—	—	Investment linked to employment creation/ protection in GLC area	—
ceptionally	Usually, but always a minority holding	Yes	Preference shares or loans: 5-10 Equity: Open	Running yield with sale if and when sought by major shareholders	Gresham director on Board to give advice and support backed by full range of merchant banking services	£60 companies— £6m
es	Preferably yes, but flexible approach, e.g. royalty income	If required	Open and flexible	Flexible— tailored to be realistic in relation to the situation	Corporate financial and acquisition and disposal advice	Company and partners investing approx £½m in around 10 companies
es	Yes	Yes	Open	Flexible	Advisory service related development capital funds available	Commenced July 1982
es	Yes	Usually	Variable	Public offering/ sale of co.		5 companies
es	Yes	Usually	5 yrs typical	USM criteria/ sale of co.		10 companies
es	Up to 40%	Exceptionally	5-10 years. 20 years for building loans	Equity by sale	Supplementary advisory and support services. Tie-up with Bank of Scotland and ICFC to form Highland Venture Capital	6,500 businesses assisted
ceptionally	Yes, minority	Not under normal circumstances. Nominee director only with mutual agreement	Fixed interest loans medium and long term	Redemption negotiated individually, no requirement to sell shares	18 branch offices, leasing and H.P. advisory services, sale and leaseback facilities management consultancy	3,800 companies— £460m
arely	Yes—minority (25 to 40%)	Yes	Equity: open Loans: 3-6 years	Sale when appropriate Repayment flexible	Management support and advice. Long term relationship Seeks capital gain not running yield	£3m— 6 companies

Vehicle for capital	Backers	Capital earmarked	Type of client or situation	Min/Max funds injected	Start up capital
INTEX Executives (UK) Ltd + E. P. Woods Investments Ltd. *Tel: (01) 831 6925/ 242-2263*	Private and institutional investors and trusts	Open	Industrial and commercial enterprises, with special reference to high technology and innovation	£10,000 to £1m	Yes
Larpent Newton & Co Ltd *Tel: (01) 831 9991*	Advisory work for leading UK institutions	Open	Unquoted companies requiring development capital and management buy-outs	£50,000–£2m	Yes with experienced management
LEDU—The small Business Agency for Northern Ireland *Tel: (0232) 691031*	Department of Economic Development	Open	Mainly manufacturing and service companies employing up to 50 people in Northern Ireland	£1,500+	Loans, guarantees and grants available
Leopold Joseph & Sons Ltd *Tel: (01) 588 2323*	Leopold Joseph & Sons Ltd and clients	Open	Good management track record, companies with growth record pre-tax profit in excess of £100,000	Open	Exceptional where entrepreneur have previous experience a can make a sound finance contribution
Lovat Enterprise Fund *Tel: (01) 621 1212*	NCB Pension Funds, Legal & General, Prudential, Electra Investment Trust, Equitable Life	£7·5m	Expansion financing, mainly private companies earning £100,000+ pre-tax	£100,000–£1m	No
Mathercourt Securities Limited *Tel: (01) 831 9001*	Private & institutional investors	Open	Private UK companies including USM candidates. Close working relationship with management	£25,000–£3·5m syndicated as appropriate	Yes
Melville St Investment. *Tel: Edinburgh (031) 226 4071*	The British Linen Bank, The Airways Pension Scheme, The Standard Life Assurance Company, Scottish American Investment Company, Scottish Northern Investment Trust, The Edinburgh Investment Trust	£8m	Profitable companies with good financial discipline and new companies with established management	£50,000–£500,000 May syndicate larger investments	Yes

scue pital	Equity stake	Seat on Board	Term of funding	Exit criteria	Special features	Portfolio
s, if viable	Usually minority only. In appropriate circumstances up to 75%	Depends upon circumstances	Equity and loan arranged according to circumstances	Not applicable	Complementary managerial and technical support and advisory services	n/a
s	Usually	Yes	Individually tailored	Flexible	Close relationship with management. General commercial and financial advice	£15m under supervision in 15+ investments
aintenance kages" are vided	Yes	Not usually	Grants/ loans/ guarantees average 5 years	Repayment of loan or grant as required under terms and conditions of offer	Financial package tailored to requirements. Business technical, marketing and accountancy and design advice	1,000 businesses assisted
	Yes	Reserve right to appoint non-executive director	Open	Dividend flow, listing on Stock Exchange	Adaptability. Full range of financial and advisory services	Cannot be differentiated from total bank holdings
	5–40%	Reserves the right to appoint non-executive director	Open	Flexible, but objective is marketability	Independent fund managed by MJH Nightingale. Minority equity shareholdings spread separately amongst the five long term institutional investors	5 companies —£2·5m
s, where uity can place debt	Yes, 3–30%	Normally. Often represented by experienced nominee	Tailored to suit circumstances	Flexible, but objective is marketability	Health care financing	Wide coverage; £10m funded in past two years
ceptionally	Minority	Retains the right to appoint a director	Long term capital	Flexible. Building up investment portfolio and does not seek to realise investments	Other merchant banking facilities available through The British Linen Bank	28 companies —£5m

Vehicle for capital	Backers	Capital earmarked	Type of client or situation	Min/Max funds injected	Start up capital
Meritor Investments *Tel:* *(01) 606 2179*	Midland Bank, Rolls Royce Pension Fund	£4m	Development situations and shareholders' needs	£100,000– £250,000 May syndicate larger investments	No
Merseyside Enterprise Fund Ltd *Tel:* *(051) 227 1366*	British Technology Group (BTG)	£1m—further funds from private sector	Start ups and small companies with growth potential	Up to £100,000— syndicate larger investments	Yes
Midland Bank Industrial Equity Holdings Group *Tel:* *(01) 638 8861*	Midland Bank	Open	Development situations and shareholders needs	£5,000–£2m	Yes
Minster Trust *Tel:* *(01) 623 1050*	Minster Assets	Open	Small and medium sized companies, public and private. Profitable private companies looking for expansion realisation of shareholders' interests, help for management for buying equity	£100,000– £250,000	Exceptionally where entrepreneur have previous experience
Montagu Investment Management Limited *Tel:* *(01) 588 1750*	Quoted Investment Trusts	Open	Small and medium sized companies, public or private, with growth potential	Normally £200,000 to £3m	Only occasionally
Moracrest Investments *Tel:* *(01) 628 8409*	Midland Bank, Prudential Group and British Gas Pension Fund	£15m	Development situations and shareholders' needs	£200,000+ May syndicate larger investments	Yes
National Westminster Bank under the terms of Capital Loan Scheme (Approach through local Branch but if guidance is needed to identify a suitable branch) *Tel:* *(01) 726 1891*		Open	Companies engaged in or planning to set up a business with good growth prospects backed by sound management; must bank or be willing to bank with National Westminster Bank	£10,000– £100,000	Yes
Newmarket Co. (1981) Ltd. (U.K. subsidiary Newmarket (Venture Capital) Ltd.) *Tel:* *(01) 638 4551*	London listed company with institutional and general public shareholders	$93m. of which a material sum is available for U.K. investment	Application of new technology or innovation	Normally U.S.$200,000– $1m but occasionally higher	Yes, but not exclusively

...escue ...apital	Equity stake	Seat on Board	Term of funding	Exit criteria	Special features	Portfolio
...o	Yes, minority	Normally	Open	Dividend flow: sale when convenient to majority shareholders	Adaptability	6 companies —£1·6m
...lo	Yes	Usually	Open	Flexible. Prepared to offer buy-back	Local fund to invest in companies located in the Merseyside area	Launched 1982 —two investments
...nly in takeover ...ituations or ...estructuring ...f CTT. ...ould back ...ew management	Yes, minority	Usual	Open	Dividend flow: sale when convenient to majority shareholders	Adaptability	109 companies —£23·5m
...xceptionally	Yes, minority	Not under normal circumstances	Open	Flexible	Complementary advisory and support services	Not stated
...Occasionally	Yes, minority	Expects the right to approve non-executive director	Open	Basis for realisation expected but flexible	Flexibility	£20m unlisted U.S. and U.K.
...lo	Yes, minority	Normally	Open	Dividend flow: sale when convenient to majority shareholders	Adaptability	16 companies —£8·7m
...Yes	An option to subscribe for shares is taken by a subsidiary, Growth Options Limited, usually for less than 25% always for less than 50%	Takes the right to appoint a director but rarely, if ever, likely to exercise the right	Up to 10 years	Flexible	Finance is provided in the form of a subordinated loan guaranteed by the directors. The other facilities of the National Westminster Bank Group are available in appropriate cases	73 companies —£3·6m
Yes, if appropriate as an investment, but likely to be confined to companies already invested in.	Never a controlling stake	Right to appoint independent director where appropriate	Primarily equity; no requirement for immediate income	As appropriate for long term investor	Group has built up substantial experience since 1972, particularly in US and UK; also invests in other countries	34 companies in U.S.—$65m. 5 companies in U.K.—£2m. 3 companies elsewhere, and approx. $25m in cash

Vehicle for capital	Backers	Capital earmarked	Type of client or situation	Min/Max funds injected	Start up capital
Noble Grossart Investments *Tel: Edinburgh (031) 226 7011*	Noble Grossart and Scottish institutional shareholders	Unlimited	Good management in growth "buy-out" or turnround situations	£50,000–£1m	Yes, if the management has good trac record in previous business
Northern Venture Capital Syndicate *Tel: 031-557-3560*	Private individuals under the Business Start-Up Scheme	£300,000	Investments qualifying for Business Start-up Scheme ie start-ups and companies trading for less than 5 years	£25,000 to £75,000	Yes
Oakland Management Holdings Limited *Tel: Hungerford Berks (04886) 3555*	A leading UK institution	£2·5m	New technology growth opportunities	£50,000– £250,000	Not normally
Oakwood Loan Finance Ltd *Tel: (01) 403 6666*	British Technology Group (BTG)	Open	Small companies with growth potential	£15,000– £50,000	Yes
PA Developments Ltd *Tel: (01) 589 7050*	Merchant Navy Officers' Pension Fund	Open	Profitable private companies requiring capital for expansion; or purchase of existing equity stakes. Particularly service industries or technology-based companies	£200,000– to £1m	No
Pegasus Holdings Limited *Tel: 01) 626 1500*	Lloyds Bank Group	Open	Management buy-out, development capital, replacement capital. For companies with proven management, pre-tax profits in excess of £50,000, and with growth potential	Minimum £100,000. No maximum, but may syndicate large investments	No
Prudential Assurance Company Ltd *Tel: (01) 405 9222*	Prudential Group	Open	Primarily development capital situations and buy-outs	Typically £50,000—£1m	Occasionally
Prutec *Tel: (01) 828 2082*	Member of the Prudential Group	Initially £20m	Development of high technology	Open	Yes

escue apital	Equity stake	Seat on Board	Term of funding	Exit criteria	Special features	Portfolio
o	Yes, usually 20–40%	Yes with active non-executive participation	Open	Flexible but no requirement to sell	Able to contribute financial and general management skills	20 companies —£10m
es (for ualifying mpanies)	Yes—up to 50%	Yes	Equity capital. Dividends not a priority	Flexible	Approved fund under Business Start-Up Scheme. Funds to be invested by April 1983.	--
es, for rowth pportunity	Yes	Yes	Flexible up to 7 years	Flexible	Strong management partnership	8 companies
xceptionally	10% to 20% by option	No	Option linked, unsecured, 5-year loan. 3-year capital repayment holiday	Flexible	Customer has right to buy out option by a formula linked to profits	35 companies —£1·6m
o	Yes, up to 40%	Yes	Equity preferably but will consider equity/loan packages	Flexible—long term	Able to offer the resources of PA Management Consultants in addition to provision of development capital	In first year invested £1m in 3 companies
lo	Yes. Usually 10–33⅓%	Reserve the right to appoint a non-executive director, but do not always exercise	Flexible	Flexible to suit company requirements	Have access to extensive clearing bank resources and ability to formulate equity/loan packages in conjunction with Lloyds branches	Started investing 1982
xceptionally	Yes	Usually	Open	Flexible	Prepared to take longer-term view	46 companies
xceptionally	Up to 49%	When appropriate	Open	To suit company and shareholders	Broad technical and financial expertise; flexible in approach and giving long-term financial support	20 investments —£10m. 28 in-house development projects in all areas of high technology

Vehicle for capital	Backers	Capital earmarked	Type of client or situation	Min/Max funds injected	Start up capital
Rainford Venture Capital *Tel: St. Helens (0744) 37227*	Pilkington Prudential, St. Helens Trust and others	Open	Entrepreneurs; start-up or rapid growth in North West	£50,000– £350,000	Yes
Safeguard Industrial Investments *Tel: (01) 581 4455*	Over 84% of shares held by 17 major insurance companies or pension funds	Open	Small or medium sized UK companies	£50,000– £250,000	Exceptionally
Scottish Allied Investors *Tel: Glasgow (041) 204 1321 (041) 226 3551*	James Finlay, Royal Bank Development Ltd, Scottish Western Trust Co. Ltd.	£3m	Profitable private companies looking for expansion capital	£50,000– £500,000	No
Scottish Development Agency *Tel: Glasgow (041) 248 2700* **Small Business Division** *Tel: Edinburgh (031) 343 1911*	UK Government	Open	Manufacturing and service businesses operating in Scotland	Open	Yes
Scottish Offshore Investors *Tel: Glasgow (041) 204 1321*	James Finlay and other financial institutions	£3m	Energy related service companies with growth prospects	£50,000– £250,000	Exceptionally
Second Northern Venture Capital Syndicate *Tel: (031) 557-3560*	Private individuals under the Business Start-Up Scheme	Fund closed 31st January 1983	Investment qualifying for Business Start-Up Scheme ie start-ups and companies trading for less than 5 years	£25,000 min.	Yes
Sharp Unquoted Midland Investment *Tel: Birmingham (021) 236 5801*	Legal & General, Royal Insurance, Sun Life Assurance Society and others	£8·5m	Successful private companies and management buy-outs	£150,000– £850,000	No
Small Company Innovation Fund (SCIF) *Tel: (01) 403 6666*	British Technology Group (BTG)	£2m	Small companies involved in technological and innovative activities	£15,000 to £60,000	Yes
Smithdown Investments *Tel: (01) 408 1502*	Private individuals	Open	Start-up situations and very small companies	£5,000–£50,000	Yes
Stewart Fund Managers *Tel: Edinburgh (031) 226 3271*	Scottish American Investment, Stewart Enterprise Investment	Open	Fast growing companies	£50,000– £500,000	Exceptionally only

Rescue capital	Equity stake	Seat on Board	Term of funding	Exit criteria	Special features	Portfolio
No	Yes, but preferably not control	Yes	Primarily equity. Loans where appropriate to agreed term	Equity—according to circumstances. Loan repayment	Backers provide on-going technical/ managerial support	7 companies —£1·1m
No	Yes	Not usually	Medium to long	Flexible	Continuing financial advice available	200 + listed and unlisted investments —£16·4m
No	Yes, between 20–49%	Yes	Medium or long term investment in equity or loan/equity package	Flexible—building up portfolio and not seeking to realise investment	Adaptability together with a management consultancy service	2 companies £520,000
Exceptionally	Where appropriate	If equity taken— right to appoint non-executive director	2–20 years equity open	By agreement with other shareholders	Advisory services. ECSC low interest funds available. Concessionary interest rates in rural areas	£23m in approx 550 companies
No	Yes, between 20–49%	Yes	Medium or long term. Equity or loan/equity package	Flexible—not seeking to realise investments	Other merchant banking facilities in UK and US	6 companies —£1·6m
Yes (for qualifying companies)	Yes—up to 50%	Yes	Equity capital dividends not a priority	Flexible	Approved fund under business Start-Up Scheme. Funds to be invested by April 1984.	—
No	10·35%	Negotiable	Open	Looking for earnings; no pressure to sell	Based in Midlands; quick decisions in principle	13 companies —£4m
Exceptionally	Yes, 10% to 35%	No	Equity plus preference shares and unsecured loan	Flexible	Ability to evaluate high technology companies	19 companies —£1m
No	Normally	By agreement	Open	Open	Financial management advice etc.	6 companies —£300,000
Exceptionally only	Yes, but always minority and can be part of a package	Not usually	Open	Flexible—but marketability is target	Finance packages of equity, preference and loans available. Experience in unquoted companies	£25m in 50 investments

Vehicle for capital	Backers	Capital earmarked	Type of client or situation	Min/Max funds injected	Start up capital
Thamesdale Investment & Finance Co Ltd *Tel: (01) 629 8322*	American and European investors	Open	Small/medium sized companies. Equity and loan facilities	£25,000 upwards	Yes, in exceptional circumstance
Thomson Clive Growth Companies Fund Thomson Clive Investments *Tel: (01) 491 4809*	Leading UK institutions	Open	Private companies requiring capital for expansion and having high quality management	£20,000–£300,000	Exceptionally if manageme of high quali and operatio within specifi areas of interest
Trust of Property Shares PLC *Tel: (01) 486 4684*	Management support with clearing bankers	Open	Small size private property companies with growth potential requiring capital for expansion	£25,000 to £250,000 Syndicate for larger investments with participation	Possibly, if management of proven calibre
UKP-EA Growth Fund Ltd *Tel: (01) 831 9991*	United Kingdom Provident Institution and the English Association Group PLC	Initially £2m	Development capital situations. Management buy-outs. Not quoted companies	£50,000–£300,000 but will lead syndicates for larger sums	Only where management has successf track record i in related or similar field
Venture Founders *Tel: (0295) 65881*	British Investment Trusts	Open	Small-medium size growth companies	£50,000–£350,000	Yes
Welsh Development Agency *Tel: Treforest (044 385) 2666*	UK Government	Open	Manufacturing and service industries in Wales	£2,000–£1m	Yes
Western Enterprise Fund Ltd *Tel: (0803) 862271*	British Technology Group (BTG) and Dartington & Co Ltd	£2m—further funds from private sector	Start ups and small companies with growth potential	Up to £100,000 —syndicate larger investments	Yes
West Midlands Enterprise Board Limited *Tel: Birmingham (021) 236-8855*	West Midlands County Council and various financial institutions	£6m	Manufacturing and productive service sector companies employing or likely to employ 100 + in the West Midlands	£100,000–£3m	Yes
West Yorkshire Enterprise Board Ltd *Tel: Wakefield (0924) 367111*	West Yorkshire Metropolitan County Council	£5·8m for 1983	Business development; plant modernisation; balance sheet reconstruction; new ventures; management buy-outs	£10,000–£500,000	Yes

Rescue capital	Equity stake	Seat on Board	Term of funding	Exit criteria	Special features	Portfolio
Yes, if viable	Yes, 10–40%	Non executive	Open	Flexible	Good overseas contacts. Facilitate export and trading situations	All activities in separate holding companies
Exceptionally	Yes, usually minority	Usually	Open	Flexible	Management support and extensive contacts particularly in US. Emphasis on technology in portfolio	£6m between the two funds in UK and US
No	Yes 10–35%	Yes	Open	Flexible Prefer dividends: Sale of equity when convenient to all shareholders	Merchant banking facilities can be introduced	Supplementary group of 6 companies
Yes	Yes, usually up to 30%. Never control	Yes	A package tailored to requirements. Loans up to 10 years	Flexible	Continuing advice and merchant banking support if required	New fund
Exceptionally	Yes prefer minority position	Yes	Open	Flexible	Seek out start-up and early stage. Strong equity orientation	8 companies— £1·5m
Only by supporting new management in takeover situation	Yes	Reserve right. Exercised for larger investments	5–15 years— equity open	Sales by agreement with other shareholders	Range of advisory services. Outside businessmen appointed directors	156 companies —£10·5m
Exceptionally	Yes. 10% to 49%	Yes	Open	Flexible. To suit shareholders and company	Local fund to invest in companies in Devon and Cornwall. Financial and general advice available	Launched 1982 —three investments
Only if viability can be proven	Can provide a flexible package of loan/equity capital	Take the right	Normal financial criteria, but prepared to wait for a long-term capital gain	Flexible	—	£2m invested
Yes	Possibly	Possibly	Medium/long as required	To suit client	West Yorkshire based companies; joint ventures; most forms of funding available	—
						—

Other sources of finance

A rather helpful and significant concession to private investors in small businesses was made in the 1980 Budget. Henceforth, investors who buy shares in small unquoted companies will be able to offset losses incurred in the disposal of such shares against taxable income, not just against capital gains. The problem, of course, is how do you find private individuals with risk capital? Surprisingly enough they do exist and, equally surprisingly, one way of getting at them is through stockbrokers. Stockbrokers have, in the past, been very coy about recommending investments of this kind, but the new legislation might, as it is intended to do, make them change their policy.

One is reluctant to suggest names of brokers because, as in the case of finance houses, there are horses for courses; but here again discreet inquiries by your accountant or bank manager might bear fruit.

Another source of information on private individuals with money to invest are solicitors and accountants in rural areas and small towns. They are often much more in touch with the situation on the availability of such funds than their brethren in larger, more imposing metropolitan offices.

Private Company, a private fortnightly subscription only magazine published by Duke Street Brokers, 35 Thayer Street, London W1, contains a regular eight-page 'marketplace' supplement which often carries information about private investors. LEntA, the London Enterprise Agency, publishes a monthly list of business propositions which occasionally includes details of a private investor.

If you are in a bigger league you might also think about talking to your advisers about going into the Unlisted Securities Market. This is a method of offering shares without the huge expense of 'going public'. However, your annual profit would have to be in the £100,000 pre-tax class for this option to be feasible.

Table 3.1 gives a comprehensive survey of sources of finance other than clearing banks, of the type of deal they offer, the criteria you must meet and the terms of the arrangement.

Using your own money

Inevitably you will have to put up at least some money of your own. Even if your form of business involves selling an intangible skill, as in the case of consultancy, you are going to need some basic equipment, not to mention the fact that you have to have enough money to live on until your business income builds up. You should bear in mind that any money of your own that you put into your firm should be earning a rate of interest comparable to what you could get outside (ie greater than its opportunity cost), and this must be reflected in your costing and estimating. This topic is dealt with in more detail in Chapter 1.7.

Apart from ready cash in the form of savings, jewellery and other liquid and saleable personal assets you will also have other, less immediate resources to turn to. The most obvious is your house and if you bought it before the huge rise in property prices which took place in the early 1970s its current value may be far in excess of your mortgage. You could take out a second mortgage on this basis, but interest rates on second mortgages are very high. Moreover, taking out a second mortgage will involve your spouse, since one person cannot obtain a second mortgage on the marital home without the other's permission. A better approach would be to take out a mortgage on anther house and sell the one you are in.

Life insurance policies are also worth bearing in mind because companies will generally be prepared to lend money against up to 90 per cent of their surrender value. Whether this yields a worthwhile amount of cash obviously varies from case to case. Interest rates on these loans, however, are generally less than on bank overdrafts.

Raising money by effective cash management

Any method of raising money from the outside costs money. In a period of high interest rates, borrowing can be so costly as to swallow up the entire profits of a business that is over reliant on it. There are instances where borrowing huge amounts of money has made sense, for instance in the property market, where the value of assets in the early 1970s increased much faster than the value of the money borrowed to acquire them. But subsequent events showed that this is dependent on the assumption that the asset does go on appreciating in value at a very rapid rate, and certainly from the point of view of the smaller business one could state as golden rules the following: never borrow more than you have to, never buy until you need to. And when you need to, consider whether hire purchase or even leasing might not make more sense for you than committing cash to an outright purchase. Remember it is cash that pays the bills, not assets or paper profits.

A surprising amount of borrowing can be avoided by effective cash management. It is not dishonest to take the maximum period of payment allowed by your suppliers, and though you do not want to get the reputation of being a slow payer once you have established a reputation of being a reliable account your suppliers may give you quite a bit of leeway before they start pressing you for payment even on an overdue sum. Nor is it dishonest to take note that some suppliers press for payment fairly quickly, whereas others are more lax. The former get paid first.

The reverse is true in the case of the customers you supply. Send out invoices as soon as the work is done. You are more likely to get paid at that point than some weeks later when the novelty has worn off and maybe quibbles have arisen. Send out statements punctually and make sure that your terms of payment are observed.

Take one simple example of how money can work for your business. If your VAT quarter is January to March you have to pay over the VAT you have billed to your customers minus the VAT you have been billed by your suppliers by the end of April. Thus, if you can send a lot of invoices out to customers on 1 January and get the money in quickly all your VAT can sit in a deposit account for nearly four months. Equally, if you are planning to buy a large piece of equipment (say, a van) on which there is many hundreds of pounds VAT for you to claim back, juggling with the precise date on which you make the purchase can minimise the damage to your cash flow.

Progress payments

In the case of work done on contract — say a design or consultancy job involving sizeable sums of money over a longer period of time like three or four months — it is worth trying to persuade your customer to make advance and/or progress payments. After all, you are going to be involved in considerable expenditure before the final sum becomes due. Whether an approach of this kind should be made depends of course on how well you know the customer and how badly you think he needs you. If you need his work more than he needs your services, you should consider a bank overdraft, though the cost of this should be reflected in your charges.

Credit factoring

Credit management is a tricky business which has sunk more than one promising new enterprise which, hungry for business, too inexperienced or simply too busy to pay attention to time-consuming detail, has let its credit index — the length of time money is outstanding — get out of control. A possible solution is to have a credit factor to look after this aspect for you. The firm using their services continues to send out its own invoices but the factor, who, of course, gets copies of the invoices, takes over the whole business of collecting the receivables. He will also generally give advice on credit limits and, if required to do so, may be able to discount the invoices, ie allow you to draw cash from him against a percentage of the amounts he is due to collect. Naturally a fairly substantial fee is charged for this service, varying with turnover, and on the whole they are not interested in firms whose annual turnover is less than £100,000, nor in those invoicing too many small amounts to small customers. Your bank should be able to advise you on the choice of a factor. Indeed a number of banks have subsidiaries who offer a factoring service. There is also now an Association of British Factors, made up of some of the largest firms in the business.

Coping with expansion

A recent British Prime Minister came in for some derisive criticism when he described the dire state of the British economy at that time as 'suffering from the problems of success'. It is, nevertheless, a phrase which would ring a bell with many a businessman caught unprepared on a tide of expansion, even though at the level of the firm the symptoms are somewhat different. They may emerge as problems with people, when the staff who were in at the beginning find it difficult to handle a larger-scale operation; or as mistakes made in interviewing and selecting people for new jobs in an expanding company; or simply when the owners are stretched in too many different directions to look at individual trouble spots in enough detail.

Most frequently these trouble spots turn out to be connected, directly or indirectly, with finance. You are producing something for which there is a demand; the world starts beating a path to your door; you appear to be selling your product profitably, and suddenly, in the midst of apparent plenty, you start running out of cash. In that case what has probably happened is that you have forgotten that in general you do not get paid until you have delivered the goods, but your suppliers and the additional staff you have taken on have to be paid out of cash flow generated by a previous and smaller scale of operations.

The way to avoid this situation is to make complete budgeting and cash flow forecasts (see Chapter 1.7) because you will then be able to select the financial package that is appropriate: short-term loans and overdrafts to meet seasonal or fluctuating demands, such as the materials to supply a big contract; long-term finance for plant, machinery or vehicles, or to make a tempting acquisition; and finance from within by tighter controls and better cash management to keep the ordinary course of expansion on an even keel. In other words, the trick is to find the right mixture, not just to grab the first jar of financial medicine on the shelf. It may not contain anything like the cure you need.

Checklist: raising capital

1. How much do you need? Have you made an initial cash flow projection?
2. Is it to finance short- or long-term financial facilities?
3. Should you be looking to your bank for overdraft facilities? If so, to what limit?
4. Should you be looking for a loan from your bank or some other commercial or official body? If so, how much and over what period?
5. Have you considered leasing or hire purchase as an alternative to raising a lump sum? If this option is open to you, have you worked out the cost of leasing and credit finance as compared to interest charges on loans?
6. If your need for cash is related to difficulties with credit control, have you considered invoice factoring?
7. Have you considered turning personal assets into cash?
8. Assuming options 5, 6 and 7 have been considered and rejected, have you worked out how to repay the loan and interest charges?
9. What security can you offer a lender, and has it been independently valued?
10. Exactly how do you propose to use the money?
11. Have you prepared a written description of your firm, what skills the key people in it have to offer, what your objectives

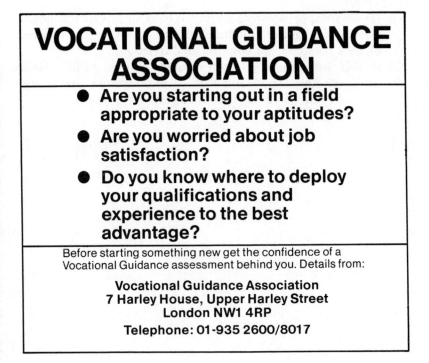
are, how your product or service compares with the competition, what firm orders you have secured and what your realistic expectations, opportunities and goals are?

12. Do you have supporting evidence on orders you have obtained or are likely to obtain?

13. Have you (and your associates, if any) made as full a commitment to your enterprise in terms of time and money as can reasonably be expected of you?

14. Have you previously obtained financial help for this or any other business? Have you repaid it within the period due?

15. If you have any loans outstanding on the business, how much are they for, for what purpose and how are they secured?

16. Can you produce an up-to-date balance sheet showing the present financial state of your company?

17. Do you have a detailed cash flow projection, monthly over the first two years and quarterly thereafter, showing cash flow over the period of the loan?

18. Do you have annual projected profit and loss accounts and balance sheets over the period of the loan?

19. If you are approaching a merchant bank or private individual for venture capital how much of the equity in and control of your company are you prepared to let go?
20. If you are raising money to enable you to fulfil a large contract, have you talked to your customer about the possibility of his paying you in stages?

1.4: Professional and Other Outside Advisers

We have already touched on the importance of the role that professional advisers, particularly accountants and solicitors, are going to play in the formation of your business, whether it is to be a limited company or some other kind of entity. You are going to be using their advice quite frequently, not only at the beginning but also later, in matters such as acquiring premises, suing a customer for payment, preparing a set of accounts or finding out what items are allowable against your or your company's tax bill. Obviously, therefore, how you choose and use these advisers is a matter for careful thought.

Making the right choice

Many people think that there is some kind of special mystique attached to membership of a profession and that any lawyer or accountant is going to do a good job for them. The fact is, though, that while they do have useful specialist knowledge the competence with which they apply it can be very variable. A high proportion of people who have bought a house, for instance, can tell you of errors and delays in the conveyancing process; and some accountants entrusted with their client's tax affairs have been known to send in large bills for their services, while overlooking claims for legitimate expenses that were the object of employing them in the first place.

So do not just go to the solicitor or accountant who happens to be nearest; nor should you go to someone you only know in a social capacity. Ask friends who are already in business on a similar scale, and if possible of a similar nature to your own, for recommendations. (If you already have a bank manager you know well, he may also be able to offer useful advice.) The kind of professional adviser you should be looking for at this stage is not a big office in a central location. He will have bigger fish to fry and after the initial interview you may well be fobbed off with an articled clerk. Apart from that he will be expensive, for he has big office overheads to meet. On the other hand, a one-man operation can create a problem if the one man is ill or on holiday. The ideal office will be a suburban one, preferably close to where you intend to set up business because knowledge of local conditions and personalities can be invaluable, with two or three partners. Apart from that, personal impressions do count. You will probably not want to take on an adviser who immediately exudes gloomy caution, or one who appears to be a wide boy, or somebody with whom you have no rapport. Some people recommend that you should make a short list of two or three possibles and go and talk to them before making your choice.

What questions do you ask?

Obviously later on you will be approaching your adviser about specific problems, but at the outset you and he will be exploring potential help he can give you. Begin by outlining the kind of business or service you intend to set up, how much money you have available, what you think your financial needs are going to be over the first year of operation, how many people are going to be involved as partners or shareholders and what your plans are for the future. An accountant will want to know the range of your experience in handling accounting problems, how much help you are going to need in writing up the books and he will advise you on the basic records you should set up. Remember to ask his advice on your year end/year start; this does not have to be April 5 to April 6, and there may be sound tax reasons for choosing other dates. He may even be able to recommend the services of a part-time bookkeeper to handle the mechanics; but, as we shall show in Chapter 1.5, this does not absolve you from keeping a close watch on what money is coming in and going out. It should be stressed at this point that certainly in the case of a private limited company the accountant you are talking to should be qualified, either through membership of the Institute of Chartered Accountants or of the Association of Certified and Corporate Accountants. Someone who advertises his services as a bookkeeper or merely as an 'accountant' is not qualified to give professional advice in the true meaning of that term, though a good unqualified man can do a very adequate job in preparing tax returns for something like a small freelance business.

A solicitor will also want to know the kind of business you are in and your plans for the future. But he will concentrate, obviously, on legal rather than financial aspects (so do not go on about money) — he is a busy man, and this is only an exploratory visit). He is interested in what structure the operation is going to have and, in the case of a partnership or limited company, whether you and your colleagues have made any tentative agreements between yourselves regarding the running of the firm and the division of profits. He will want to get some idea of what kind of property you want to buy or lease and whether any planning permissions have to be sought.

How much is he going to charge?

This is rather like asking how long is a piece of string. It depends on how often you have to consult your adviser, so it is no use asking him to quote a price at the outset, though if you are lucky enough to have a very clear idea of what you want done — say, in the case of an accountant, a monthly or weekly supervision of your books, plus the preparation and auditing of your accounts — he may give you a rough idea of what his charges will be. Alternatively he may suggest an annual retainer for these services and any advice directly concerned with them, plus extra charges for anything that falls outside them, like a complicated wrangle with the inspector of taxes about allowable items. When calculating the likely cost of using an accountant remember that his fees are tax deductible.

An annual retainer is a less suitable way of dealing with your solicitor because your problems are likely to be less predictable than those connected with accounting and bookkeeping. A lot of your queries may be raised, and settled, on the telephone: the 'Can I do this?' type. Explaining that kind of problem on the telephone is usually quicker and points can be more readily clarified than by writing a letter setting out the facts of the case (though you should ask for confirmation in writing in matters where you could be legally liable in acting on the advice you have been given!). However, asking advice on the telephone can be embarrassing for both parties. You will be wondering whether your solicitor is charging you for it and either way it could inhibit you from discussing the matter fully. You should, therefore, check at the outset what the procedure is for telephone inquiries and how these are accounted for on your bill.

A guide — not a crutch

For someone starting in business on their own, facing for the first time 'the loneliness of thought and the agony of decision', there is a temptation to lean on professional advisers too much. Apart from the fact that this can be very expensive, it is a bad way to run a business. Before you lift the telephone or write a letter, think. Is this clause in a contract something you could figure out for yourself if you sat down and concentrated on reading it carefully? Would it not be better to check through the ledger yourself to find out where to put some item of expenditure that is not immediately classifiable? Only get in touch with your advisers when you are genuinely stumped for an answer, not just because you cannot be bothered to think it out for yourself. Remember, too, that nobody can make up your mind for you on matters of policy. If you feel, for example, that you cannot work with your partner, the only thing your solicitor can or should do for you is to tell you how to dissolve the partnership, not whether it should be done at all.

Your bank manager

The other person with whom you should make contact when you start up in business is your bank manager. The importance of picking a unit of the right size which we have mentioned in connection with professional advice also holds true in this case. A smaller local branch is more likely to be helpful towards the problems of a small business than one in a central urban location with a lot of big accounts among its customers. You might also discuss, with your accountant, the possibility of going outside the 'big five'. It is necessary to be careful here because there have been some notorious failures of 'fringe banks', but there are a number of solid smaller banking houses who are more accommodating about charges on handling your account and loans. If you are changing banks, as opposed to merely switching branches, it will be difficult for you to get a sizeable overdraft until the manager has seen something of your track record.

You must inform your bank manager of your intention to set up in business, providing him with much the same information as you gave to your accountant. Indeed, it is quite a good idea to ask your accountant to come along to this first meeting, so that he can explain any technicalities.

You may be operating a small-scale freelance business that

does not call for bank finance. It is very important, in that case, to keep your personal and business accounts separate, with separate cheque and paying in books for each one. Mixing up private and business transactions can only lead to confusion, for you as well as your accountant. Even if you are simply, say, a one-man freelance consultancy it is worth keeping your bank manager well-informed about your business. Your cash flow as a freelance might well be highly erratic and unless he knows you and your business well he will be firing off letters about your unauthorised overdraft.

Insurance

If you are setting up a photographic studio and an electrical fault on the first day destroys some of your equipment you are in trouble before you have really begun. If you are a decorator and a pot of paint falling from a window sill causes injury to someone passing below you could face a suit for damages that will clean you out of the funds you have accumulated to start your business. Insurance coverage is, therefore, essential from the start for almost all kinds of business.

Insurance companies vary a good deal in the premiums they charge for different kinds of cover, and in the promptness with which they pay out on claims. The best plan is not to go direct to a company, even if you already transact your car or life insurance with them, but to an insurance broker. Brokers receive their income from commissions from the insurance companies they represent, but they are generally independent of individual companies and thus reasonably impartial. Here again, your accountant or solicitor can advise you of a suitable choice, which would be a firm that is big enough to have contacts in all the fields for which you need cover (and big enough to exert pressure on your behalf when it comes to making a claim), but not so big that the relatively modest amounts of commission they will earn from you initially are not worth their while taking too much trouble over, for instance, when it comes to reminding you about renewals. Apart from these general points you will have to consider what kinds of cover you need and this will vary somewhat with the kind of business you are in. The main kinds are:

1. Insurance of your premises.
2. Insurance of the contents of your premises.

3. Insurance of your stock.

(The above three kinds of cover should also extend to 'consequential loss'. For instance, you may lose in a fire a list of all your customers. This list has no value in itself but the 'consequent' loss of business could be disastrous. The same is true of stock losses. If a publisher loses all his books in a fire it is not only their value that affects him, but the consequent loss of business while they are being reprinted, by which time the demand for them may have diminished.)

4. Employer's liability if you employ staff on the premises, even on a part-time basis.

5. Public liability in case you cause injury to a member of the public or his premises in the course of business. You will also need third-party public liability if you employ staff or work with partners.

6. Legal insurance policies cover you against prosecution under Acts of Parliament which relate to your business (eg those covering unfair dismissal and fair trading).

7. Insurance against losing your driving licence, important if your business depends on your being able to drive.

Your broker will advise you on other items of cover you will need. Some professions, for instance, need professional liability cover, but do not leave the whole business of insurance in his hands. Read your policies carefully when you get them and make sure that the small print does not exclude any essential item.

Insurance is expensive (though the premiums are allowable against tax inasmuch as they are incurred wholly in respect of your business), and you may find that in the course of time you have paid out thousands of pounds without ever making a claim. However, it is a vital precaution, because one fire or legal action against you can wipe out the work of years if you are not insured. For this reason you must check each year that items like contents insurance represent current replacement values and that your premiums are paid on the due date. Your broker should remind you about this, but if he overlooks it, it is you who carries the can.

The National Federation of Self-employed and Small Businesses now includes automatic legal insurance in its membership subscription. This covers professional and legal fees of up to £10,000 for appeals to VAT Tribunals, defence of Health and Safety at Work prosecutions, 90 per cent of the cost of an

Industrial Tribunal Award and defence of private and business motoring prosecutions. The NFSE also runs a voluntary top-up scheme to supplement this basic legal cover.

Other advisers and suppliers

In the course of transacting your business, you will probably need the services of other types of people: builders, to maintain and perhaps refurbish your premises; printers, to produce letterhead, advertising material, etc; surveyors and valuers to assess your property; and so on. You should apply the same criteria to these as to your professional advisers. Their services should be reasonably priced, and the service performed to the required standard. If the service is of a professional nature, the consultant should be a member of the relevant professional body. If this does not apply, it may be worth asking for recommendations from the local Chamber of Commerce or Small Firms Centre.

Checklist: professional advisers

Solicitors

1. How well do you know the firm concerned?
2. What do you know of their ability to handle the kind of transactions you have in mind?
3. Is their office convenient to the place of work you intend to establish?
4. Do they know local conditions and personalities?
5. Are they the right size to handle your business affairs over the foreseeable future?
6. Have you prepared an exhaustive list of the points on which you want legal advice at the setting-up stage?

Accountants

1. Have they been recommended by someone whose judgement you trust and who has actually used their services?
2. Are the partners members of one of the official accountants' bodies? If not, are you satisfied that they can handle business on the scale envisaged?
3. Is their office reasonably close by?
4. Does it create a good and organised impression?

5. Can they guarantee that a member of the firm will give you personal and reasonably prompt attention when required?
6. Have you thought out what sort of help you are going to need?
7. Have you prepared an outline of your present financial position and future needs?
8. Have you considered, in consultation with your solicitor, whether you want to set up as a sole trader, a partnership or a limited company?

Bank manager

1. Is your present bank likely to be the right one for you to deal with in this context?
2. Have you informed your bank manager of your intention to set up a business?
3. Have you established a separate bank account for your business?
4. Have you discussed with your bank manager the possibility of switching your account to a local, smaller branch?

Insurance

1. Do you have a reliable reference on the broker you intend to use?
2. Is he efficient, according to the reports you receive, about reminding you when policies come up for renewal?
3. Has he any track record of paying promptly on claims?
4. Have you prepared a list of the aspects of your proposed business which require insurance cover?
5. Are you fully insured for replacement value and consequential loss?
6. Have you read the small print on your policies or checked them out with your solicitors?

1.5: Simple Accounting Systems and Their Uses

Any bank manager will tell you that at least 80 per cent of all business failures are caused by inadequate record keeping. Unfortunately this fault is by no means uncommon in small businesses because the entrepreneurial person who tends to set up on his own is often temperamentally different from the patient administrative type who enjoys paperwork and charting information in the form of business records. He is apt to feel what really keeps the show on the road is obtaining and doing the work, or being in the shop to look after customers. However, unless you record money coming in and going out, owed and owing, you will never have more than the haziest idea of how much to charge for your products or services, where your most profitable areas of activity are (and indeed whether you are making a profit at all), how much you can afford to pay yourself and whether there is enough coming in to cover immediate commitments in the way of wages, trade debts, tax or professional fees, rent, rates, etc.

Legally, in fact, only a limited company is obliged to keep proper books of account: the definition is that they have to do so 'with respect to all receipts and expenses, sales and purchases, assets and liabilities and they must be sufficient to give a true and fair picture of the state of the company's affairs and to explain its transactions'. This is actually no bad objective for anyone carrying on a business on a full-time basis; the only trouble is that keeping and entering up a full set of books is very time-consuming, and, though not inherently difficult, does require a certain amount of training and some natural aptitude for organising facts and figures if you are to avoid getting into a muddle.

As a rule of thumb, if your scale of operations is big enough to come within the orbit of VAT (that is, if your turnover is, or is likely to be, over £18,000 a year) we suggest you get qualified help with bookkeeping. But first of all, let us look at the very basic records you ought to keep if you are in business for yourself at all, even as a part-time freelance.

Two starting points

At the small scale sole trader end, one reason why you need to keep records is to justify your expenditure claims to the tax inspector. For this purpose you may find that your most useful investment is a spike on which incoming receipts, invoices, statements and delivery notes can be placed. This ensures that essential documentary evidence of expenditure is retained and kept together, not used to put cups on or carried around in your wallet for making odd notes on the back. As your business grows you may find that the spike should be supplemented by a spring loaded box file in which all such items should be placed in date order.

However, not all expenditure can be accounted for in this way. Fares, for instance, are not generally receipted, nor is postage, or you may be buying items for personal use at the same time as others that are directly connected with your business. Thus it is a good idea to carry a notebook around with you and enter up any expenses that you have incurred that are not documented. You will find that the taxman will accept a certain level of claims of this kind provided they bear a credible relationship to the business you are in. For example, if you are earning income from travelling round the country giving lectures he will accept a fairly high level of claims for fares, but not if the nature of your business is carrying out a local building repair service.

For larger outlays you may find credit cards a useful record keeping aid. Apart from the fact that when card companies render their account for payment they provide a breakdown of where, when, and how items were purchased they also, in effect, give you six weeks' credit. During periods of high inflation, this is a real consideration.

Keeping a cash book

The next stage is to keep a cash book. It does not have to be anything elaborate. The object of the exercise is to provide a record from which an accountant or bookkeeper can write up a proper set of books and to save him the time and trouble (which you have to pay for) of slogging through dozens or possibly hundreds of pieces of paper in order to do this. Since your professional adviser will have to work off your records it is a good idea to ask him what the most convenient way of setting them out is. He may suggest that you buy one of the ready-made books of account like the *Complete Traders Account Book* or the *Self-employed Account Book*, though such books are not suitable for every kind of self-employment. If you find it difficult to follow his instructions, or you are using a ready-made book and are having trouble with it, here is something very simple you can do (see Table 5.1).

Buy a large (A4) rule notebook and open it up at the first double page. Allocate the left-hand page to sales and the right-hand page to expenditure. If sales and expenditure fall into further categories which you want to keep track of, say if you want to keep travel costs separate from the cost of materials, or if you are registered for VAT, divide up the page accordingly. You should also rule up columns for the date, the invoice number and the details of the invoice. Enter these details up at the end of each day's trading and you will find that it works both as a discipline in checking that all your sales and purchases are logged and that you now have a further record in addition to the documents on your spike or in your box file.

More elaborate systems

This sort of record is fine as far as it goes and in a small business engaged mainly in cash transactions your accountant may not need very much more than this to produce a set of accounts. In a larger concern, or one that operates extensively on taking and giving credit, it has some obvious limitations. For example, keeping track of when payments are made or received can become rather messy and difficult, and you will need to have a separate record, called a ledger, of the customers and suppliers with whom you do business so that you can see at a glance how much you owe or are owed in the case of individual accounts. Such details will be taken from further books — purchases and sales day books and a more elaborate kind of cash book than the simplified one we have described above. Though we have recommended that you leave the details of this kind of book-keeping to a qualified person, let us look briefly at what is involved.

1. *Cash book*. Shows all payments received and made, with separate columns for cash transactions and those made through the bank (ie payments by cheque). Amounts received from customers are credited to their account in

INCOME							EXPENDITURE						
Date	Invoice No	Date paid	Details	Amount (£)	VAT (£)		Date	Invoice No	Cheque/ Credit card	Details	Amount (£)	VAT (£)	
2.5.83	8061		Six tables	112	16.80		3.5.83	—	911112	Wooden Top timber yard	425	63.75	
6.5.83	cash		Desk	200	30.00		4.5.83	Petty cash voucher 23	cash	Stamps	3	—	
10.5.83	8062		Dining table	162	24.30		5.5.83	Petty cash voucher 24	cash	Expenses: trip to Harwich to inspect timber	20	3	
12.5.83	cash		Repair of wooden chest	83	12.45		13.5.83	—	911113	Electricity bill	44	6.60	

Table 5.1 Sample entries from the cash book of a cabinet maker

the ledger (see below). Payments made to suppliers are debited to their account in the ledger.

2. *Petty cash book*. Shows expenditure on minor items — postage, fares, entertainment and so forth, with a column for VAT.

3. *Sales day book*. Records invoices sent out to customers in date order, with some analysis of the goods or service supplied and a column for VAT.

4. *Purchases day book*. Records similar information about purchases.

5. *Ledger*. Sets out details, taken from sales and purchases day books, of individual customers' and suppliers' accounts and serves as a record of amounts owed and owing. Details from the analysis columns of the sales and purchases day books are also transcribed, usually monthly, under corresponding headings in the ledger. This enables you to see at a glance where your sales are coming from and where your money is going.

6. *Capital goods ledger*. If you own expensive capital equipment — cars, lorries, machine tools, high class film or photographic equipment, etc — you should have separate accounts for them in the ledger because the method of accounting for them is somewhat different. Capital items depreciate over a period of time (as you will know if you have ever sold a car) and this fact must be reflected both in your balance sheet and profit and loss account, and in the way you price your goods and services.

Writing down capital goods affects your tax liability. With some items you can write down the full value in the year of purchase, but it may not pay you to take advantage of this concession. How you deal with depreciation is very much an area where you are dependent on your accountant's expert advice.

Trading and Profit and Loss Account

From the books described above, your accountant can draw together the information needed to compile the trading and profit and loss account (see Table 5.2). The function of the account is to tell you whether you have been making a gross profit and a net profit on your trading. It must be compiled annually and preferably more often than that, quarterly for instance, to enable you to measure your progress and make your VAT return.

Trading and Profit and Loss Account for year ended 31.12.82		
	£	£
		20,000
Sales		
Purchases	12,000	
Opening Stock	2,000	
	14,000	
Less Closing Stock	3,000	11,000
Gross Profit		9,000
Rent and Rates	1,000	
Salaries	2,750	
Heat, Light	200	
Phone	120	
Travel	300	
Repairs	200	
Depreciation	650	
Professional Advice	150	
		5,370
Net Profit		3,630

Table 5.2 *Example of a trading and profit and loss account*

To put together the account he begins by identifying the period you want to cover. He then totals up the value of all sales, whether paid for or not. Then he takes your opening stock and adds it to the purchases (but not expenditure like rent or repayment of interest on loans). From this he takes the value of your stock (based on cost or market value, whichever is lower) at the end of the period you want to cover. Deducting the value of opening stock plus purchases from the value of sales will give him your gross trading profit (or loss) over the period.

Using this information he can work out the net profit and loss over the same period. The gross profit figure from your trading account appears at the top and he sets against it all the items from the various expenditure accounts in the ledger. He also includes in this figure the depreciation on capital equipment, but not its actual cost (even if you purchased it during the period in question) because that crops up later, in the balance sheet.

Deducting these from the gross profit gives you your profit over the period. If the total expenditure exceeds the gross profit you have obviously incurred a loss.

The balance sheet

We have mentioned in the previous section that capital equipment does not figure in the profit and loss account, but goes into the balance sheet. The balance sheet is a picture, taken at a particular point in the year (usually at the end of a company's financial year) of what the firm *owes* and what it *owns* (see Table 5.3). (This is not the same as a profit and loss account, which covers a period of time.)

In a balance sheet the assets of the firm used to be set out on the right and the liabilities on the left but it is modern practice to display them as below. However, all the assets and all the liabilities are generally not lumped together, but distinguished qualitatively by the words 'fixed' and 'current'.

'Fixed assets' are items which are permanently necessary for

Balance Sheet as at 31.12.82			
	£	£	
Fixed Assets			
Vehicles	1,600		
less depreciation	400	1,200	
Fixtures and fittings	1,000		
less depreciation	250	750	
		1,950	
Current Assets			
Stock	3,000		
Debtors	900		
Cash	75		
		3,975	
Less Current Liabilities			
Trade Creditors		795	
Net Current Assets		3,180	
Total Assets		5,130	
Represented by		Authorised	Issued
Capital (1,000 shares at £1 each)		1,000	500
Loan repayable 1984			1,000
Profit			3,630
			5,130

Table 5.3 *An example of a balance sheet*

the business to function, such as machinery, cars, fixtures and fittings, your premises or the lease on them. 'Current assets' on the other hand are things from which cash will be realised in the course of your trading activities. These include amount owed to you by your debtors (from the customers' accounts in the ledger), and the value of your stock (from the trading account). It also, of course, includes cash at the bank (from the cash book).

With liabilities, the position is reversed. 'Fixed liabilities' are those which you do not have to repay immediately, like a long-term loan from a kindly relative. What you do have to repay promptly, however, is the interest on that loan and this goes under current liabilities if it is due, but has not been paid at the time the balance sheet has been prepared. The same is true of any amounts you owe to your suppliers' accounts in the ledger. Another item that goes on the 'liabilities' side is the share capital in the business and the profit from the trading account because both these amounts are ultimately owed by the company to the shareholders. Where, on the other hand, the company has been making a loss, the amount is deducted either from profits retained from earlier periods or from the shareholder's capital.

What should you be looking for in your records?

You will want to know whether you are making or losing money, but there are many other useful bits of information to be gleaned as well. If you are making a profit, what relationship does it bear to the capital employed in the business? You can calculate this by subtracting total liabilities from total assets. If you are making less than a 15 per cent return on capital, you are not, on the face of things, making much progress, though, of course, you could be paying yourself a very handsome salary before the profit figure was arrived at.

The percentage return on capital can be calculated by the following sum:

$$\frac{profit}{capital\ employed} \times 100$$

Another thing you can work out from your balance sheet is whether you are maintaining sufficient working capital to meet your requirements for new stock or materials or to pay for wages and rent. Here you look at current assets and current liabilities. The calculation:

$$\frac{\text{current assets}}{\text{current liabilities}}$$

gives you your *current* ratio. If you have, say, £1000 of each you are said to have a current ratio of 1:1. Clearly in that case you would be in trouble if a major debtor were to go bankrupt. So it may be that you should cut back on some item of expenditure you were planning on. Furthermore, the current ratio includes certain items, like stocks, which may not be immediately realisable. If your current ratio is low, and you are still in two minds whether or not to buy that new machine you might apply what is known as the *acid test ratio*, which shows your ability to meet liabilities quickly if the need arises. Here you simply deduct stock from your figure for current assets to give you a figure for liquid assets, ie debtors and cash. If the ratio liquid assets : current liabilities is too low you may have more money tied up in stock than you should have.

Even the acid test ratio assumes that your debtors are going to pay you in a reasonable period of time: most likely within the terms of trade you are allowing. But is this assumption really correct? Look at the annual sum:

$$\frac{\text{debtors}}{\text{sales}} \times 365$$

If your sales are £10,000 and your debtors owe £1000, they are near enough to meeting net monthly terms for you not to worry about it. But if your debtors, on the same sales turnover, are running to £3000, there is something wrong with your credit control and you are probably heading for serious trouble.

Another important ratio is profit to sales. What this should be depends on the sort of business you are in. Your accountant should be able to advise you here on the basis of his knowledge of similar traders. If your percentage is on the low side you may be buying badly, failing to pass on cost increases, or possibly incurring losses from pilferage.

There are other ratios to look out for, but we hope that you will now be clear that the balance sheet and trading and profit and loss accounts are not just a financial rigmarole you have to go through, but very valuable indicators of the way your business is going, or some other business you are thinking of buying. They are also useful for:

1. Assisting the bank manager to determine the terms of an overdraft.

2. Selling your business to a proposed purchaser.

3. Agreeing tax liabilities with the inspector of taxes.

Checklist: simple accounting systems

1. Do you carry a notebook to record smaller items of business expenditure, such as taxi fares, as soon as they are incurred?

2. Have you considered using credit cards for larger outlays?

3. Do you have a system for filing incoming invoices as soon as they are received?

4. Have you asked your accountant what books and records he advises you to keep?

5. Do you know and understand the procedures involved?
   If not, have you asked your accountant to recommend someone who can help you on a regular basis — at least once a week or once a month, depending on your scale of operations?

6. Do you have any idea of the ratios current in your type of business, so that you can measure your performance against the norm?

1.6: Invoicing and Credit Control

Time is money, as an old saying goes. It ought to be written large in the minds of anyone giving credit, that is, any business that supplies goods and services which are not on a strictly cash-on-the-nail basis.

In these days of tight money there is a tendency for many customers, including large and reputable firms, to delay payment as long as possible; because, as noted in Chapter 1.3, taking credit long — and preferably giving it short — is one way to maintain a flow of cash in the business. The supplier who does not demonstrate that he is in a hurry for payment, therefore, is the one who comes last in the queue.

Sending out invoices and statements

The first step towards ensuring that you are not in this position is to issue an invoice for work done or goods supplied as soon as possible after you deliver. On the invoice you should give the customer's order number. If it was a telephone order and you forgot to get an order number, you should at least give the date of the order. You should also state when you expect to receive payment. The usual period is between seven and 30 days after delivery. Many private individuals, in fact, pay on receipt of an invoice. Business firms, on the other hand, expect to receive a statement of their account at the end of the month, setting out invoices due or sent during this period: their dates, invoice number, the nature of the goods and the amount. You can have statement forms printed, but if you are not a limited company you can use your letterheads for this purpose, simply typing the word STATEMENT at the top. Every customer who has received an invoice and not paid at the end of the month when it is due should get a statement, which should repeat your payment terms.

The particulars of the invoice(s) are drawn from your customers' ledger, though it is essential to keep copies of the actual invoices as well, filed in date order. You are going to need them for VAT purposes, or to check queries. When you receive payment, check that it tallies with the amount due on the customer's ledger entry, mark off the details against each individual item as shown in the previous chapter and enter the amount in the cash book. If the customer requires a receipt, ask him to return the statement (or the invoice if he has paid on that) with his remittance — otherwise you will be involved in time-consuming typing — tick off the items paid, and attach a receipt form or bang on a rubber stamp, 'Paid'. Be uniform about your systems. If you have two different ones for the same part of your operation you are going to waste a lot of time looking in the wrong place when you come to check a document.

Do not neglect the process of checking payments because any amounts unpaid must go into next month's statement. Some invoices which have appeared on your statement will not be paid because they are not yet due for payment. For example, if your terms are 30 days and you have invoiced an item on the 20th of the month, a business customer is unlikely to pay you until the month following. Quite often he only activates payments at the end of the month, unless he is unusually punctilious, efficient or being offered extra discount for quick settlement.

What happens if payment becomes overdue? This is extremely annoying, because at best it is going to involve you in extra correspondence. You must be tactful and patient if you want more business from your clients, and remember that some large organisations are slow in paying, not by choice but because they are dictated to by their computer accounting systems. But if your patience is exhausted, there are usually three stages. The first is a polite reminder of the amount due, how long it has been due and of your terms of supply. This should be coupled with asking the customer whether he has any queries on any of the invoices which might explain the delay. If there is not a reply by the end of that month, write again, referring to your first reminder and setting a deadline for payment. A telephone call to the customer is often opportune at this stage. If that deadline is not met, you will have to write again, referring to your previous reminders and threatening legal action unless a new and final deadline is met. (If you have a large number of credit accounts, it may pay you to have sets of blank letters for each stage prepared in advance.)

In most cases the threat of legal action will do the trick, but whether you actually carry out your threat will depend on the amount involved. Sums under £75 are not really worth pursuing because your solicitor's services are going to cost you money; and it is not worth taking matters to court — that is, to the stage beyond a solicitor's letter — unless quite a sizeable sum is involved. Your solicitor will advise you on the best course of action. Alternatively, there are firms of debt collectors who are geared to this kind of work and who will endeavour to collect debts for a percentage of the amount due. Five per cent is the norm. But there are some doubtful operators and a good deal of tricky legislation in debt collecting, and you would be well advised to check out any agency that has not been personally recommended with the National Association of Trade Protection Societies, 8 New Street, Leicester LE1 5NF.

You can, of course, ask for references before giving credit though this is a matter which has to be approached with some delicacy; but if you receive a sizeable order out of the blue from some business firm with whom you have not previously dealt, it is advisable to ask for a couple of references in acknowledging the order. Ask the referees to what amount they give credit to this particular customer, how long they have been doing business with him and whether he pays promptly.

If your business consists of making or repairing goods to order — tailoring, for instance — it is not unusual to ask the customer to pay up to 50 per cent on account where an estimate of over £50 or so has been given. This helps cash flow as well as protecting you against possible default. Equally, if goods of resaleable value are left with you for repair you should display a notice reserving the right to dispose of them if the customer does not come to collect them within a reasonable time of completion of the work.

A common delaying tactic, or it may be a perfectly legitimate query, is for the customer to ask for copy invoices on receipt of your statement. Do not part with your file copy. You will have to send a photocopy if you do not keep duplicates for this purpose.

Credit cards

For larger personal transactions and for items such as the settlement of restaurant bills credit cards are becoming an increasingly popular method of making payment. A typical scheme is the one operated by the Joint Credit Card Companies, which include Access. A business which wants to offer credit card payment facilities to its customers has to make application to join the scheme to the Joint Credit Card Companies, General Sales Office, 30-31 Newman Street, London W1P 4LJ. The Joint Credit Card Companies then set a money limit to the transaction per customer for which the business in question can accept payment on the cards of JCC member companies. Above that limit, which is based roughly on the applicant's average transaction per customer, the sale has to be referred back to JCC. This can be done over the telephone.

Each sale, as it is made, is entered up on a voucher supplied by the credit card company. The voucher is paid into the bank by the seller and the amount is debited to the card holder's bank account. The advantage of credit cards from the seller's point of view is that he gets guaranteed payment. Against this, he has to pay a small percentage on every transaction to the bank, the amount of this percentage being negotiated at the time he joins the scheme.

Most credit card companies operate on lines very similar to the scheme we have just outlined. Diner's Club vouchers, for instance, though not paid into a bank are sent to the Club organisation on certain specified dates, whereupon payment is made to the seller.

Checking incoming invoices and statements

Unless you transact your business by paying in cash or by cheque on the spot (which is likely in only a few business spheres), you will also be at the receiving end of invoices and statements from your suppliers. The moment they come in, put them on the spike. Then, daily if possible, enter the details in the supplier's ledger, as described in Chapter 1.5. File incoming invoices in date order, for you will need them for VAT purposes.

When you receive your statement make sure it tallies with the amounts and details which you have entered in the suppliers' ledger, mark off all the items paid and write up the amount in the cash book.

If you are paying by cheque there is no need to ask for a receipt (which only adds to the paperwork) since an honoured cheque is itself a receipt. Make sure, though, that you enter up the stubs, unless you write up the cash book at the same time as you draw the cheques.

Checklist: invoicing and credit control

Invoicing

1. Are you invoicing promptly, on or with delivery?
2. Do your invoices clearly state your terms?
3. Do you ensure that the customer's name, address and order number (if any) or date is correctly stated on your invoice?
4. Are your statements sent out promptly at the end of the month? Do they state your payment terms?
5. Are they clear and easy to follow? Would they make sense to you if you were the recipient?
6. Are you checking payments received against ledger entries?

Credit control

1. Does every account have a credit limit?
2. Is it based on first-hand knowledge of the customer as a credit risk or personally, his track record as a payer with you or others in your line of business, on representatives' reports or reliable trade references, or on bankers' references, in that order of usefulness?
3. Do you exercise special vigilance on new accounts?
4. Do your statements show the age of outstanding balances and do you or your credit controller look at outgoing statements to check on customers whose payments situation seems to be deteriorating?
5. Do you have a system for dealing with customers who exceed their credit limit?
6. Do you have a sequence of reminder procedures for dealing with overdue accounts by telephone calls and/or letters?
7. Do you check orders received against a list of customers who have exceeded their credit limit or who are proving to be reluctant or non-payers?
8. Does the person in charge of credit control liaise with those responsible for supplying the account in question to make sure that there are no special reasons for non-payment before sharper warnings are delivered?
9. Do you regularly check on the debtor : sales ratio to make sure you are not heading for a liquidity problem by being too generous about extending credit?

1.7: Budgeting and Cash Flow Forecasting

One principle that it is vital to grasp is the importance of liquid cash in running a business. This should not be confused with profitability. Because of the way the profit figure is arrived at on the trading account (see Chapter 1.5), it is perfectly possible for a business to be trading profitably and yet be quite unable to pay the tax bill or the rent because its resources are tied up in stock or, even worse, in equipment.

Failure to understand the distinction between profit and cash flow is not uncommon and it can be disastrous. For example, you may be offered very persuasive financial inducements to carry or manufacture additional stock. If it is a good product and one for which there is a consistent demand you may say to yourself that you are going to need more anyway in six months' time, so why not stock up for a whole year at a bargain price? This can be a valid argument, but before you accept it consider that when the bills come in they have to be paid with money, not with stock. Profitability means very little unless cash is there when it is needed.

This is true even for businesses that do not carry stocks, like a photographic studio producing goods only to order, or a design consultancy selling more or less intangible skills. You are still going to have outgoings on travel or materials; and even if your premises are a back room in your own house there are still rate demands to be met, apart from the matter of needing money to live on.

Planning your cash requirements

Planning your cash requirements is crucial from the outset of your career as a self-employed person. It will determine much of your policy towards what kinds of work you take on. It is far better, if you are short of liquid capital, to take on a number of small jobs which will keep money coming in than one big, tempting, potentially profitable one where you might run out of cash three-quarters of the way through. For, unless you make provision to get progress payments from your customer backed up, possibly by a bank overdraft, your suppliers are going to be pressing you for payment before you are in a position to send your bills to the customer. Even at best, in most businesses which are not taking cash across the counter there is going to be a lag between the time you are being asked for payment and when your customer pays you.

In order to estimate what your needs for cash are going to be you should set up and revise at three- or six-monthly intervals, a cash flow budget; and in order to refine it, you should also check it back against what actually happened. Indeed, before you begin you should have (and the bank manager will want to see) a fully worked out cash flow projection for the first 12-18 months.

The words 'cash flow budget' sound intimidatingly technical, but mean simply that you should make a realistic forecast of money coming in and going out over the period. Again, how accurate you can be depends somewhat on the circumstances and the type of business you are in. If you have bought a going concern there may be regular contracts that you hope to maintain, or in the case of a retail business or a restaurant some kind of predictable pattern of trade which can be established from the cash book or general ledger. If you have started a new business of your own, on the other hand, you may not have much to go on in the way of facts on cash coming in. You might only have enough certain information on the next two or three months, though if you have asked yourself the questions we outlined in Chapter 1.1 you will have ensured, as far as possible, that there is a continuing demand for your product so that orders will go on arriving while you are completing the work you have already lined up. But even in cases where you do not know where the penny after next is coming from, at the very least the cash flow budget will tell you what commitments you have to meet and, therefore, what volume of sales should be your target to this end. You can include this sales target in your budget, but do not forget that in order to achieve it costs of materials and additional overheads will also be involved. Moreover, both in cases where income is firmly expected and where it is only a forecast of expectations the cost of materials and wages will have to be met before you actually get paid.

Let us take a hypothetical case here to illustrate a cash flow budget in operation over the first four months of the year, for a small offset printing business with two partners and one employee. Over these months they have a contract to print the spring catalogue from a local firm of nurserymen, a monthly list from a firm selling militaria by mail order and a booklet on the town for the Chamber of Commerce. They also have some orders for what is known as 'jobbing' — small jobs such as wedding invitations, brochures, printed labels and the like — with the prospect that a regular flow of such work can be picked up. Against this, they have to meet wages, rent, PAYE, VAT, telephone, the running of a van, the purchase of materials, rates, electricity, National Insurance contributions, etc.

As you will see from the forecast (see Table 7.1) the partners budgeted for a deficit in the first two months, but they were not worried because they knew that in March and April they could expect a couple of big payments from Rosebud Nurseries and from the Chamber of Commerce. However, in order to keep solvent they had to borrow £2000 from the bank, interest payments on which had to be paid at intervals. They also had to plan the purchase of their most costly item, paper, as close as possible to the month in which they would actually be using it for their two big jobs. There is no point in holding expensive stock which cannot be used at an early date. Even though, with inflation, it might actually have been cheaper for them to have ordered all their paper for the first four months back in January, their bank overdraft would not have been sufficient to meet the bill.

In March they had to allow for three quarterly items, electricity, telephone and their VAT return, and as the year progresses they will have to make plans to meet such major items as rates and taxes. Note also that expenditure which is central to the activities of the business, in this case paper, has to be forecast more carefully than incidentals such as postage where a monthly average has been extended. If postage was a more crucial factor, as might be the case with a mail-order firm, this part of the cash flow budget would have to be worked out in more detail.

Regarding the revenue part of the forecast, the partners had enough orders for jobbing work to budget fairly accurately for the first two months. For March and April they guessed a figure, hoping spring weddings and a general upturn of business after the winter would lead to a modest growth in incoming funds after that point.

The overall March and April figures look quite rosy, but after that it was clear that they would have to turn up some more

Income (£)

	January	February	March	April
From	December Statement	January Statement	February Statement	March Statement
	Militaria Ltd 500	Militaria Ltd 500	Rosebud Nurseries Ltd 5,300	Chamber of Commerce 2,000
	Other work 400	Other work 250	Militaria Ltd 500	Militaria Ltd 500
			Other work 500	Other work 500
	900	750	6,300	3,000

Expenditure (£)

	January	February	March	April
Wages, salaries, PAYE, National Insurance	750	Wages, etc 750	Wages, etc 750	Wages, etc 750
Rent	100	Rent 100	Rent 100	Rent 100
Maintenance contract	20	Maintenance 20	Maintenance 20	Maintenance 20
Petrol	40	Petrol 40	Petrol 40	Petrol 40
Postage	20	Postage 20	Postage 20	Postage 20
Travel and Entertainment	40	Travel, etc 40	Travel, etc 40	Travel, etc 40
Paper	1,500	Materials 100	Materials 150	Materials 100
Other materials	200	Bank Interest 60	Electricity 70	Paper 1,500
			Telephone 40	
			VAT 300	
			Paper 1,000	
	2,670	1,130	2,530	2,570

Cash surplus (deficit)

January	February	March	April
(1,770)	(380)	3,770	430

Table 7.1 An example of a cash flow budget

jobs like Rosebud Nurseries and the Chamber of Commerce booklet because the overheads — wages, rent, the maintenance contract on their machines, bank interest — plus the cost of paper and materials needed to fill forecast work were running slightly above the expected income. So even though they are running well ahead of the game at the end of April, they would be unwise to start reducing that bank overdraft just yet.

There are many other lessons to be learned from your cash flow budget. They vary from business to business, but the essential points are that it is an indispensable indicator in making your buying decisions both of stock and materials, that it helps you decide your priorities between getting work (and what sort of work) and devoting all your energies to executing it and points to the importance of getting the maximum credit and allowing the minimum!

Checklist: budgeting and cash flow

1. Is the forecast of money coming in based on firm orders or at least reasonable expectations or does it include an element of fond hope?
2. Are the customers concerned likely to pay you at the times forecast?
3. Can you persuade any large customers to offer you progress payments to help you over difficult months?
4. Have you included everything in the outgoings section of the budget, including allowing for things like VAT and the heating of premises in winter months?
5. Do you have the resources to see you through deficit months, or have you secured finance to this end?
6. Is there any way you can cut down on the expenditure element by delaying or staggering buying decisions of stock or leasing rather than buying equipment?

1.8: Costing, Pricing and Estimating

How much should you charge your customers? Or, to put it more searchingly, on what factors should your charges be based? It is surprising that many self-employed people would be hard put to it to give a clear answer to that question. There are such things as 'going rates' and 'recommended' (or generally accepted) prices, but often these are in the nature of broad guidelines and unless you know what all your costs are, not just the cost of materials, or how long the job took you, you are sooner or later going to be in the position of either undercharging or making an actual loss.

There are some self-employed occupations where the scope for how much you can charge is either narrow or non-existent. This applies particularly to many areas of the retail trade, where goods tend to have recommended prices printed on them by the suppliers; but even there you may want to consider *reducing* some prices in order to undercut a competitor and the question arises whether you can afford to do so. This depends on your overall costs — rent, rates, power supplies and many other factors. Equally, some freelance jobs are subject to generally accepted 'going rates' and the more commonplace such jobs are (ie the smaller the degree of service or expertise that is involved) the more strictly you have to keep within that rate. But the corollary of this statement is also true: the more unique your product or service, the more you can afford to charge for it.

This can apply even in the ordinary retail trade where, on the face of things, the prospect of getting away with charging more than the competition is not promising. Recently a small supermarket opened near my house. It is open late at night, on Sundays and on public holidays and, quite rightly, it charges for that extra time. Most things cost a penny or two above what they do in the larger shops down the High Street, but it is offering something more than they are, and meets competition not by charging less, but by providing more — a much-needed neighbourhood service for out-of-hours shopping.

The same principle can be applied to even rather routine

freelance jobs. Provide a straightforward typing service and you will have to stick pretty much to the going rate; but offer something special, like accurately typing mathematical material or unusually high turnround speeds, and you can move into a different price bracket.

Determining your costs

You could say to yourself: 'I'm going to charge as much as I can get away with' or, 'I'm going to charge the standard rate for the job'. These are quite sensible guidelines to be going on with, but at some point you are probably going to be in the situation of wondering whether you should be charging a little more, or perhaps whether you can afford to reduce your price in order to land some work that you badly want. It is then that you have to get to grips with what your costs really are.

The most obvious one is your own time, and curiously enough it is an element that self-employed people are often confused about, because they tend to regard it as being somehow different from the time taken by employees. If a job involves your working flat out for a 100-hour week, you are underpricing the product of that work if your remuneration is less than that of an employed person doing the same kind of work at full overtime rates. There may be a reason why you *should* be undercharging: you may want a 'loss-leader' introduction to a particular customer, or to undercut a competitor, or you may simply need the money that week. But if you undercharge, you should be clear in your mind why you are doing so.

Another factor that is sometimes overlooked is that in most cases there are overhead costs incurred in running your business, irrespective of whether you have work coming in or not. We will deal with these overheads in more detail in a moment, but the point to be made here is to correct any misconception that the margin between what you charge and your basic costs in time and/or materials represents your profit. True, it is a profit of a kind — gross profit. But the real profit element in a job, the net profit, only emerges when the overhead costs have been met. So the right way to work out your price to the customer, or to determine whether a job is worth taking on, is to establish whether it will pay for materials, overheads, wages (if you employ others) and still leave you with a margin of net profit that adequately reflects the time and skill you are putting into it.

Once you have been in business for a few months you should have accumulated enough facts and figures to establish what your overhead costs are. To what extent you can control the situation beyond that depends, again, on what sort of business you are in. If you are running an ordinary retail shop, operating on margins that are more or less fixed by the supplier, there is not much you can do about pricing your goods, but at least you will know whether you can afford to spend more on extra fittings or take on more staff, or whether you should be staying open longer to attract extra trade. But if you are manufacturing something, then you can work out a rule-of-thumb method in the form of a percentage to add on to your materials costs in quoting prices; or in the case of a service, an average hourly rate. It is important, though, to keep on monitoring these rule-of-thumb procedures against what actually happened, so you should keep a record detailing the specification of each job, in which actual costs can be compared against your original estimate. Over a period of time you should in this way be able to build up a reliable set of costs which can be referred to when an assignment which sounds similar comes up.

At the beginning, though, you will have very little to go on, so let us look in more detail at the factors you will have to take into account.

Costs connected with your premises

Rent, heat, light, telephone, rates, insurance, finance (if you own or have bought a lease of the premises), cleaning and maintenance contracts.

Costs of finance

Interest charged on overdrafts or loans. You should include in this calculation interest on any money you yourself have put into the business, because it should be earning a rate of return equivalent to what you could get on the open market.

Costs of equipment

If you are renting equipment or buying it on hire purchase this item of expenditure presents no problems. The issue is more complicated if you have bought equipment outright, because you have to figure out some way of recovering the purchase price and this is done by bringing in the concept of 'depreciation'. What this means is that you gradually write off, over a period of time based on the item's useful life, most of the amount you paid initially; not all, because it will have some resale value at the end of the depreciation period.

Supposing you bought a van for £3000 and you think it will last you for four years, at the end of which time you could expect to get £1000 for it. This leaves you with £2000 to depreciate over four years — £500 per annum. There are also a number of other ways to calculate depreciation and your accountant will advise you on the method most advantageous to your kind of business. The important point to bear in mind, though, is that depreciation is a real factor, not just an accountancy device. Assets like motor cars and equipment do wear out and have to be replaced. Reserves should be built up to enable you to do this.

Administrative costs

Running your business will involve general expenditure which cannot be directly related to particular assignments: stationery, publicity, travel, postage, entertainment of clients, fees to professional advisers, and so forth.

Salaries and welfare

Salaries are best calculated as an hourly rate, based on an average working week. In the case of employees these rates are usually determined by the market for that particular kind of employment. The problem is deciding how much you should pay to yourself. Again, this obviously varies with the kind of business you are in, but as a rough guideline you should, after meeting all your expenses, be earning at least as much as an employed person with the same degree of skill and responsibility. It is most important to cost your time properly; let us, therefore, look at a worked example of what might be involved in the case of a person in full-time self-employment.

Supposing you were aiming to earn £10,000 a year. To start with you would want to take into account four weeks' annual paid holiday (three weeks, plus statutory holidays) and you would assume an eight-hour day and a five-day working week. However, not all your time would be directly productive: some of it would be spent travelling, on administration and on getting work. So let us say your productive time is 32 hours a week. That would give you an hourly rate based on 32 x 48 hours a year: 1536 hours. Divided into £10,000 that means a rate of about £6.51 per hour. On top of that you have to allow for welfare items: your National Insurance stamp, possible contributions to a retirement pension scheme and certainly insurance against sickness or death. Let us assume this comes to another £800 a year. Divided by 1536 working hours, this adds another 52 pence to your hourly rate.

Similarly, when costing the time of any full-time staff working for you, it is not just a question of calculating basic rates of pay. You have to allow for holidays, the employer's contribution to National Insurance stamps and to the graduated pension scheme. These items can add 6 to 8 per cent to the cost of wages.

Variable costs

All the costs we have just described are fixed costs. You incur them whether you have work coming in or not. Variable costs are items like materials which can be attributed to specific jobs. There are circumstances in which what we have described as fixed costs can vary slightly. If you are running a lot of overtime, this will mean an increase in your fuel bills and extra payments to your staff or to yourself. But the benefit of achieving properly costed increases in productivity, for example, in the case of a shop staying open late to attract more trade, is that, provided you are able to keep fixed overheads stable, this element will form a smaller proportion relative to your turnover; and that means a more profitable business.

Establishing your prices

You now have a set of basic data on costs which can be applied to your prices when you are asked to quote for a job or in making up your invoice. If you are supplying a service, the best way to do this is to take all your fixed costs, establish an hourly rate based on your usual working week and then estimate how long the job will take you. The effect of this is that if jobs do not materialise in the way the 'usual working week' concept implies you yourself are going to be carrying the can for the fixed overheads which are being incurred during all the hours in that week when you are not working. And if you only get

113

20 hours' work during a week in which you had budgeted for 40, loading your charges to the customer to make up for the shortfall could mean that you will come up with an unacceptable quotation or a price that will discourage your customer in the future.

The other lesson to be learned is that fixed overheads should be kept as low as possible. For instance, if you are planning a freelance design service to earn extra money in the evenings you should be chary of acquiring expensive equipment. In the limited hours of work which a part-time freelance operation implies you may never be able to charge enough money to do more than pay the overheads. As far as possible, keep your costs in the variable category by hiring or renting equipment only when and for as long as you need it.

This is also true of businesses that produce manufactured articles (and activities which operate on lines similar to manufacturing like a restaurant, where the product is created in the form of a meal), though in these cases some machinery and equipment are usually essential. The price here will be based on a unit per item rather than on an hourly rate, but the principle is the same. Instead of fixing an hourly rate based on an expected working week, calculations should be made on a projected volume of costs spread over the number of units sold. Thus, if you aimed to sell in a week 20 chairs which cost you £5 each in materials your variable costs would be £100. If your fixed overheads, including your own remuneration, came to £300 a week, you would have to charge £20 per chair. And do not forget that even if your object is only to make a living wage out of your business, you should still be putting aside reserves to replace equipment as it wears out, and that the cost of doing so will, in periods of inflation, be a great deal higher than its original cost.

Preparing quotations

With many jobs, whether they are a service or a commission to manufacture something, you will be asked to supply a quotation before a firm order is placed. Once that quotation has been accepted it is legally binding on both parties, so it is important not only to get your sums right but to make it clear in the wording attached to them what exactly you are providing for the money. In the case of a decorating job, for example, you should specify who is providing the materials and, if you are, to what standards they are going to be. Consider also whether any out-of-pocket expenses will be involved (travel, subsistence) and whether these are to be met by your customer or whether they have been allowed for in your quotation.

Apart from variable factors such as these, every quotation should set out the conditions of sale under which it is being offered. Different businesses will involve different kinds of conditions, but here are some basic points to bear in mind:

1. Particularly in times of inflation, you should make it clear that the prices quoted are current ones and may have to go up if costs rise during the course of the job.

2. Terms of payment should be set out, for example 30 days net.

3. You will have to cover the not uncommon situation of the customer changing his mind about the way he wants the job done subsequent to his accepting your quotation. You should leave yourself free to charge extra in such circumstances.

4. If you have agreed to complete a job within a certain length of time, set out the factors beyond your control which would prevent you from meeting the agreed date.

5. You should make it clear what circumstances of error, loss or damage will be your responsibility and what would fall outside it.

6. You should stipulate that, once the quotation is accepted, the order cannot be cancelled except by mutual consent and that the customer will be liable for all charges up to that point.

7. You should mention that the total is subject to VAT at the rate ruling at the date of invoice. This is particularly important when the customer is a private person who is unable to claim back his VAT inputs. (See Chapter 1.11 for details of VAT.)

Having gone to all the trouble to set out the quotation and conditions of sale, you should not neglect to check, before you start work, that the customer has actually accepted it in writing! It is all too easy to forget this or to imagine that an amicable verbal OK is sufficient. If a dispute arises, however, you will be very thankful to have carried out all the formal steps of documentation.

Every few months sit back for half an hour and consider your pricing policy. If you have set up as a consulting engineer and have no wish to get involved with renting offices and employing others, then your workload capacity is limited to the number of hours you put in. To start with you will probably be glad of work at any price but as your business builds up to the point where you are working all hours the only way you will be able to increase your real income is to increase your prices. So if you have a reliable supply of work coming in which is giving you a reasonable income, do not be afraid to put in some highish quotes for new work. It is not always the case that the lowest tender wins the job, particularly in the field of consultancy.

Checklist: costing, pricing and estimating

1. How unique is your product or service? If it is not particularly uncommon, how can you make it more so?
2. How essential is it to the customer?
3. What is the competition charging for the same or similar product or service?
4. How badly do you need the job or order?
5. Is your customer likely to come back for more if the price is right, or is it a one-off?
6. Will doing business with this customer enable you to break into a wider market, and thus enable you to reduce your unit costs?
7. What is the element of risk involved (ie is the customer, to your knowledge, a quick and certain payer)?
8. Do you have any idea how long the job will take you?
9. Can you relate the time element to your fixed costs?
10. Have you made a full assessment of all your fixed costs?
11. Do you have any idea what your materials are going to cost you?
12. Have you costed your own time properly?
13. Will the job leave you a margin of net profit? Or should you forgo this in the interest of meeting fixed costs?
14. Have you prepared a quote, specifying exactly what you are going to provide or do, including terms of payment?
15. Has the customer accepted your quotation?
16. Are you keeping records of what the job cost you so that you can adjust your prices or quote more accurately next time?

1.9: Marketing Your Work

Good ideas, it is sometimes dismissively said, are ten a penny; the implication being that the really difficult part is putting them into effect. Apart from the obvious virtues of persistence, hard work and technical know-how, this also requires a modicum of marketing skill. In other words, you will have to know whether there is a big enough demand for your product or service at the price you need to charge to make a living and how to identify and reach your potential customers.

Manufacturers

You may be the world's most skilful maker of hand-carved model sailing ships, but unless enough people want them, you are going to have a hard time trying to make a living out of producing them commercially. So before you start in business, look around. Go to gift shops, luxury stores or wherever it is that the kind of item you are aiming to produce is being sold and find out about prices, quality standards and the extent of the demand. Any intelligent shop manager or assistant will be glad to give you such information, provided you do not buttonhole them at a busy time of the day. It may be that by modifying your idea in quite a minor way, you will come up with a much more saleable article than the one that was originally in your mind.

Another point to watch out for is whether there is a long-term future for your product. This is particularly true with regard to fashion goods. There may be a craze for some particular kind of accessory and for a while you will be able to sell everything you produce. But before long some large manufacturer will come along and make the same thing much more cheaply and distribute it more effectively than you can. When the craze dies down he will get off the bandwagon and on to something else. Are you going to be able to keep a step ahead of him by being in a position to meet the next craze before the big manufacturers become aware of it?

You also have to keep an eye on competitors of your own size. If you are making and selling pottery, consider how many other craft potters are active in your area and whether your work is so good and so competitively priced that it does not matter how many there are; or whether you can produce something commercially viable that they are not doing.

But no matter how good or unique your product may be, the ultimate key to success lies in effective sales and distribution. At the smallest level you might be selling direct to the public through your own shop, as is the case with many craft goods, but you have to bear in mind that you need to achieve a considerable turnover for a shop in a good location to be viable. This is difficult if the range of specialisation is very narrow, and many small-scale manufacturers, therefore, combine having their own shop with direct mail and mail order (which we shall come to in a moment) and with marketing to other retail outlets. Shop and workshop premises can be combined in the same floor area, so that you can switch readily from the sales counter to the workbench when the shop is empty. This requires permission from the local planning authority if a 'change of use' of what were originally shop premises is involved.

Starting-up costs will eat deeply into your capital, so unless you have enough experience of the marketing (as opposed to the manufacturing) end of your specialty to be absolutely convinced that you can sell it, it is a good idea to begin by making a few prototypes of the product and its packaging and by trying to get orders from retailers. Though your friends and family may think your idea is wonderful, the acid test is whether it will survive in the marketplace. In the course of investigating this, the natural conservatism of most branches of the retail trade may at times depress or irritate you, but it is worth listening to what people who are involved in it have to say. If the same criticisms keep on cropping up you should think seriously of modifying your prototype to take them into account.

Distribution can be another big headache and your premises should be big enough to enable you to hold roughly as many days' or weeks' supply of stock as it takes to replace it at its rate of demand. If a business is selling 10 chairs a week and it takes two weeks to get that number of replacements there should, ideally, be space for something like 20 chairs. A customer might be prepared to wait a week for delivery, but he is unlikely to wait a month.

Accessibility of non-selling areas is important too. Adequate entry for goods and materials at the rear or side of the premises is often essential and will always save time and energy.

Dealing with large companies

Winning an order from a large company can put a small business on its feet at a stroke, not only directly but in terms of gaining credibility with other customers. But pursuing orders of that kind is not without its perils. For one thing large firms are not necessarily rapid payers; nor, as some recent bankruptcies have shown, is a household name inevitably a sign of financial soundness. Careful checks with your bank are essential.

The implications of a big order also need to be thought out very fully in cash flow terms and if progress payments are not offered, other forms of finance will have to be found. A further point to consider is that it is highly likely that a major customer will seek to impose conditions not only of price, but of quality and delivery. Fair enough; but in combination these three can make what seems like a high value order look much less tempting on the bottom line of profitability.

The whole thing becomes even more complicated if you find you have to sub-contract part of the job, as is often the case when a small business lands in the big time. Unless you can control the sub-contractor's work very tightly by writing and being in a position to enforce a very clear set of specifications you can land yourself in the position one small book publisher got into not long ago. They won an order from a major chain of multiples for many tens of thousands of copies of a number of titles. For cost reasons these had to be manufactured in the Far East and when they were delivered they did not match up to the very strict merchandising standards that had been stipulated. What had looked like a wonderful stroke of good fortune turned into a horrifying, litigation laden loss.

Of course, large companies are anxious to avoid this sort of thing, so they seldom deal with small companies whose approach is less than 100 per cent professional. A lot of them, by all accounts, fall down at this first hurdle. However good your idea or product, it will never even come up for discussion unless your letter is clearly and neatly presented, reasonably well-written and, above all, sent to the right person. Firms are full of stories of letters being sent to executives who had long left the company and whose names had been gleaned from some out-of-date directory. One phone call would have done the trick.

The lesson that small things make big impressions is also worth remembering when the big customer you have been courting finally sends his inspection team or his purchasing officer round. Nothing looks worse than a scruffy reception area or sounds worse than badly briefed staff. Indeed you yourself should make sure that you can answer convincingly all the questions you are likely to be asked on such things as capacity, delivery, the quality of your work force and whatever is connected with the business you are trying to win.

Shops and service industries

The first large shopping centre built in Britain was a flop because, among other disadvantages, it had no parking facilities and was situated in a working class area a few minutes' walk away from a large, long-established and very popular street market. The developers, for all their vast financial resources, had ignored hotel magnate Conrad Hilton's three factors in siting a business serving the public: location, location and location. If you are thinking of setting up a shop, restaurant or some other service outlet, find out as much as possible about the area. What sort of people live there? Is the area declining economically or on the up and up? What is the range of competitors? How efficient do they look and how well are they doing? If you are thinking of opening a high-class restaurant and there are nothing but fish and chip establishments in the neighbourhood, does this mean that there is no demand for a good restaurant or a crying need for one?

Taking the case of a bookshop. You would want to conduct some rule-of-thumb market research about the area before going any further. For example, you would want to know whether there were enough people in the area to support such a venture, whether they were the sort of people who regularly bought books, and how good the local library was. You would also want to know what impact the result of your market investigations might have on your trading policies. Thus, if there were a lot of families with young children around, you should be considering getting to know, and stocking, children's books; or, if there were a lot of students in the neighbourhood, it would be worth your while finding out what textbooks were being used in local educational institutions. Alternatively, if your bookshop is highly specialised — medicine, academic history, chess, or some other specific activity — an expensive High Street location is likely to be wholly inappropriate. You will want to be near the centre of that activity, or, more likely, will want to sell to your well-defined audience through direct mail.

The same broad principles apply to almost every kind of retail or service outlet and you will have to conduct this kind of research, which is really just plain commonsense — whatever your venture. Do not be tempted to overlook it just because you are buying what is supposed to be a 'going concern'. One reason why it is up for sale may be that, despite the owner's or agent's protestations to the contrary, it was doing badly. If that was because the previous owner was a poor manager or stocked the wrong kind of goods for the neighbourhood, you might be able to turn the business around; but if there was simply too much competition in the area from similar shops and there is no chance of trading viably in something else from the same address, you would be well advised to forget about those premises, however good a buy they may seem from a purely cost point of view. You will also be able to check on the vendor's assertions by looking, preferably with your accountant, at his profit and loss accounts, not just for the past year's but the previous three to five years', to get a picture of the general trend of things. On the whole, buying a going concern has to be approached with great caution, particularly by the inexperienced, because of the difficulties of valuing stock and goodwill with any accuracy. See Chapters 2.2 and 2.4 for more detailed treatment of these points.

Freelance services

Most freelances agree that the way you get work is by knowing people who are in a position to give it to you. That sounds rather like a chicken and egg situation, and to begin with, so it is. You would be ill-advised to launch into freelance work, certainly on a full-time basis, until you have built up a range of contacts who can provide you with enough work to produce some sort of living for at least the first few months. Often these are people whom you have got to know in the course of a full-time job, or while doing temporary work. Many advertising agencies, for instance, have been started by a breakaway group taking a batch of clients with them when they start up.* And it

* To combat this trend many firms now include clauses in their employment contract expressly stating that it is not permissible to work for a client of the employer for two years after leaving that employer.

may even be that your employer, having been compelled to make you redundant, will still be willing to put work out to you on a freelance basis.

Once you have got going and established a reputation for doing good, reliable work, things get much easier. For one thing, word-of-mouth recommendations have a strong effect in the freelance world. Moreover, you will be able to produce examples of work sold, or be able to refer prospects to other clients who have engaged you successfully. Evidence, for instance, that your fashion photographs have actually been used by national magazines generally impresses more than a folder of prints, no matter how good they are. In freelance work, as in other spheres, nothing succeeds like success.

One problem with freelance work, though, is that clients often want something done in a hurry — over a weekend or even overnight. This can be highly inconvenient at times, but it is generally a bad idea to turn work down simply for this reason. If you have to be selective, turn away the smaller, less remunerative jobs or commissions from people who are slow to pay their bills. One thing you should never do, though, is to let a client down. If you cannot, or do not want, to take on an assignment, say so immediately.

Press advertising

Advertising is a marketing tool and like any other tool you have to use it in the right place, at the right time and for the right job if it is going to be of any use to you. If you are a local building contractor, there is no point advertising in national newspapers, because most of the circulation, which is what you are paying for in the rates charged, will be outside the geographical area you are working in. On the other hand, if you are making a product to sell by mail order, the bigger the circulation the better. There are, however, still provisos: there is, for example, no point in advertising a product aimed at 'top people' in a mass-circulation tabloid.

The first rule is to pick the right medium for the product or service you have to sell. Do not be dazzled by circulation figures. What matters is the *quality* of the circulation in relation to your marketing needs, and a trade or local paper may often provide the best value for money. A few years ago the author was responsible for marketing a very expensive American book on Japanese flower arranging. It turned out that there was a small journal with a circulation of a few hundred copies to devotees of this arcane hobby and a full-page advertisement (which then cost a mere £15), combined with an order coupon, produced a quite extraordinary response. Of course, full-page advertisements normally cost a good deal more than that and in the nationals they can run to thousands of pounds. A small, regular insertion in a local or specialist paper is what you should be thinking of; and the keyword is 'regular'. People's needs change from week to week, and unless you happen to hit them in the week they need your product, you will not hit them at all.

Regular advertising need not be expensive. An advertisement in the 'classified' section (but be sure to specify the right classification!) costs only a few pounds, and there may be bulk rates for regular insertions. You can also have a display advertisement. These are charged by column inches (or centimetres) rather than by line as is the case with classified. It costs more, but the advantage is that you may be able to control the position in which your advertisement is to appear. The top and outside edges are more eye-catching than, say, the inside corners. 'Facing matter' advertisements, particularly when they are facing a feature article relating to your kind of product, can also be very effective. It is a good idea to get a graphic designer — you will find plenty of addresses in Yellow Pages or your Thomson local directory — to do a layout for you. It will only cost you a few pounds and the result will be infinitely more attractive and eyecatching than if you leave it to the printer's typesetter.

Some days are reckoned by admen to produce a better response than others, although there are divided opinions on what these days are. The best advice is to experiment with different days. It is worth experimenting with the wording, too. Try several variations on the same theme and use the one that brings you the best response. But avoid trying to cram in too many words. People do not, on the whole, respond to over-crowded ads.

One important feature is that your advertisement should be very specific about how the goods and services advertised can be obtained. Your address should be prominent and if you are only available at certain times of the day or in the evenings this should be stated. If you are selling a product, an order coupon (stating price *and* postage) reinforces this point. It will also enable you to measure the extent of the response. You should, in fact, keep a close eye on where most of your sales or assignments come from: the type of customer and how he is getting to hear about you. This will enable you to concentrate future marketing efforts in the most rewarding sectors.

Public relations

It may be possible, particularly if you have a specialist line of business, to obtain free coverage in trade journals and local newspapers by sending them press releases to mark events such as the opening of an extension or the provision of some unique service. You simply type the information on a slip marked PRESS RELEASE; 'embargo' it — ie prohibit its use — until a date that suits you, and send it to newspapers and magazines you choose as the likeliest to use it. Newspapers and other news media — don't forget about local radio and even local TV — are, however, only interested in *news* and the mere fact that you have opened a business may not interest them much. Try to find a news angle, for instance, that you have obtained a large export order, or are reviving a local craft or are giving employment to school leavers. If you have any friends who are journalists ask their advice on the sort of information that is likely to get the attention of editors. Better still, ask them if they will draft your press release for you.

There are many other PR activities — sponsorship, stunts, celebrity appearances at your premises, public speaking, and so on. All are designed to publicise who you are and what you do, and suggest to the public that you provide a worthwhile and reliable service. PR for the small business is covered throughly in Michael Bland's *Be Your Own PR Man* (published by Kogan Page).

Direct mail and direct response promotion

Direct mail selling is a considerable subject in its own right. It differs from mail order in that the latter consists of mailing goods direct to the customer from orders engendered by general press advertising, whereas in the case of direct mail selling the advertising is a brochure or sales letter specifically directed at the customer. Direct response promotion consists of an ad plus coupon placed in a newspaper or journal, to be posted to the manufacturer as an order. If you use these methods, remember to allow for postage in your pricing and since the response to direct mail averages around 2 per cent, the postage cost per sale is quite a considerable factor. It can, however, be a very effective way of selling specialised, high-priced items (£10 is around the viable minimum these days) or of identifying people who are likely to buy from you regularly if you are selling variations on the same product. Unless you are very skilful at writing brochures or sales letters you should get this done for you by an expert. Such people are employed by mailing list brokers (you will find those in the Yellow Pages) who will often provide a complete package: they will sell to you, or compile for you, specialised lists, address and stuff envelopes and produce sales literature.

Their services are not cheap and before you plunge into a direct mail campaign there are relatively inexpensive ways of testing the market for yourself. Pick 100 specialist addresses of the type you want to reach on a bigger scale — again, you may find them in the Yellow Pages. A small want ad in one of the advertising industry's trade papers will soon raise the services of freelance copywriters and designers if you need such help. From the percentage reply to the sample mailing you will be able to gauge whether a bigger campaign is worth mounting and you will also get some idea of how to price the product to take into account the likely mailing costs per sale. It is generally essential, by the way, with direct mail advertising, to include a reply paid card or envelope with your sales literature. Details of how to apply for reply paid and Freepost facilities are available from the Post Office.

Checklist: marketing your work

Manufacturers

1. Have you tested your idea by discussing your proposed product with potential customers? Or, better still, showing it to them?
2. Is the market for it big enough? How accessible is it?
3. Can the customers you have in mind afford a price that will produce a profit for you?
4. Have you studied the competition from the point of view of price, design quality, reliability, delivery dates, etc?
5. Should you modify your produce in some way so as to get the edge on the competition? Have you worked out what this will do to your costs?
6. Is there a long-term future for your product? If not, do you have any ideas for a follow-up?

125

7. Can you handle distribution? Do you have access to a van if the market is local? Do you have adequate parking facilities if it requires despatching?
8. In the latter case, have you taken post and packing costs into account in working out how much the product will cost the customer?
9. Do you have adequate space to hold stock, taking into account production time?
10. Do you have someone who can deal with customer queries and complaints? Or have you allowed for the fact that you will have to take time out yourself to deal with them?

Shops and service industries

1. How much do you know about the area?
2. Is the location good from the point of view of attracting the kind of trade you are looking for?
3. What competitors do you have?
4. How are they doing?
5. Based on your study of the area, and the people who live in it, how does this affect the type of goods or the nature of the service you are going to offer?
6. If you are buying a going concern, have you checked it out thoroughly with your professional advisers?

Freelance services

1. Do you have any contacts who can give you work?
2. Have you made a realistic appraisal of how much you can expect to earn over the first six months?
3. Have you allowed for the fact that you will need a good deal of spare time to go around looking for more business?
4. What evidence can you produce of your competence to do freelance work in your proposed field?
5. Have you shown that evidence to the sort of person who might be a customer to get his reaction on whether it is likely to impress?
6. Who are your competitors, what do they charge and what can you offer that is superior to their services?

Advertising and promotion

1. Have you chosen the right medium to promote your product or service?

2. Do you have any idea of the circulation and how this is broken down, geographically or by type of reader?
3. Have you worked out any way of monitoring results, for instance by including a coupon?
4. Have you included the cost of advertising and promotion in your cash flow budget and in costing your product?
5. Have you worked out how many orders you need to get from your advertising/promotion campaign to show a profit?
6. In the case of a display advertisement, have you specified a position in which it is to appear?
7. Again, in the case of a display ad or a brochure have you had it properly designed?
8. Does your advertising/promotion material state where your product or service can be obtained and, if relevant, the price?
9. Is the wording compelling? Does it clearly describe the product or service and does it motivate the customer? Would you buy it, if you were a customer?
10. In the case of a classified advertisement, have you specified under which classification it is to appear?
11. Are all the statements and claims you are making about your product or service true to the best of your knowledge and belief, bearing in mind that untruths can leave you open to prosecution under the Trade Descriptions Act?

1.10: Employing People

A fairly common observation about employing people has always been to say that this is when your troubles begin. Today this is truer than ever, because apart from the difficulty of finding Mr or Ms Right — a task which even experienced personnel people admit, in their more candid moments, is something of a lottery — a mass of legislation has been enacted in recent years which, it is thought by some, favours the rights of employees at the expense of employers. Though the aim of this legislation has mainly been to protect the workforce of larger companies from arbitrary hiring and firing, it embraces even the smallest employer and to a large extent it covers part-time as well as full-time employees. Whole books could be and have been written about the legal technicalities involved, but all we can do in this section is to draw the reader's attention to some of the major pitfalls you should look out for when you start employing people.

The contract of employment

The contract of employment statement which has to be issued in writing to every employee who is going to work for you for 16 hours or more per week within 13 weeks of joining is in fact not a pitfall, but a rather sensible document which clarifies right from the outset what the terms of employment are. From the employer's point of view, the necessity of drafting a contract of employment statement should concentrate the mind wonderfully on issues about which it is all too easy to be sloppy at the expense of subsequent aggravation, such as hours of work, holidays and, above all, exactly what it is the employee is supposed to be doing. The following points have to be covered in the contract, and you must say if you have not covered one or other of them:

☐ The rate of pay and how it is calculated
☐ Whether it is paid weekly or monthly

THE GUARDIAN GUIDE TO RUNNING A SMALL BUSINESS

THIRD EDITION
Edited by Clive Woodcock

This book is based on a collection of useful and informative articles which have appeared in the **Small Business Guardian**. It begins by explaining the first steps towards establishing a business and goes on to discuss in detail all aspects of general business organisation: choosing offices, employing staff, controlling cash flow, dealing with the vast amounts of governmental legislation and administrative procedures, legal and financial options, marketing, sales promotion and the tax benefits which may be gained through intelligent use of the existing system. It provides a clear and practical outline of how to approach problems which may arise in these areas and a guide to where expert advice on solutions to all these matters can be obtained.

For this edition, certain sections have been heavily revised and new ones have been added to keep up with recent innovations and changes within the world of business. Computers, for example, are now more widely used in all sizes and types of organisations. Consequently, a new chapter has been included to assist the small businessman in choosing new technology of this kind.

Despite technological change and the shift towards fully computerised systems, employees are still crucial to the success of any new venture and a chapter on employees, their rights and those of the employer, has been written as a guide to help both parties make the best of the opportunities available.

'Pithy, clear . . . and full of good practical advice' British Business

Clive Woodcock is editor of the *Small Business Guardian* and the *European Small Business Journal*. He has also written *Raising Finance*.

£9.95 Hardback 0 85038 619 5
£5.95 Paperback 0 85038 620 9
256 pages 216x138mm

Kogan Page, 120 Pentonville Road, London N1

Available from Booksellers or, in case of difficulty direct from the publisher

- ☐ The normal hours of work and the terms and conditions relating to them
- ☐ Holidays and holiday pay
- ☐ Provision for sick pay
- ☐ Pension and pension schemes
- ☐ Notice required by both parties
- ☐ The job title
- ☐ Any disciplinary rules relating to the job
- ☐ Grievance procedures.

A further requirement is that employers must issue on or before each pay day and for each employee an itemised statement showing:

- ☐ Gross wages/salary
- ☐ Net wages/salary
- ☐ Deductions and the reasons for them (unless these are a standard amount, in which case the reasons need only be repeated every 12 months)
- ☐ Details of part-payments, eg special overtime rates.

Unfair dismissal

Probably the area of legislation which it is easiest and most common to fall foul of is that relating to unfair dismissal. Every employee, including part-timers if they work for you in other than a freelance capacity for more than 16 hours a week, who has been on your staff continuously for 52 weeks or more (104 weeks or more in the case of a new business) must be given a written statement of your reason if you want to dismiss him. You must also give him one week's notice (or payment in lieu) if he has been with you continuously for four weeks or more and, after two years, one week's notice for every year of continuous employment. Fair enough, you might say, particularly as, on the face of things, what the law regards as fair grounds for dismissal are perfectly reasonable: incompetence, misconduct or genuine redundancy. The problem is that the employee is at liberty to disagree with you on the fairness issue and to take his case to an industrial tribunal, which stipulates that the employment grounds for dismissal must be *reasonable*.

The 1980 Employment Act made four changes of particular relevance to small businesses employing staff:

1. The qualifying period for alleged unfair dismissal claims

was extended from six months to 12. For firms with 20 employees or less it has been extended to two years in respect of new employees; an important simplification since redundancy has a similar two-year qualifying period.

2. Industrial tribunals are directed to take account of the size and resources of employer. For example where an employee proves unsatisfactory in one job, a large employer might be able to offer him another position, but a small employer would find this more difficult in most cases.

3. Post-maternity reinstatement is waived for firms of five employees or less, if re-instatement is not practicable.

4. Frivolous claims are to be deterred by a liability to costs.

If the employee has been guilty of gross misconduct, such as persistent lateness, you will probably win your case, provided you warned him in writing to mend his ways well before you dismissed him. The point here is that you must not only have good reasons for dismissing him, but you must also have acted reasonably in the dismissal situation. This means that you have got to follow a proper sequence of written warnings, not less than three is the number generally recommended, stating his inadequacies, telling him what he has to do to put them right and spelling out the consequences if he fails to do so.

When it comes to matters of competence, though, things are rather less clear-cut, particularly if the task involved is not one where performance can be readily quantified or where there are many imponderables. It would be relatively easy to argue a case against a machine operator who was consistently turning out less work than his colleagues on similar machines, but far more difficult in the case of a salesman who could plead that a poor call-rate was the result of difficulties in finding car parking or inefficient back-up from the office.

The fact is that in all matters affecting competence you really have to do your homework very carefully before dismissing someone. The inexperienced employer may unwittingly contribute to a judgement by the Tribunal going against him by such steps as including the person concerned in a general salary rise not long before informing him he is not up to the job.

There may be cases where you, as the employer, are satisfied that dismissal is fair, but where the law does not agree with you. One where you have to be very careful is dismissal on medical grounds. No reasonable employer would dismiss anyone in such circumstances if he could help it, but if you get stuck with someone who is persistently off sick and is able to provide satisfactory medical evidence you would have to show proof that the absences were of such a nature as to cause disruption to your business before you could discharge him. Even more tricky is the case of employees who are engaged in public duties, such as being on the local council. You have to give them reasonable time off to attend those duties, though not necessarily with pay.

We have used the word 'he' of employees so far (in the interests of brevity, not for sexist reasons) but, of course, all these provisions extend to women as well. The Sex Discrimination Act and the Equal Pay Act mean that women have in all respects to be treated on an equal footing with men, though since 1982 firms with fewer than five employees have been exempt from the former provisions. There are also occupations where discrimination is legal on commonsense grounds — for instance, lavatory attendants! For firms employing more than five people, there are some additional hazards to employing women of child-bearing age. Provided she works until 11 weeks before her confinement a woman who has been continuously in your employ for two years or more is entitled to take 40 weeks off if she becomes pregnant and to return to her original job, without loss of seniority, at the end of that time. Furthermore, she is entitled to remuneration at nine-tenths her normal salary less NI maternity allowance, for the first six weeks of her absence, although the employer can recover the money from the Department of Employment. And if you bring in a replacement for her, or any other employee who is off for any longer period of time, be very careful. Her replacement could sue you for unlawful dismissal unless you notify him or her in writing that the appointment is a temporary one and give notice when it is coming to an end.

The penalties for losing an unfair dismissals case can be ruinous for a small firm. In the most extreme instances you could be in for a compensation award of £7000, plus any redundancy pay to which the employee is entitled, plus a basic award related to age and length of service of up to £4050. On top of all this, in the most aggravated cases, there is a further additional award of £7020. Thus if you are in any doubt at all about a dismissal you should consult a solicitor who is versed in this aspect of the law.

Redundancy

Redundancy is a ripe area for misunderstanding. Redundancy

occurs when a job disappears, for example, because a firm ceases trading or has to cut down on staff. It does not have the same restrictions as dismissal, but nevertheless does involve some financial penalties for employers if the employee has been continuously employed by the firm concerned for two years or more. In that case he will be entitled to redundancy pay on a formula based on length of service and rate of pay. About half of this can be recovered from the Department of Employment, which you should notify if you intend to make anyone redundant. As usual, there is a good deal of form filling involved. The law also requires you to give advance warning to the relevant unions if any of their members are to be made redundant.

What happens if you buy a business, lock, stock and barrel, together with the staff? You may find that you do not like some of the people the previous owner took on, or that you want to change or drop some of the things he was doing, with the result that staff will be made redundant. Irrespective of the fact that you did not hire the people concerned, you are still stuck with your responsibility towards them as their current employer, so that being the proverbial new broom can be a very costly exercise. Before buying a business, therefore, it is very important to look at the staff and at the extent of any redundancy payments or dismissals situations you could get involved in.

In the same context, another Act of Parliament you should keep an eye open for when buying a business is the Health and Safety at Work Act which lays down standards to which working premises have to conform. Before putting down your money you should check with the inspectors of the Health and Safety Executive that any premises you are buying or leasing as part of the deal meet those standards.

Recruitment

The cost of discharging staff, whether because of redundancy or by dismissal, makes it imperative that you should make the right decisions in picking people to work for you in the first place. We have said that the sphere of personnel selection is something of a lottery. It could equally be described as a gamble and there are ways in which you could cut down on the odds against you.

The most obvious question to ask yourself is whether you really do need to take someone on permanently at all. The principle we have put forward for the purchase of equipment —

never buy anything outright unless you are sure you have a continuing use for it and that it will pay for itself over a reasonable interval of time — also applies to personnel. The legal constraints that cover part-time or full-time employees do not extend to freelances, personnel from agencies or outside work done on contract, and this could well be the best way of tackling a particular problem such as an upward bump in demand until you are sure that it is going to last.* It is worth remembering, too, that when you take on staff you take on a good many payroll and administrative overheads in addition to their salary. These can add quite significantly to your costs.

Sooner or later, though, if you want your business to grow (and growth of some kind seems to be an inevitable concomitant of success) you are going to need people. But even then you should ask yourself what exactly you need them for and how much you can afford to pay. Clarifying these two issues is not only important for itself, but it will also give you the basis of a job description which you can use in your press advertising or approach to a recruitment agency, at the interview and, finally, in the contract of employment. Around it you should also build a series of questions to ask the interviewee that should give you some indication of his competence to do the job. Such questions should call for a detailed response rather than a 'yes' or 'no' type of answer. For example, if you are interviewing a sales representative, asking him how long he has been in the business will tell you something, but not nearly as much as the answer to a question that tries to elicit which buyers he knows and how well he knows them.

Competence is part of the story. Equally important is the interviewee's track record: how many previous employers he has had and whether his progress has been up, down or steady. Too many job changes at frequent intervals can be a bad sign and it is fair to ask searching questions about this if it is part of the employment pattern. It is also wise to be cautious about people who are willing to take a large drop in salary. In these days when good jobs are hard to come by there can be a perfectly good reason for this, but you ought to tactfully find out what it is.

---

*However, in some cases freelances have successfully argued retrospectively that since they were subject to the same conditions as the ordinary employees of a firm, they were covered by employment law. It is not enough to say that 'A' is a freelance and 'B' is not; there must be recognisable differences in the way they work. The freelance must not be under your direct supervision and control, or he will be likely to be classified (for the purposes of redundancy pay, etc) as an employee.

Possibly the references will give you a clue and you should always ask for and check references. They are not always reliable — most employers are reasonable people and they will not speak ill of an ex-employee if they can help it (though they should be aware that it is illegal to misrepresent the abilities or overstate the capability of an employee or ex-employee to another employer) — but they will generally alert you to real disaster areas. Telephone reference checks are widely reckoned to be more reliable than written ones because referees are nearly always more forthcoming in conversation than in a letter, since the law of libel and industrial relations law looms large in any written deposition.

Conditions of work

Numerous regulations affect working conditions and you should be conversant with those relevant to your area, particularly if it is a potentially dangerous trade. Length of hours, minimum wages, employment of young persons, etc will tend to apply to all businesses, and, though you may escape persecution for a while, to fall foul of the law is likely to be embarrassing and expensive.

Checklist: employing people

1. Do you really need to take on staff? Will there be enough to keep them busy a year from now?
2. Have you worked out a job description which sets out the purpose of the job, the duties involved and who the person appointed will report to?
3. Have you decided how much you can afford to pay?
4. Do your advertisements or approach to a recruiting agency spell out the job description, the salary and the approximate age of the person you are looking for?
5. Does it in any way contravene the Sex Discrimination Act or the Race Relations Act?
6. Have you prepared a series of questions that will throw some light on the interviewee's competence, personality and previous record of employment?
7. Have you taken up and checked references?
8. Are you satisfied, before making the appointment, that you have seen enough applicants to give you an idea of the quality of staff available for this particular job?

1.11: Taxation

How you are affected by taxation depends on the nature of the commercial activity in which you are engaged. Virtually everyone pays tax on income from some source, whether this be from full-time employment, from dividends or interest or from self-employment or from a combination of several of these elements. The various kinds of income are assessed under several headings or schedules and the ones we will be particularly concerned with are:

1. Schedule D. Case I and Case II: Income from trades, professions or vocations. (In the interests of simplicity we will refer to this as Schedule D, though there are four other 'Cases' of Schedule D income.)
2. Schedule E: Wages and salaries from employment.

There are also other ways in which you may be involved in tax matters. You may be paying capital gains tax on the disposal of capital assets. If you are employing people full-time, you will be responsible for administering their PAYE payments; also, in certain circumstances, your own PAYE. If you are a shareholder in a limited company, it will be paying corporation tax on its profits. Lastly, you may — and if your turnover exceeds £18,000 a year, you must — for the supply of certain goods and services collect VAT from your customers and pay it over to Customs and Excise, less any VAT on goods and services supplied to you in the course of business.

One cannot, in a book of this nature, deal with a subject as complex as taxation exhaustively. But, with this proviso, let us look in broad outline at some of its principal implications. There are certain income tax advantages in working for yourself, or even in earning a supplementary income from part-time self-employment. To some extent these advantages were eroded by the National Insurance contributions for the self-employed (Class 4) which came into force in April 1975 and imposed what was, in effect, an additional and much resented tax on the self-employed. The amount of the contribution is subject to a certain amount of annual tinkering. It is payable by men under 65 and women under 60 and it currently stands as a levy of 6.3 per cent on profits/gains between £3800 and £12,000.

There have also been some changes in real terms in the flat-rate weekly (Class 2) National Insurance contribution additionally payable by people who have an income from self-employment as well as a salary from another source. The earnings rate from self-employment above which this additional contribution has to be paid has been raised to £1775 a year and the weekly contributions have been raised from £3.75 to £4.40 for 1983. There is, however, a maximum on the total contributions due and if your contributions exceed that maximum then the excess is refunded. Alternatively you can apply to defer your weekly contribution until the end of the year when your potential contribution is known. Your accountant should be able to advise you on the best course of action to take. Details of what you have to do to get deferment are given in a government leaflet, NP 18.

The reasoning behind what remains a somewhat doctrinaire piece of legislation appears to be that self-employed people are obtaining tax concessions that are not offered to the rest of the community. There is therefore a correspondingly strong case for taking the fullest possible advantage of these concessions in so far as they are indeed available.

Like the income of employed persons, the income from self-employment in its various forms is subject to an ascending rate of tax, starting at a flat 30 per cent up to the first £14,600 per annum and rising to a maximum of 60 per cent. These figures are subject to certain personal tax reliefs, such as allowances for dependent relatives, for part of the premiums on life assurance policies, etc, which you can deduct from your total income in arriving at the rate at which you pay tax.

Where income from self-employment or even part-time employment differs from ordinary wage- or salary-earning status is that you are allowed, in assessing your earnings, to deduct from your profits any revenue expenditure 'wholly and exclusively incurred' in carrying on your trade or profession. Under the heading of revenue expenditure comes business expenses, and since your profits and your earnings will be either synonymous or closely related, the first point to observe is that you must claim all the business expenses to which the taxman entitles you.

Principal allowable business expenses

1. *The cost of goods bought for resale and materials bought in manufacturing.* This does not include capital expenditure like cars or machinery, though certain minor items like small tools or typewriters may be allowed under this heading.

2. *The running costs of the business or practice.* Under this concession come heating, lighting, rent, rates, telephone, postage, advertising, cleaning, repairs (but not improvements of a capital nature), insurance, the use of special clothing. If you are using your home as office you can claim up to two-thirds of the running costs of the premises as a business expense — provided you can convince the taxman that you are indeed using as high a proportion of your house as this exclusively for business purposes. In the past some people have been advised not to make this type of claim at all, because of the probability that, on selling, they might have to pay Capital Gains Tax on the 'business' part of the sale, thus outweighing any income tax advantage. This situation was altered in the 1978 and 1980 Budgets (see section below on Capital Gains Tax).

3. *Carriage, packing and delivery costs.*

4. *Wages and salaries.* Any sums paid to full-time or part-time employees. You cannot, however, count any salary you and your partners are taking from the business, but you can pay your wife a salary (provided she is actually doing a reasonably convincing amount of work for you). This is an advantage if her income from other sources is less than £1785 a year, because that first slice of earnings is free of tax — one of the reliefs we mentioned earlier.

5. *Entertaining.* Entertainment of overseas customers. The tax office may want to establish some correlation between the amount of export business you do and the sums you are claiming for entertainment in this connection. You are also allowed to claim for entertaining your own staff.

6. *Travel.* Hotel and travelling expenses on business trips and in connection with soliciting business. You are not, however, allowed the cost of travel between home and office, if you

have a regular place of work. In addition to these expenses you can claim for the running costs of your car (including petrol) in proportion to the extent to which you use it for business purposes.

7. *Interest.* Interest on loans and overdrafts incurred wholly in connection with your business. This does not include interest on any money you or your partners have lent to the business.

8. *Hire and hire purchase.* Hiring and leasing charges and hire element in hire-purchase agreement (not the actual cost, because this is a capital expense).

9. *Insurance.* Every kind of business insurance, including that taken out on behalf of employees, but excluding your own National Insurance contributions and premiums paid on your personal life insurance (though these premiums are subject to 17.5 per cent personal tax relief).

10. *The VAT element in allowable business expenses (unless you are a taxable trader for VAT purposes).* This would include, for instance, VAT on petrol for your car. The VAT on the purchase of a motor car is allowable in all cases, since this cannot be reclaimed in your VAT return.

11. *Certain legal and other professional fees.* You are allowed to claim for things like audit fees or court actions in connection with business, but not for penalties for breaking the law (eg parking fines!).

12. *Subscriptions to professional or trade bodies.*

13. *Bad debts.* These are bad debts actually incurred, though provision is generally allowed against tax in the case of specific customers whom you can show are unlikely to meet their obligations, for instance if their account is overdue and they are failing to respond to reminders. A general provision for a percentage of unspecified bad debts is not allowable against tax, however sensible it may be to make such provision in your accounts.

Trade debts owing to you are counted as income even if they have not been paid at the end of the accounting period.

Likewise, debts owed by you are counted as costs, even if you are not going to pay them until the next accounting period.

14. *Gifts.* Business gifts costing up to £2 per recipient per year (but excluding food, drink and tobacco). All gifts to employees are allowable, but generous employers should remember that the employee may have to declare them on *his* tax return if their value is substantial.

Capital allowances

The business expenses listed above are all revenue expenditure items, incurred in the day-to-day running of your affairs. There are also capital expenditure outlays, such as the acquisition of motor cars, large items of machinery and permanent fixtures and fittings. Although these cannot be deducted from your profits as normal business expenses, there are concessions available on them under another heading. In Chapter 8 we dealt with the subject of depreciation as an element to be allowed for in considering the cost to the business of acquiring capital equipment.

1. The depreciation on a motor car can be deducted from your profits at the rate of 25 per cent a year as a 'writing down allowance'. However, in the case of cars costing more than £8000 this is limited to £2000 a year.
2. A writing down allowance is also given for other capital equipment (but not buildings). You can, in fact, take a 'first year allowance' which enables you to write off 100 per cent in the tax year of acquisition. It may, of course, not pay you to do it this way if you do not have profits to set it off against. In that case you can claim your allowance at the rate of 25 per cent a year. Each year, of course, the 25 per cent is claimed on the proportion that has not yet been written off. Thus, if you buy an offset machine for £500, in year one you claim 500 x (25/100) = £125; and in year two £375 x (25/100) = £94, and so on.
3. Equipment bought on hire purchase is eligible for the writing down allowance in respect of the capital element. The hire charges themselves can be claimed as business expenses, spread over the period of the agreement.

In calculating your writing down allowances you will have to take into account whether or not you are a taxable trader for VAT purposes, which depends on whether your annual turnover exceeds £18,000. If you are, you will already have reclaimed the VAT on your purchase in your quarterly or monthly VAT return. Thus capital allowances will be calculated on the net amount excluding VAT (except in the case of motor cars).

Stock valuation

If you are in a business which involves holding stock (which may be either finished goods for resale, work in progress or materials for manufacture), it must be valued at each accounting date. The difference in value between opening stock and closing stock represents the cost of sales. Obviously, therefore, if you value your closing stock on a different basis from the opening stock, this will affect the profit you show. If you value the same kind of items more highly it will depress the cost of sales and increase the apparent profit. If you value them on a lower basis the cost of sales will be increased and the profit decreased.

Example A			Example B		
Sales		£150	Sales		£150
Opening Stock			*Opening Stock*		
100 Rose bushes			100 Rose bushes		
@ £1.00:	£100		@ £1.00:	£100	
Closing Stock			*Closing Stock*		
50 Rose bushes			50 Rose bushes		
@ £1.50:	£75		@ 60p:	£30	
Cost of Sales		£25	Cost of Sales		£70
Profit		£125	Profit		£80

Table 11.1 *An example of stock valuation*

Plainly, then, it does not make sense for you to upvalue your closing stock in order to show a paper profit. Equally, you are not allowed to depress it artificially in order to achieve the reverse effect. However, if you can make a genuine case that some stock will have to be sold at a lower margin than the one you normally work to in order to be able to sell it within a reasonable time, then a valuation in the light of this fact will generally be accepted by the taxman.

Stock relief

In times of high inflation it becomes almost inevitable that your stock appreciates in value, at least on paper. The snag is that when you come to replace it you will have to pay correspondingly more so that your profits, assuming you go on trading, are rapidly wiped out. It would be unjust as well as damaging to many businesses if these paper profits were taxed and in 1974 a provision was introduced to give tax relief in such cases. Initially, this was a temporary measure, but it has now achieved more permanent status. The 1981 Budget established that from November 1980 the relief given is based on a percentage of the opening stock (and work in progress) for the period of account. The first £2000 of stock do not qualify for relief. As far as the pre-November 1980 situation is concerned it could, of course, have happened that your stock actually decreased in value, for example, because you had decided to carry less inventory. In that case you would be liable to repay any corresponding relief previously granted, but there are quite generous provisions for deferring such repayments on which your accountant should be able to advise you.

Computing taxable profit

Normally your accountant will prepare a set of accounts for you for each year you are in business. Your accounting date need not coincide with the tax year (ending 5 April). The profits shown in these accounts will be the basis of your assessment.

As we stated earlier, certain costs which are genuine enough from the point of view of your profit and loss account are nevertheless not allowable for tax purposes, for example, entertaining customers other than foreign buyers or their agents. You are also not allowed to charge depreciation against your profit (though remember that you will receive a writing down allowance which, in the end, has a similar effect). These and other non-allowable expenses, therefore, must be added back to the profits.

Equally certain profits which you have made are to be deducted for the purposes of Schedule D assessment because they are taxed on a different basis and are subject to a return under another heading. Examples are gains from the disposal of capital assets, income from sub-letting part of your premises or interest paid by the bank on money being held in a deposit account.

143

In the 1980 Budget some new kinds of business spending came in for tax relief, notably incidental costs of raising loan finance and start-up costs incurred before you began trading.

Losses

If your business or professional occupation has made a loss on its accounting year (and remember that from the tax point of view non-allowable expenses are added back to profits and you will have to do the same in your return), you can have the loss set off against your other income for the tax year in which the loss was incurred and for the subsequent year. The set-off has to be made first of all against earned income and then, if you are still 'in credit', against unearned income. This is laid down because unearned income (income from investments) may be subject to a higher tax rate than the earned variety. However, you cannot set off business losses against liability for capital gains tax.

If your income for the year in which you made the loss and that of the subsequent year still does not exceed that loss, you can set off the balance against future profits; or you can carry the loss back and set it against earlier profits.

An important concession was made in the 1978 Budget to sole traders and partnerships. Since 1978 losses incurred in the first four years of a business can be carried back against income from other sources, including salary, in the three years before commencing business as a self-employed person or partner. However, it should be noted that this does not apply to losses incurred by a limited company of which you are a shareholder — such losses can only be set off against profits chargeable in the form of corporation tax. Even if you invest your money in your own company and it fails, you can only set off your loss against capital gains from other sources — not against income tax.

The basis of assessment

Schedule D tax is normally assessed on the profits for the preceding tax year. Thus your tax assessment for the tax year ending 5 April 1983, and which you have to pay in 1983, will relate to the accounting year which ended in the tax year finishing 5 April 1982. Your *accounting* year, as we have just said, need not coincide with the taxman's year: 6 April to

5 April. You can, if you like, run it to the anniversary of your commencing business, or on a calendar year. However, in the first year of operations, you will be assessed either on the proportion of profits for the accounting year represented by the time from your starting date to 5 April, or the actual profits during those months. You cannot, in respect of the first year, ask to be assessed on a preceding year basis.

Thus, if you commenced business on 1 October 1982 and your profit for the year ending 30 September 1983 is £1000, you will be taxed on the basis of six months' profit (1 October 1982 to 5 April 1983). This assessment will have to be met in 1983. It is not on a preceding year basis.

In the second tax year, in this instance, the one ending 5 April 1984, your Schedule D tax will be based on the actual profit for the first 12 months of business: here, £1000.

In the third tax year you will be assessed on your declaration for the preceding year which, as we have seen, is still the profit in your first 12 months of operations: in this case again £1000. Thereafter you will be paying tax on the normal basis of the preceding year's profits.

The object of these somewhat tortuous manoeuvres is to put you into phase for paying tax on the latter basis; but it has the disadvantage that if your profits are high in the first twelve months and thereafter shade off, you will be paying more tax than you should be in the second and third year. You can, therefore, elect to be taxed on your actual profits for those years. You should take your accountant's advice on the best course of action. He may also be able to demonstrate technical advantages, in terms of taxation, in starting business just after, rather than just before, 5 April in calculating the basis of assessment over the opening three-year period of a business.

Spare-time work

Even though you have a full-time job which is being taxed under Schedule E and thus being taken care of under your employer's PAYE scheme, you may also have earnings from part-time employment in the evenings and weekends which you have to declare. Your employer need not know about this second income because you can establish with your tax inspector that the tax code which fixes the amount of PAYE you pay (see below) only relates to the income you receive from your employer.

Your spare-time income is also eligible for the allowances on expenses 'wholly and exclusively incurred' for business purposes. This means that it is most important that you should keep a proper record of incomings and outgoings. If your spare-time activities are on a small scale, you will not need to keep the kind of detailed books of account described in Chapter 1.5; but you should certainly maintain a simple cash book, from which at the end of the year you or your accountant can prepare a statement to append to your income tax return.

Tax on spare-time work is payable in two half-yearly assessments: on 1 January within the year of assessment and on 1 July following the end of it.

Probably the largest item you will be able to set off against spare-time income is any sums you can pay your wife for her assistance up to the level of her tax-free allowance of £1565 and provided she is not earning as much as this from another source.

Partnerships

Partnership income is assessed between the partners in the same ratio as that in which they have agreed to split profits. However, the ratio will be the one that actually exists at the time the assessment is made which, since the tax is on a preceding year basis, may not necessarily be the same as that which obtained the year the profits were established.

Salaries, and interest on money put into the business by partners, are considered as profits for tax purposes and have to be added back as such in order to arrive at taxable profits.

For the purposes of assessment, the partnership is treated as a single entity, so the tax will be collected from the partnership as a whole, not from the individuals that constitute it.

Corporation tax

Corporation tax is payable by limited companies. Its provisions are somewhat complicated and it must be assumed, for the purposes of this brief chapter on taxation, that readers who are intending to set up businesses in this form will seek professional advice on tax aspects. However, the salient points are as follows:

1. Corporation tax is charged at a rate of 55.5 per cent on profits of between £100,000 and £500,000, though for companies with profits under £100,000 the rate is 38 per cent.

2. Dividends are paid to shareholders without deduction of tax, but 30/70ths of the dividends must be handed over to the Inland Revenue by the company within three months of the date of payment of the dividend. This is known as 'advance corporation tax' and is set off against corporation tax payable on profits.
3. Unlike Schedule D income tax, corporation tax is normally payable nine months from the end of each accounting period.
4. Allowable expenses against profits for corporation tax purposes are roughly the same as those for other forms of revenue expenditure, with the important addition that salaries paid to employees (who include the owners of the company, if they are working in it) are deductible. However, in certain circumstances, the interest on loans made to the company by directors will not be treated as an allowable expense, but as a distribution of income on which advance corporation tax is payable.

If you are a director of a limited company, your income from this source will not be liable to the National Insurance levy of 6.3 per cent on income between £3800 and £12,000 a year. Your National Insurance contributions will be at the employed rate and you will be paying PAYE on your salary.

Capital transfer tax

Capital transfer tax was introduced in 1974 to replace estate duty and was potentially disastrous for many small businesses, which, having no liquid assets with which to pay the tax, would ultimately have been faced with no alternative but to sell out, when their proprietors would have come up against the further hurdle of capital gains tax.

The effect of CTT was mitigated in the 1978 and 1980 Budgets. It has been recognised that small businesses are, in current jargon, a 'special case'. So, for the purposes of CTT, the value of a business is reduced by 50 per cent when it comes to assessing it for this tax. In the 1983 Budget the threshold above which CTT is payable was raised to £60,000. Thus on a business with assets of £120,000 no CTT is now payable. Furthermore, if its value exceeds that figure, payment can be spread over eight years, thus diminishing the possibility of forced sales of assets simply to pay CTT.

Capital gains tax

This tax is of longer standing than CTT and has therefore acquired the inevitable battery of judgements of what is and is not a capital gain. But, in essence, the situation is that if you sell or give away assets, which are usually cash, shares, property or other valuables, and your real or notional gain in any tax year from such transactions is more than £5300 (a figure set in the 1983 Budget) you are liable for capital gains tax at a flat rate of 30 per cent on the difference between the price at which you acquired the asset and its current net value.

Two loopholes have been created in this particular tax fortress which may benefit small businesses. First, if you sell a business and buy another one within three years you can defer payment of the tax until you finally dispose of the one you have bought and cease trading. Second, people who have been owners of a business for more than 10 years can, at the age of 60, obtain relief from CGT if they do sell their assets, up to a maximum of £100,000.

This last benefit could be of particular value to people who have been using part of their private house as business premises and claiming tax relief on the charges incurred (heating, lighting, rates, etc) on a proportionate basis. Before 1978 they would have had to pay CGT on that proportion when they came to selling the house and this deterred quite a number of people from making such a claim, understandably when you consider the level of capital gain reached on house prices through the 1970s. Furthermore, in the 1983 Budget the first £10,000 capital gain relief on the sale of a private residence, part of which had been let, was increased to £20,000.

Appeals

Every taxpayer, be he an individual or a corporation, has the right to appeal against his tax assessment, if he has grounds for believing he is being asked to pay too much. Such appeals have to be made in writing to the Inspector of Taxes within 30 days of receiving an assessment. They are usually settled by more or less amicable correspondence, but ultimately can be taken to a hearing by the General or, in more complex cases, Special Commissioners.

PAYE

If you employ staff you will be responsible for deducting PAYE from their wages. The same applies to your own salary from a partnership or a limited company. The sums have to be paid monthly to the Inland Revenue by the employer.

You will receive from the tax office a tax deduction card for each employee, with spaces for each week or month (depending on how they are paid) for the year ending 5 April. On these cards, weekly or monthly as the case may be, you will have to enter under a number of headings, details of tax, pay for each period and for the year to date. You will know how much tax to deduct by reading off the employee's tax code number, which has been allotted to him by the tax office, against a set of tables with which you will also be issued. Without going into technicalities, the way the tables work is to provide a mechanism, self-correcting for possible fluctuations of earnings, of assessing the amount of tax due on any particular wage or salary at any given point of the year.

At the end of the tax year you will have to make out two forms:

1. Form P 60 issued to each employee. This gives details of pay and tax deducted during the year.
2. Form P 35 for the Inland Revenue. This is a summary of tax and graduated National Insurance contributions for all employees during the year.

When an employee leaves, you should complete another form, P 45, for him. Part of this form, showing his code number, pay and tax deducted for the year to date, is sent to the tax office. The other parts are to be handed by the employee to his new employer so that he can pick up the PAYE system where you left off.

VAT

If the taxable outputs of your business, which for practical purposes means what you charge your customers for any goods or services that are not specifically 'exempt', exceed, or are likely to exceed £18,000 in a year (or £6000 in any quarter) you will have to register with the Customs and Excise (not the tax office, in this case) as a taxable trader for VAT purposes. This means that you will have to remit to Customs and Excise,

149

either monthly or quarterly, 15 per cent of the price you charge on your 'outputs', this being the current standard rate of VAT. However, you will be able to deduct from these remittances any VAT which you yourself have been charged by your suppliers — your 'inputs'. This item covers not only materials used in producing the goods or services you supply to your customers, but everything which you have to buy to run your business, including such things as telephone charges.

Not all goods and services carry VAT. Some are 'zero rated' — basic foodstuffs, newspapers and exported goods being notable examples. Full details are contained in VAT Notices 700 and 701, issued by Customs and Excise, Kings Beam House, Mark Lane, London EC3, and you should obtain these from them, together with any other Notices about VAT which are relevant to your trade or profession. The significance of zero rating is that even though you do not charge VAT on goods of this nature that you supply, you can still claim back VAT on all your inputs, excluding the purchase of cars and business entertainment of domestic customers.

Zero rating is not, however, the same as 'exemption'. Zero rating carries a theoretical rate of VAT, which is 0 per cent. Exemption means that no rate of VAT applies at all and examples of exempt suppliers are bookmakers, persons selling or renting land and buildings, and various types of medical services. The exempt status is not particularly desirable, because if you are exempt you still have to pay VAT on all your inputs but have no outputs to set the tax off against.*

In this sense exempt traders are like private individuals and the question, therefore, arises as to whether you should, as you are entitled to do, ask to be registered as a taxable trader even though your outputs are less than the mandatory £18,000 a year level. Customs and Excise may, of course, refuse to register you on the grounds that your outputs are too low, though no hard-and-fast minimum figure for this has been fixed. Your accountant should be able to advise you on this point, but the main consideration would be the level of your taxable inputs. Thus if you are a part-time cabinetmaker you would be buying a lot of materials which carry VAT. But, if you were doing

---

* The distribution between zero-rated goods and exempt goods is important in determining whether you should be registered for VAT. Exempt goods do not count towards total 'turnover' for this purpose, but zero-rated goods do. Thus, if your turnover is £17,000 *with* exempt goods but only £12,000 without them, you are not liable to pay VAT.

something like picture research, the VAT inputs might be quite low and the administrative work involved in being a taxable trader might not be justified by the amount of VAT you could claim back against your outputs.

The point to be realised is that if you register as a taxable trader, voluntarily or otherwise, you are going to be involved in a fair bit of extra administration. At the end of each VAT accounting period (quarterly or monthly, the latter being more usual with traders in zero-rated goods), you will have to make a return of all your outputs, showing their total value and the amount of VAT charged. Against this you set the total of your inputs and the amount of VAT you have paid. The difference between the VAT on your outputs and that on your inputs is the sum payable to Customs and Excise. This obviously causes problems for retailers making a great many small sales and particularly for those supplying a mixture of zero-rated and standard-rated goods (eg a shop supplying sweets, which are taxable and other items of foods which are mostly zero rated). It also underlines the vital importance of keeping proper records and retaining copy invoices of all sales and purchases, because although your VAT return need only show totals, Customs and Excise inspectors are empowered to check the documents on which your return is based. There is obviously, therefore, a link between the records you have to maintain for ordinary accounting purposes and those that are needed to back up your VAT return.

There is also a close connection between VAT and the problem of cash flow. When you receive an invoice bearing VAT, the input element can be set off against the VAT output on your next return, irrespective of whether you yourself have paid the supplier. Therefore, if you are buying an expensive piece of capital equipment it will make sense for you to arrange to be invoiced just before your next return to Customs and Excise is due.

The boot is on the other foot, though, when you yourself are extending credit to a customer. The sale is reckoned to have taken place when the invoice has been rendered, not when you have received payment. Therefore you will be paying VAT on your output before you have actually received the cash covering it from your customer. This also means that except in some special cases no relief is given in respect of bad debts.

The black economy

One cannot these days write about taxation without some reference to the 'black economy'. There is a good deal of evidence to suggest that the response to the way inflated wages and salaries are pulling an increasing number of people into higher tax brackets has been tax evasion on a large scale by a variety of means such as straightforward non-declaration of earnings, making or receiving payments in cash, arranging remuneration in kind or, simply, barter deals. Some of these methods are easier for the tax inspectors to spot than others, but this is not the place to give advice on a highly contentious topic, except to say that all forms of tax evasion are illegal. In fact, there are enough loopholes and 'perks' available to self-employed people with a good tax consultant at their elbow to render law breaking an unacceptable and unnecessary risk.

The challenge to self-employed status

In recent years there has been an increasing tendency for the Inland Revenue to challenge taxpayers' claims to be assessed under Schedule D and to try to bring them within the PAYE scheme. The challenge hinges round the nature of the relationship between the provider of work and the performer of it. If the provider of work is in a position to tell the performer the exact place, time and manner in which the job is to be done, then the relationship between them is, to use an old-fashioned phrase, a master-and-servant one and clearly does not qualify for Schedule D taxation. On the other hand if the performer of the work is merely given a job to do and is absolutely free as to how he or she does it, except in so far as it has to be completed within certain specifications of time, quality and price, then the performer can be regarded as self-employed. There are, however, some potential grey areas here; for instance, a freelance working mostly for one client may be straying into a master-and-servant situation — or at least the Inspector of Taxes could take that view. If you are not satisfied with such a decision you, or better, your accountant, can ask to take the matter to an Independent Appeals Tribunal.

1.12: Introducing Microcomputers

Microcomputers

In the last couple of years microcomputers have come into the same price range as the fancier, but by no means the most expensive and outlandish bits of gadgetry which a self-employed person or a small office might consider getting; a far cry from the fairly recent past, when installing a computer was a major undertaking for any company with a turnover of less than a couple of million or so.

Computers have become easier to operate ('user friendly', as the jargon has it) as well as much cheaper; the National Computing Centre estimates that computing costs only 1 per cent of what it did a decade ago. Nonetheless, the possibilities of making expensive mistakes, both in purchasing and in application, still abound. The only difference is that whereas large businesses can afford to make mistakes, there is much less margin for error in the case of small ones.

Selling computers has become a big and competitive business and at some point you may be tempted by an advertisement or by an eager salesman, either of whom will try to convince you that a micro is the answer to your problems and that it costs a lot less than the annual salary of a junior member of staff. How will you be able to tell whether or not you should take the plunge?

Getting to know computers

If you are already 'into' computers, by virtue of your education or training or because you have an interest in electronic gadgets, you obviously start with a big advantage. But if, like the vast majority of people over 40, your knowledge of computers is limited to having seen the odd print-out, it would probably pay you to read a simple book on the subject. If this thought fills you with terror, it should be stressed that there is no need whatever to get involved with the technicalities of how

153

computers work or how to write a program — all you need to know are the basics of what they can do. An excellently down to earth introduction to the subject is *The Good Computing Guide for Beginners* (ECC Publications £1.95). It consists of a brief, clear text and a long glossary of 'buzz words', ranging from the essential to those which are employed by computer salesmen to blind you with science.

It is not our intention to go into detail on computers here, but for the benefit of readers who know absolutely nothing about the subject, a few terms and concepts do need to be explained at this stage.

First of all, any computer system has two components — hardware and software. Roughly they mean what they describe. The hardware is the machine itself and the software is the program or programs which instruct it to carry out a range of tasks. These begin with information being put in (eg a customer's account number) and this stage is called *input*. The next thing to happen is *processing*, when the input is acted on by the current program (eg the program instructs the computer to turn the customer's account number into his full name and address and maybe to check that her/his account is up to date). If a transaction has taken place the details would go into *storage* in the computer's *memory*; in this case, it might be the information that the customer's account should be debited with the value of the transaction. Finally, the whole transaction itself should be displayed on a screen and/or printed out as hard copy: this is known as *output*.

In order to carry out these processes the computer employs various pieces of hardware and software. The input is typed on a *keyboard*, which looks much like the keyboard of a typewriter. It is processed in what might be called the brain of the computer, but for which the technical name is the *central processing unit*. Some of the basic programming instructions are built into this unit but most of the programs which carry out the tasks you want the computer to do are stored on floppy disks, much like a 45 rpm record, and these respond to and interact with the instructions you type on the keyboard.

An example would be the case of a program which included order processing. The operator types in a customer number; the program converts this into an actual name and address which would appear on the TV-like screen (properly called a *VDU* — Visual Display Unit). The operator then types in a number for the item ordered and if it is out of stock or nearing a re-order

THIRD EDITION

Law for the Small Business
The Daily Telegraph Guide
Patricia Clayton

Law for the Small Business covers every aspect of the law affecting the small business, explaining how to start a business, how to keep it going and how to avoid all the legal pitfalls. Each subject – taxation, insurance, employment law, liability in the event of bankruptcy, and so on – is treated clearly and succinctly, providing in one volume a complete reference guide. This new edition has been revised and updated to include recent legislation. There are additional chapters covering litigation, enforcement of court judgements and orders, and debt collection. There is also fuller treatment of current taxation provisions, especially fringe benefits, a complete updating of the law, and an enlarged glossary.

Contents
Preface 1. Starting out: sole trader, partnership or company *2.* Establishing the business *3.* Capital and profits *4.* Running the business *5.* Premises *6.* Taxation *7.* Insurance *8.* Employment law *9.* Trading *10.* Cash and credit at home and abroad *11.* Intellectual property: patents, copyrights and trademarks *12.* Litigation *13.* Collecting your debts *14.* Bankruptcy and liquidation *15.* Takeovers and mergers
Appendices
1. Useful addresses *2.* Further reading *3.* Glossary *4.* Draft county court pleadings *Index*

Patricia Clayton is a qualified solicitor and barrister. She lectures and writes on business law, and is in practice as a solicitor in London. She is the author of *Consumer Law for the Small Business*.

'a first class guide' Accountancy Age

'clearly written' The Director

£9.95 Hardback *0 85038 606 3*   **£5.50 Paperback** *0 85038 607 1*
286 pages 216x138mm

Kogan Page 120 Pentonville Road, London N1

Available from Booksellers or, in case of difficulty direct from the publisher

point and appropriate instructions have been written into the program by the supplier of the software, it will inform the operator accordingly. Furthermore, and again if the program allows for it to be done, the fact that the item in question should be re-ordered will be stored in the memory to be called up by the operator when he or she is running the re-order part of the program. This transaction will most likely be printed out as hard copy on the *printer*.

Cans and can'ts of computing

The moral of all this, sometimes overlooked by eager buyers, not to mention eager salespersons, is that the computer can only do the things which the programs running at the time will allow it to do. An analogy might be hiring a secretary. She might be the most decorative lass that ever walked through your door, but if you want a shorthand-typist and she has not been trained (or programmed, if you like) to carry out either of these functions, she will not be a success.

In the case of a secretary, or any other person you take on to the staff, you will have analysed at least to some extent what you want him or her to do and you will look for someone who by virtue of a mix of experience, track record and qualifications can carry out those tasks. In essence this is what you should do if you are contemplating buying a microcomputer. In fact it is much more necessary to have a clear 'job description' for a machine like a computer, because unlike a human being it is not flexible: you cannot say to it (unless of course the program allows you to do so); 'Hey, wait a minute. While you're doing x, could you also check on y and z?'

As we have said, a computer can be programmed to do all sorts of tasks, but this requires writing special programs, which can be very costly indeed. It has to be done by experts – and the stories of experts getting it wrong, at vast expense to their client, are legion – and it will usually cost you several times what you paid for the computer in the first place. There are, however, standard tasks which are common to most types of business and for these program packages are available which cost only a hundred or so pounds. Such programs carry out, at the operator's instructions, tasks like invoicing, preparing statements and reminders, stock control and sales analyses of various kinds. They cannot, however, do more than they have been programmed to do and if your kind of business has lots of one-offs and exceptions, you will either have to adapt your transactions to fit in with what the computer can do, get some software specially written or stick with your manual systems.

Consultants

If you are serious about getting a computer, the plan of campaign recommended by nearly everyone who has had any experience in the matter is to get in a consultant. This need not necessarily mean an expenditure of thousands. At this stage all you need is to get someone to have a look over your operation to tell you whether computerisation is the right answer for you. There are lots of computer consultants advertising in the yellow pages, but a word of mouth recommendation is always better than pulling a name out of the telephone book. It is also best to find a local firm rather than one that has to travel a long way to come and see you.

If someone can give you a recommendation, make sure you get the name of the actual consultant he or she saw, because the quality of advice depends not so much on the firm as on the person. Failing personal recommendations, you should ask the consultants you are approaching to name a couple of their customers and check them out. You should also ask whether the consultants in question are tied in with any particular manufacturer. The roles of consultants and salesman do not always mix to the advantage of the customer, to put it mildly.

As we have recommended in the case of other kinds of advisers in Chapter 1.4, you should specify exactly what you want them to do and ask them to quote a price on it. This will not only give you an idea of how much you will be paying for, it will also simplify the consultant's task and should hence make his services cheaper for you. For this purpose you will have to break down the nature of your operation and set out what you want done by the computer. For instance, a typical trading operation might fall into such headings as these:

- ☐ *Input:* order, and returns from customers.
- ☐ *Processing:* invoicing and updating stock records.
- ☐ *Storage:* lists of customers and their credit limits.
- ☐ *Output:* creating the physical invoices, credit notes, statements, reminders, etc.

As well as the routine items and their present and expected volumes, you should have an idea of exceptions and over-rides, how often they occur and what particular problems you have. Finally, but by no means least important, you should have a clear idea of how much you can afford to pay for the system, both initially and by way of annual service charges.

Quis custodiet custos ipse? (Who guards the guardian?), as the Romans pertinently asked. Or, in this case, how will you know whether the consultant knows his stuff? One way to do so is to get to know more about computers yourself and the National Computing Centre offers some good introductory courses for small businessmen. Failing your being able to do that, there are some key questions the consultant ought to answer in making his report — here are some of them:

Checklist: key computing questions

1. The cost of the system.
2. What extras are required, why and how much they will cost.
3. Delivery time for hardware and software.
4. Whether hardware and software are being supplied by the same firm or not (the reason for this question is that where the two are being supplied separately, it is all too easy for the one to blame the other for failures, leaving you as piggy-in-the-middle.
5. Whether additional software is needed and how long it will take to create.
6. Guarantees.
7. Availability and cost of induction courses.
8. Storage/memory capacity (the less the computer has, the less it will be able to do, which is why very cheap computers like the £69 Sinclair are not suitable for business purposes, whatever their educational virtues may be).
9. Capacity for expansion (adding on more VDUs as your business expands may slow up the memory hopelessly, unless additional storage/memory capacity can be added).
10. Availability and cost of additional functions, like word processing.
11. Arrangements for security of data (this does not mean theft so much as the existence of inbuilt precautions against damage to programs or loss of vital data — too bad if you accidentally deleted all your accounts receivable, for instance).
12. Maintenance and servicing costs (who pays for what).
13. Maintenance and servicing efficiency (how long will it take

for someone from the supplier to turn up if something goes wrong).

14. Written commitments (what written commitments, as compared to verbal promises and assurances, is the supplier prepared to make about performance and after-sales back-up).

15. How many of the make recommended are installed and working? For how long?

16. Whether it is being used by other companies similar to yours and what the problems, if any, are likely to be.

17. Whether the suppliers will let you 'play with' the micro for a reasonable period of time (and without obligation) so that you at least get to grips with the most basic difficulties.

Satisfactory answers to these questions will not, of course, in themselves guarantee that your computer will be a success. But they should protect you from some of the more grievous and expensive errors that have been, and continue to be made, by businesses large and small.

1.13: Legal Basics

Going to law is a process where the cure, in money terms, is often worse than the disease — which is why so many settlements are made out of court. Even seeking legal advice is an expensive business: £30 to £50 an hour is now the going rate depending on where you are and few legal bills come to less than this minimum, even for a short consultation. In complex disputes or where larger sums of money are involved legal action may ultimately be the only course open. But at the more basic levels of trading law there are some straightforward principles laid down, though they are sometimes blurred by old wives' tales — for instance that a shopkeeper is obliged by law to sell anything he displays for sale. Knowing what the law actually says about this and other everyday trading transactions will help you sort out minor disputes and, very often, save costly legal fees.

The Sale of Goods Act 1979

This Act places some clear but not unfair obligations on you as the seller once a contract has taken place, an event which occurs when goods have been exchanged for money. Nothing needs to be written or even said to make the contract legally binding and you cannot normally override it by putting up a notice saying things like 'No Refunds' or limiting your responsibilities in some other way. This is prohibited under the Unfair Contracts Act of 1977.

The Sale of Goods Act has three main provisions concerning what you sell.

1. The goods must be 'of merchantable quality'. This means that they must be capable of doing what the buyer could reasonably expect them to do — for instance an electric kettle should boil the water in it within a reasonable length of time.
2. The goods are 'fit for any particular purpose' which you make known to the buyer. For instance, if you are asked

whether a rucksack can carry 100 lbs without the strap breaking and it fails to match up to your promises of performance, you will have broken your contract.

3. That the goods are 'as described'. If you sell a bicycle as having five speeds and it only has three, then again you are in breach of contract — as well as of the Trade Descriptions Act, if you do so knowingly.

But what happens if you yourself have been misled by the manufacturer from whom you bought the item in question? You cannot refer the buyer back to him: the Sale of Goods Act specifically places responsibility for compensating the buyer on the retailer, no matter from whom the retailer bought the goods in the first place.

Thus, if the goods fail on any of the three grounds shown above, you will have to take them back and issue a full refund, unless you can negotiate a partial refund, with the buyer keeping the goods about which he or she has complained. However, they need not accept such an offer, nor even a credit note. Furthermore, you may be obliged to pay any costs the buyer incurred in returning the goods, and even to compensate him if he had a justifiable reason to hire a replacement for the defective item, for instance if he had to hire a ladder to do an urgent DIY job because the one you supplied was faulty.

The only let-out you have under the Act — which also covers second-hand goods — is if you warned the buyer about a specific fault, or if this was so obvious that he should have noticed it. In the case of the bike, he probably would have found it difficult to spot that a couple of the gears were not working, but he could reasonably be expected to notice a missing pedal.

Obligation to sell

Contrary to some widely held beliefs, there is no obligation on you to sell goods on display for sale if you don't want to. For instance, an assistant in an antique shop might wrongly price a picture at £2.50 rather than £250. The intending buyer cannot force you to sell at that price, even though it is publicly displayed. However, once the goods have been sold at £2.50, even in error, a contract has taken place and cannot be revoked without the agreement of both parties.

This also applies when the buyer has paid a deposit and this has been accepted. Supposing he had paid £1 and offered to return with the balance, a bargain would have been made which you would be obliged to complete. It is, however, binding on both parties. If the buyer, having paid a deposit, decided to change his mind you would be within your rights in refusing to refund the money.

Estimates and quotations

Self-employed people supplying services such as repairs are often asked for a quote or an estimate. How binding is the figure you give?

This is a grey area in which even the Office of Fair Trading finds it difficult to give a legal ruling. They recommend, however, that a 'quote' should be a firm commitment to produce whatever the subject of the enquiry is at the price stated, whereas an 'estimate', while it should be a close guess, allows more leeway to depart from that figure. Therefore, if you are not sure how much a job is going to cost you should describe your price as an estimate and say it is subject to revision. This may, of course, not satisfy the customer, in which case he would press you for a quote. If you really find it difficult to state a fixed sum because of unknown factors, you can either give some parameters (eg between £x and £y) or say that you will do £x-worth of work — which is what on present evidence you think is what it would take — but that you will notify the customer if that sum is likely to be exceeded to do the job properly. In general, though, an itemised firm quotation is the document that is least likely to produce disputes.

Completion and delivery dates

If you give a time for completing a job you will have to do it within that time — certainly if it is stated in writing.

In the case of delivery of goods ordered by customers the same is true. If you give a date you have to stick to it or the contract is broken and the customer can refuse the goods and even, in some cases, ask for compensation. Even if no date is given, you have to supply the article within a reasonable period of time, bearing in mind that what is reasonable in one case, such as making a dress, may not be reasonable in another — obtaining some ready-made article from a wholesaler, for example. The relevant law here is a new one — the Supply of Goods and Services Act 1982.

Trading Associations

In addition to legal obligations you may also belong to a trading association which imposes its own code of conduct. Such codes sometimes go beyond strict legal requirements, on the principle that 'the customer is always right'. This is not a bad principle to observe, within reason, whatever the legalities of the case. A reputation for fair dealing can be worth many times its cost in terms of advertising.

Leases

Apart from trading law, the other area where it is important to be aware of the basics is in looking at the terms of your lease if you plan to trade from rented premises. This would include your own home. There are likely to be restrictive covenants in the lease which will prevent you from carrying on a trade in premises let to you for domestic use. This may not be an insuperable obstacle, but you would certainly have to get the landlord's permission if you wanted to use your home for any purpose other than just living there.

Even when you rent commercial premises there are likely to be restrictions on the trade you carry on in them. An empty flower shop, for instance, could probably be used as a dress shop without complications, but its use as a furniture repair business might be disallowed because of the noise involved in running woodworking machinery. You and your solicitor should examine the lease closely for possible snags of this sort.

Equally important is the existence of any restrictions which would prohibit you from transferring the lease to a third party. This would mean that the purchaser would have to negotiate the lease element in the event of the sale of the business with the landlord, not with you, and this could drastically affect the value of what you have to sell. For instance, if you took a gamble on renting premises in an improving area which fulfilled your expectations by coming up in the world, you would not be able to reap the benefit of your foresight and courage if you could not transfer the unexpired portion of the lease.

Commercial leases, unlike most domestic ones, run for relatively short periods: usually between three and seven years, with rent reviews at the end of each term or sometimes even sooner. This adds an unknown factor to the long-term future of any business in rented premises and is one you need to take into account in buying a business — again, particularly in an improving area. In Covent Garden, for instance, a number of small shops which moved in when it was a very run-down part of central London with correspondingly low rents were hit by huge increases when these rents were reviewed in the light of the improved status of the area subsequent to the re-development of the market building and its surroundings.

The other point to watch for in leases is whether you are responsible for dilapidations occurring during the period of your lease. If you are, you could be in for a hefty bill at its end and for this reason it is advisable to have a survey done, and its findings agreed with the landlord, before you take on the lease.

1.14: Pensions and the Self-employed

It is scarcely possible these days to open the financial pages of any newspaper without seeing at least one advertisement for self-employed pensions. It is also a fair bet that these are studied more closely by financial advisers than by the self-employed at whom they are aimed, unless of course the latter are nearing the age at which pensions begin to become of immediate interest — by which time it may be too late to do anything about it. The trouble is that the self-employed, by temperament, are more interested in risk than security and tend to place provisions for retirement rather low on their scale of priorities.

However, there are compelling reasons why you should take self-employed pensions seriously and find out what they involve: to outline which is the object of this chapter. In urging you to read it, we promise to avoid the mind boggling pension jargon which generally sends readers of newspaper articles on the subject straight to the less demanding pastures of the sports pages.

State schemes

Everyone in the UK now has a pension provision of some kind, by law. You either belong and contribute to the state scheme (even if you are self-employed — through your NI contributions) or to a scheme set up by your employer which has to provide benefits at least equal to those offered by the state. The state scheme provides a small basic pension topped up by an earnings related amount and it has a number of serious disadvantages. One is that the earnings related element is calculated on a formula based on your earnings over 20 years from the start of the scheme and without going into the details of this, the effect is that you cannot get the full benefit of it if you retire before 1998. A second disadvantage is that there is no lump sum provision on retirement or death, as is the case with most private schemes. A third drawback is the top limit on earnings, on which the earnings related benefit is limited to £220 a week.

Thus, the more highly paid you are on retirement, the worse your benefit is in comparison.

However, from the point of view of the self-employed, the biggest drawback of the lot is that you are not eligible for earnings related benefit at all, on the grounds that the fluctuating nature of self-employed earnings makes it difficult to set up such a scheme. All you are entitled to is the basic pension, which is generally admitted to be quite inadequate on its own.

Tax benefits

This is in itself a reason why you should make additional arrangements as soon as you possibly can, but for the self-employed there is another compelling incentive. Investing in a pension scheme is probably the most tax beneficial saving and investment vehicle available to you at this time. Here are some of its key features:

1. Tax relief is given on your contributions at your top rate of tax on earned income. This means that if you are paying tax at the top rate of 60 per cent, you can get £1000 worth of contributions to your pension for an outlay of only £400.
2. Pension funds are in themselves tax exempt — unlike any company in whose shares you might invest. Thus your capital builds up considerably more quickly than it would do in stocks and shares.
3. When you finally come to take your benefits — and you can take part of them as a lump sum and part as a regular pension payment (of which more later) the lump sum will not be liable to capital gains tax and the pension will be treated as earned income from a tax point of view; as distinct from investment income which is regarded as 'unearned' and taxed much more severely.
4. Lump sum benefits arising in the event of your death are paid out to your dependants free of Capital Transfer Tax. This may enable you to build up pension funds to the extent where liability to CTT is reduced quite drastically on other assets from which income has been siphoned to provide a pension.

The advantages of all this over various DIY efforts to build up a portfolio of stocks and shares — even if you are more knowledgeable about the stock market than most — should be obvious; you are contributing in that case out of taxed income, the resultant investment income is taxed at unearned rates and capital gains tax is payable on the profits you make from selling your holdings.

The convinced adherent of the DIY road may at this point say: ah, but under my own provisions I can contribute as, when and how much I can afford and I am not obliged to make regular payments to a pension plan when it might be highly inconvenient for me to do so. Pensions, however, are not like life insurance, though misguided salesmen sometimes try to make out that they are. You need not contribute a regular amount at all. You can pay a lump sum or a regular amount. In fact you need not make a payment every year. There are even a number of plans now available under which you are entitled to borrow from your pension plan.

The only restriction that is put on you is imposed by the government and relates to tax benefits. In order for self-employed pensions not to become a vehicle for tax avoidance, the amount you can contribute to them is limited to 17.5 per cent of your income. You are however allowed to 'average out' your contributions over any six year period to arrive at an overall percentage per year of 17.5 per cent.

There is also now a further concession for older people making their own pension plans. If you were born between 1916 and 1933 you can contribute 20 per cent of your relevant earnings. The concessions are even higher for people older than that (up to 24 per cent for those born back in 1912) but in that case your interest in pension plans might be somewhat academic.

Since an increasing number of self-employed people — and their financial advisers — have come to recognise the merits of these schemes, a great many companies have moved into the market for self-employed pensions. Under a fair amount of jargon and an often confusing lineage of fine print, the plans they offer boil down to the following options.

1. *Pension Policy with Profits.* In essence this is a method of investing in a life assurance company, who then use your money to invest in stocks, shares, government securities or whatever. As we said earlier, the advantage from your point of view is that pension funds are tax exempt, so the profits from their investments build up more quickly. These profits are used to build up, in turn, the pension fund you stand to get at the end

of the period over which you can contribute. There is no time limit on this period, though obviously the more you do contribute the greater your benefits will be and vice versa; and you can elect to retire any time between 60 and 75.

At retirement you can choose to have part of your pension paid as a lump sum and use it to buy an annuity. This could in some circumstances have a tax advantage over an ordinary pension, but the situation on it is quite complicated and you should seek professional advice in making your decision. What happens with an annuity, however, is that you can use it to buy an additional pension, the provider of which takes the risk that if you live to a ripe old age he might be out of pocket. Equally you might die within six months, in which case the reverse would be true. The statistical probabilities of either of these extremes have been calculated by actuaries and the annuities on offer are based on their conclusions.

One important point about a conventional with-profits pension that often confuses people is that it is not really a form of life insurance. If you die before pensionable age, your dependants and your estate will not usually get back more than the value of the premiums you have paid, plus interest. The best way of insuring your life is through term assurance, of which more later.

2. *Unit Linked Pensions.* Unit linked policies are a variant of unit trust investment, where you make a regular monthly payment (or one outright purchase) to buy stocks and shares across a variety of investments through a fund, the managers of which are supposed to have a special skill in investing in the stock market.

Combining investment with a pension plan sounds terribly attractive and much more exciting than a conventional with-profits policy and it is true that in some instances unit linked policies have shown a better return than their more staid rivals. However, as unit trust managers are at pains to warn you (usually in the small print) units can go down as well as up and if you get into one of the less successful unit trust funds — and there are quite wide variances in their performance — you may do less well than with a conventional policy.

There are also, of course, fluctuations in the stock market itself which affect the value of your holdings. Over a period of time these fluctuations should even themselves out — you can get more units for your money when the market is down, and fewer when share prices are high. The only problem is that if your policy terminates at a time when share prices are low you will do worse than if you cash in on a boom. However, there is nothing to compel you to sell your holdings when they mature. Unless you desperately need the money you can keep it invested until times are better. Remember, though, since this policy is for your pension, you may not be able to delay using the funds for too long.

Most unit trust companies run a number of funds, invested in different types of shares and in different markets; for instance there are funds that are invested in the US, Australia or Japan, or in specialist sectors, like mining or energy. If you find that the trust you are in is not performing as well as you had hoped (prices are quoted daily in the press) most trusts will allow you to switch from one fund to another at quite a modest administration charge.

3. *Term Assurance.* While this is not a form of pension at all, it may be attractive to add term assurance to your pension policy for tax purposes. Term assurance is a way of insuring your life for a given period by paying an annual premium. The more you pay, the more you (or rather your dependants) get. If you do not die before the end of the fixed term (eg 20 years) nothing is paid out. As with any other form of insurance, your premiums are simply, if you like, a bet against some untoward event occurring.

There is one indirect but useful connection between pensions and term assurance. The tax people allow you a scheme under which you pay term assurance premiums along with your pension premiums, both of them being relieved of tax at your top earned income rate. If you pay your term assurance premiums separately, they are still relieved of tax, but at the much lower rate of 15 per cent.

The one thing that all types of pension schemes have in common is that their salesmen are all eagerly competing for the self-employed person's notional dollar. They will be anxious to extol the virtues of their own schemes, to withhold any unfavourable information about them and to make no comparisons, which could be odious, with other schemes. Your best plan in making your selection is to work through a broker and to let him or her make the recommendation, but that does not mean that you can abdicate responsibility altogether. For one thing, in order for a broker to make the right selection of pension plans appropriate to your circumstances, you have to describe what your needs and constraints are:

1. Can you afford to make regular payments?
2. Does the irregular nature of your earnings mean that the occasional lump sum payment would be better?
3. Do you have any existing pension arrangements — eg from previous employment?
4. When do you want to retire?
5. What provision do you want to make for dependants?

Very likely he or she will come up with a mix of solutions — for instance, a small regular payment to a pension scheme, topped up by single premium payments. The suggestion may also be made that you should split your arrangements between a conventional with-profits policy and some sort of unit linked scheme; certainly you will be recommended to review your arrangements periodically to take care of inflation and possible changes in your circumstances.

Brokers have to be registered nowadays, so it is unlikely that you will be unlucky enough to land up with someone dishonest. Check that the person you are dealing with really is a *registered* broker — not a consultant, because anyone can call themselves that. Some very big household names among brokers are not, in fact, registered but the majority are. Whoever you deal with though, there are, as in other things in life, differences in the quality of what you get, which in this case is advice. It is as well to have a few checks at your elbow which will enable you to assess the value of the advice you are being given. For instance, national quality newspapers like the *Telegraph, Guardian* and the *Financial Times*, as well as some specialist publications such as the *Economist* and *Investor's Chronicle* publish occasional surveys of the pension business which include performance charts of the various unit trust funds, showing those at the top and bottom of the league table over one, five and ten year periods. There are also tables of benefits offered by the various life companies showing what happens in each case if, for instance, you invest £500 a year over ten years. There are quite considerable differences between what you get for your money from the most to the least generous firms. If your broker is advising you to put your money in a scheme that appears to give you less than the best deal going, you should not commit yourself to it without talking to your accountant; but with brokers, as with many other professional advisers, the best recommendation is word of mouth from someone you can trust and who can vouch for the ability of the person in question.

1.15: Retirement and the Self-employed Person

Fred Kemp, *FCIS, FBIM, former director of the Pre-Retirement Association*

Introduction

Since 1975, when the first edition of this book appeared, the way of life for millions of people has been affected by the economic recession. The official unemployment figures in the UK now exceed three million but the true figure is much larger if one takes into account those now engaged on various government financed job creation and re-training schemes. In times of high unemployment the older employed person is much more vulnerable and retirement has come to many earlier than expected. Companies needing to shed staff have encouraged early retirement as an alternative or a prelude to enforcing redundancy schemes. These changed circumstances have brought countless problems, but they have also created openings for those with vision and adaptability to exploit them. Many of those who have volunteered for early retirement or opted for redundancy benefits are determined to launch their own businesses.

For the fifth edition of *Working for Yourself* it has therefore been decided to divide this chapter into two sections:

1. The essentials for a successful retirement.
2. Self-employment within retirement as a means of increasing both income and life interest.

The six basic needs

Professor Alastair Heron, the founder Vice President of the Pre-Retirement Association, suggested in an early PRA booklet that there were six essentials for a successful retirement.

He suggested we must give thought to:

1. Good physical and emotional health.
2. Adequate income, substantially beyond subsistence level.
3. Suitable accommodation.
4. Congenial associates and neighbours.

5. One or more absorbing interests.
6. An adequate personal philosophy of life.

His original guidelines have stood the test of time and gained international acceptance.

Health

Before anyone seeks to invest his capital in any type of business, he should first invest in good health. Paying insufficient attention to the guidelines for preserving good health can render valueless all paper profits from one's own business. Loneliness, and the depression it brings with it, can be a bugbear in retirement. Self-employment which enables contact to be kept with other people provides mental stimulation, companionship and status in society.

Everyone should remain as active and lively in retirement as possible. Take as much exercise as your body will permit. This does not mean a sudden conversion to a health and exercise 'kick'. It would be foolish at the age of 60 to start leaping about a squash court after an abstention of 20 years. It would be equally stupid to try to dig in a huge vegetable garden or allotment if you have not wielded a spade for ages.

Your retirement survival kit should include a regular mixture of physical activities. Your local library stocks a variety of health books which contain suggestions for a daily exercise routine to keep your muscles toned up. Acquire a dog if you don't already have one: brisk walks at least twice a day at a pace sufficient to work up a gentle sweat are an excellent basis to preserve the discipline of regular exercise.

There are facilities provided by the local authorities within reach of everyone's pocket. (Isn't it time you benefited from those rates you always complain about?) Local adult education centres provide, for example, yoga, keep-fit and old time dancing classes. Many courses are available at reduced fees for pensioners. Swimming is an excellent exercise for using muscles and is recommended for back pain sufferers. If your district boasts a heated swimming pool, why not use it?

Weight should be continuously monitored so that you remain within ten per cent of the weight appropriate to your height. Over-loading the heart by carrying excess weight can be compared with towing a caravan behind a 1000 cc motor car. Both examples can lead to trouble!

Any person of retirement age would be wise to have a full medical examination before investing his capital in a business. Where appropriate, the same advice applies to the marriage partner.

Finance

The subject which concerns people most, before retirement, is money. Despite persistent inflation, most of those who have retired find that the situation is not as bad as they had anticipated.

Sit down (with a large sheet of lined paper) and write in column one your present pre-retirement budget, then in the next column show the pluses and minuses expected in retirement. Profits or salary, car and expenses from the business will be a minus; pluses will be private pensions plus the state pension, and income from investments. Outgoings which will be reduced in retirement include travel costs and lower income tax. At home you may have more meals, lighting and heating. Take into account your mortgage which you may have planned to complete at retirement date and endowment insurances which may mature.

Many people approaching retirement age, worried about their future income, fail to appreciate the savings which will become available. National Insurance contributions are no longer payable after 65 (men) and 60 (women) even if you continue to work. Obtain from the local Department of Health and Social Security office the leaflet NP 32 *Your Retirement Pension* and complete a 'Certificate of Age Exemption' if you intend to continue to work. If you need to supplement your income, remember to check the current amount of the 'Earnings Rule' with the DHSS. If you are a man of 65 or a woman of 60, the government will reduce your state retirement pension if you earn more than the approved level. At the age of 70 (men) and 65 (women) restrictions on earnings are lifted.

An unusual privilege is allowed concerning the 'Earnings Rule' as certain expenses, such as fares to and from work, are taken into consideration. Needless to say, another form from the DHSS needs completion (BR 356 LO). Do this as soon as you take up fresh employment.

Those leaving paid employment on retirement will cease to contribute to their occupational pension scheme. When completing your income tax return, remember that the Special

Age Allowance can be claimed from the beginning of the income tax year in which you reach the age of 65. Your local tax office will supply you with the leaflet IR4 (*Income Tax and Pensioners*). Your net income in retirement should reflect these savings.

In addition, other privileges become available such as free National Health Service prescriptions, and travel concessions including reduced rail fares.

At the end of your budgeting exercise you will have a fair idea of how your finances will look, and you will be better able to decide whether you need to set up a small business or look for a part-time job.

Living arrangements

Where to live in retirement? The cottage by the sea or the country may represent a lifetime's dream but do not be carried away by memories of 20 holidays spent in August at your favourite seaside resort. Go and visit the area in mid-January when half the shops are shut. Do not go to see the town's Director of Tourism. Seek out the Director of Social Services and ask if his area qualifies for the label 'Costa Geriatrica'. Ask him what are the social services and health services for the elderly. You must be practical and accept that eventually you might need such assistance as a home help, especially if by moving away from your home area you will be cutting yourself off from family and friends. Because many south coast areas have a high population imbalance caused by the retirement migration, the social services, working with limited funds, are unable to meet all the calls made upon them. Similar considerations apply to country areas. With the high cost of petrol an isolated cottage with one bus a day to town could become a virtual prison, and many rural areas now have no bus service at all.

Consider then staying in the area where your family and friends are and which is convenient (but not too convenient!) for grandchildren.

Do no necessarily stay in that large house where you reared the family. Choose a modern bungalow and move into it before you retire. While you are still earning money get all the essentials installed, including double glazing and roof insulation. If you cannot find or afford a modern bungalow (for you really should plan to avoid stairs in old age), look around for a suitable property to modernise, remembering that your local authority can dispense handsome grants towards modernisation and improvement. Make inquiries with the housing department of your local council, estate agents and the Citizens' Advice Bureau.

The essentials for the retirement home are economic central heating, privacy, good lighting, sensible electric wiring with waist-high power points, and proper working levels. Make it a safe place to live — more people kill themselves in the home than on the roads! If you find such a home in an area where you are likely to have congenial neighbours and former business associates so much the better.

At long last specially designed retirement communities offering support services to residents are becoming available in the UK. 'Supported independence in retirement' is the central theme of the Retirement Homes Association.

At Elmbridge, at Cranleigh in Surrey, for example, you can become a resident by buying a lease for a capital sum. If you decide to leave, the original capital sum is refunded in full to you or to your estate. An annual service charge covers the cost of a resident caretaker, nursing and administrative staff. The Social Centre includes a restaurant, bar, TV lounge and billiards room. Purpose-built accommodation includes one and two bedroom apartments and bungalows set around attractively landscaped areas. An inspection visit is recommended, for if you decided to move from your home area such a community does offer trouble free living in congenial surroundings.

Leisure interests

Leisure is most valuable when it is in short supply. The average man or woman retiring from full time work, however, immediately has an extra 2000 additional hours a year available as 'free time'. No longer is there a clear cut distinction between work/travel time and leisure hours.

Variety is the spice of life and now is the time to explore new interests. When the author chaired the Council of Europe Working Party on Preparation for Retirement, its report referred to leisure in retirement as the time 'to preserve creativity and curiosity, the ability to marvel, and the capacity to listen and learn.'

Visit your local adult education centre. The centre may conduct a pre-retirement course covering in detail the aspects mentioned here. Such a course will give you an opportunity to discuss problems with the lecturers and other participants. Moreover, reduced rates for pensioners will mean you can take up such things as pottery, painting or old-time dancing for a nominal outlay, and you will meet people of all ages who live near you. Develop the hobby you have been thinking about for years and preferably also take up a completely new one – one that will challenge you and keep that trained mind active. At 60 you can acquire a degree through the Open University while studying at home.

If your retirement income is such that you do not need a supplement, offer your services to an organisation that is looking for voluntary help. Be committed to some job or some person. A garden or a golf course will not get you out of bed, dressed and shaved at 10 am on a frosty January morning, but if you are responsible for driving a car with its boot full of food for a 'Meals on Wheels' service for the aged you will be there! You will enjoy it and you will get tremendous personal satisfaction from knowing you are being useful to others.

Your retirement survival kit needs a mixture of interests, and voluntary work can be one way of putting shape or routine back into your week once you have retired. Do not be in a hurry, however, to over-commit yourself. Consult your local Citizens Advice Bureau or Voluntary Workers Bureau for suggestions and advice.

Self-employment

The dangers

For the former employee now retired, or whose job has vanished, the desire to be one's own boss and join the self-employed is often very strong after a lifetime spent obeying orders and taking instructions in a large organisation. Ideally, for the person on the verge of retirement, the aims and objectives of running one's own business are to make it relatively trouble-free, to provide a secure additional income and allow it to be sold easily after his death for the benefit of his or her spouse. Such businesses cannot be bought at a modest price and anyone with capital to invest who thinks otherwise is a likely target for the professional confidence trickster.

The person retiring from paid employment who is perhaps commuting part of his pension as a lump sum, or the redundant employee who is collecting his severance payment, must exercise extreme caution in investing the fruits of perhaps a lifetime's work. Any offers of franchise arrangements or purchase of stocks for resale should be viewed with due suspicion, and the advice of both your bank manager and solicitor should be sought before any contract or agreement is signed. This seems plain common sense, but an article in the *Sunday Times* Business News on confidence tricksters stated that 'Phineas Barnum's dictum that there is a fool born every minute was a gross underestimate!' Certainly such warnings regarding investment cannot be repeated too often.

For the man or woman who has been an employee throughout life, the risks and stresses of running one's own small business full-time at the age of 60 plus can be hazardous. Take the typical local shopkeeper. He is working six or seven days a week. He has to meet ever rising costs: for rates, staff wages, electricity, heating and insurance. He must keep detailed accounts and VAT records. It is unlikely that he will be able to go on holiday with his family, and he dreads being ill. Should he die, his widow would have to cope with the business single-handed, and may decide to try to sell it at a time when prospective buyers will realise she wants to sell out quickly. If she has been living on the business premises she will have to buy a house and face the upheaval of moving at a time when she is still suffering from the shock of bereavement. This is no legacy for any person to force on his spouse.

If you are on the verge of retirement you should be looking forward to a period of purposeful activity, and possible the initial step for someone who still cherishes such ambitions is to take a part-time job in the type of business which interests him. He will then be able to sum up, on the basis of practical experience, the opportunities and problems of buying or starting an enterprise before risking precious capital.

The opportunities

It *is* possible for the employed person to choose a business opportunity to provide an income and interest in retirement provided he plans far enough ahead. There is, for example, a definite need in many places for boarding kennels where people can leave their animals when going on holiday or into hospital. There is also a steady demand for long-term quarantine homes for animals being brought to the UK by owners returning from

177

work overseas (4100 dogs and 2000 cats a year). But do not underestimate the amount of work or capital involved. In the first place contact your local authority. Any kennel or cattery which wishes to keep animals in quarantine must be licensed by the Ministry of Agriculture, Fisheries and Food and the Animal Health Division of the Ministry handling this is at Government Buildings, Hook Rise South, Tolworth, Surbiton, Surrey KT6 7NF. If you write to this address, the Ministry will supply you with the relevant information and give details of the standards specified for the buildings including the types of materials. Also seek out the local veterinary surgeons. They might well know of a business for sale or suggest where one might be started.

One of the advantages with this type of business is not having to invest capital in holding a large stock! Such an enterprise could be started on a small scale by the wife while the husband continues his normal occupation until he reaches retirement age. The business could then be expanded when he is available full time to assist his wife. However, rather more capital is required for a quarantine home than for boarding premises.

Suburban houses and gardens are *not* suitable for kennels. A semi-rural area is essential as well as planning permission to run kennels.

Costs of pet foods are always increasing and these must be reflected in regular reviews of fees charged. Food costs can be offset by bulk buying. Frozen tripe is recommended by kennel owners and can be purchased in 50 lb cartons. Remember that one member of the family must be on duty seven days a week.

The retailing business

If you are approaching the age of 60 consider any retail business with a jaundiced eye. As a rough yardstick, we may say that today a business with a turnover of less than £50,000 a year is not economically viable because of the meagre profit margins and cost of overheads. Any retailer with a turnover of more than £17,000 a year must register for VAT. A supplier will rarely be able to deliver to a small retailer the goods he actually ordered. The haberdasher may request that 75 per cent of men's shirts he orders should be supplied in size 16½. In practice he is likely to receive only 10 per cent in that size. Often there is only part delivery of orders. Prices change frequently. The retailer must keep up to date with new fashion demands and tastes. He is at the mercy of TV advertisements. The public will expect him to have in stock next day any item they may have seen advertised the previous evening. A newsagent was swamped with orders for a particular book on football which was advertised one evening. Six months later he was still awaiting supplies. The small shopkeeper, despite recent efforts to merge with other small shopkeepers, will always have difficulty in competing with the huge multiple organisations, shopping precincts and DIY warehouses. The days of many small shops are numbered. Read the chapter on retailing in Part 2 and, above all, remember the three golden rules which dictate your choice: *location, location* and *location.*

Partnerships and consultancy

If you are considering entering a partnership, discuss any projected arrangement in detail with your solicitor and bank manager. If you have been employed in say the clothing industry and wish to set yourself up as a textile consultant, do not underestimate the cost of keeping yourself up to date. You will have to buy all the specialist trade journals (see Appendix 3) and not until you leave a large organisation will you fully appreciate the value of having all the secretarial and back-up facilities. Technology is advancing at such a pace that you may soon find yourself left behind.

If you have a particular expertise, it may well be preferable to join an existing organisation as a consultant rather than attempting to build up a new connection from scratch. (The ground work for a new organisation should be prepared several years ahead.)

If you are well known and respected in your profession, you may be able to earn fees on a regular basis acting as:

☐ 'Trouble-shooter' or quality control inspector for a manufacturer having difficulties.
☐ Arbitrator for a retail trade association or Testing Bureau which handle complaints from the general public.
☐ An inspector on an independent basis on construction/ building work.
☐ A non-executive director for a company which is keen to make use of your contacts.

Companies which have reduced permanent staff to an absolute minimum are finding it increasingly useful to be able to call on experienced personnel to handle 'one-off' situations.

New horizons

Nevertheless, the old maxim 'find a demand and meet it' holds good in a rapidly changing world. If you, approaching retirement age or already at retirement age, can earn an income doing something you enjoy, then your life will be enriched.

The following case histories may encourage you to consider whether similar opportunities exist in your area:

☐ A man's hobby was repairing cane-bottomed furniture for his friends. His wife dreaded his being at home all the time when retirement came, but he advertised for work in local shop windows and now spends three full days a week in his garden workshop. His wife is equally content!

☐ The wife of a departmental store manager enjoyed growing exotic fruits and vegetables in a large greenhouse. She 'test-marketed' her produce through the Women's Institute produce stall. This was so successful that her husband took early retirement to help her in the business, and added another greenhouse.

☐ A group of enterprising housewives pooled their resources and set up an organisation which advertises the following services: home-minding, private catering, escort service for school children, home help during convalescence, transport service for small items, and guided tours with foreign language guides!

☐ A fishmonger introduced a mobile van service to Surrey villages which lacked fresh fish shops. He calls regularly one morning a week; sells fish direct from Billingsgate; uses a public house car park and works non-stop serving a queue. He probably sells as much in one morning as he would in a week if he had a shop with all its overheads. Business has built up by word of mouth and a one inch advertisement in the local church magazine!

☐ A retired school music teacher now supplements her income by playing the piano for children's dancing and ladies' keep fit classes. She works on Saturdays at the local music shop demonstrating electric organs on a salary plus commission basis.

Hobbies for pleasure and profit

Here is a selection of some three dozen hobbies and interests which can be turned to profit. Adult education classes can be

TAKING UP A FRANCHISE

Godfrey Golzen, Colin Barrow and Jackie Severn

It is reckoned that ninety per cent of all businesses fail whereas ninety per cent of new franchises succeed. Setting up one's own business may be the only feasible alternative to unemployment and franchising is an attractive option for someone who has money to invest but does not wish to take the obvious risks involved in 'going it alone'.

For anyone contemplating taking up a franchise this book is essential reading. It is packed with vital facts and invaluable information which will enable you to make the right decisions. Apart from explaining exactly what franchising is and how it operates, it gives financial and marketing data on around 100 franchisors. There is detailed advice on evaluating a franchise proposal and how to finance a franchise, plus lists of useful organisations and publications.

Taking up a Franchise aims to eliminate the notion that franchising is an easy way to riches by alerting you to the potential pitfalls. It clearly indicates that, as well as the numerous advantages, there are stresses and dangers in some of the compromises franchising offers between self-employment and working for someone else.

Godfrey Golzen was a publisher and is now a freelance journalist. He is also the author of several highly successful *Daily Telegraph/Kogan Page* guides: *Working for Yourself, Working Abroad* and *Changing Your Job* (with Philip Plumbley) and writes frequently for The Daily Telegraph.

Colin Barrow is director of the Small Business Research and Development Unit at Thames Polytechnic and runs his own management consultancy business. He is also programme consultant to the BBC television series 'Business Club' and has written the book that accompanies the programme.

Jackie Severn, FCA, qualified with a major international firm of accountants and has subsequently specialised in advising small businesses, particularly on taxation problems.

£11.95 Hardback 0 85038 633 0

£5.95 Paperback 0 85038 653 5

256 pages 216x138mm

Kogan Page, 120 Pentonville Road, London N1

Available from Booksellers or, in case of difficulty direct from the publisher

181

used to brush up old skills. You will also meet other people with similar interests living in your area. These contacts can also replace the social links lost when full time work ceases.

Art — painting, sculpture, wood carving
Basketry
Bee-keeping
Bookbinding
Car maintenance, repair and restoration
China restoration and decorating
Clock and watch repairs
Cookery (continental, haute cuisine, patisserie)
Crochet
DIY home repairs and decorating
Dressmaking
Embroidery
Enamelling
Furniture repair and renovation
Gardening
Genealogy
Glass decorating and engraving
Home made preserves
Jewellery making
Lace making
Lacquer work
Lecturer — Adult Education/ Workers' Educational Association/Technical College
Marquetry
Photography
Picture framing
Pottery
Printing
Public speaking
Rug making
Tailoring
Tapestry work
Toy making
Upholstery
Weaving
Woodwork
Writing

TOPS (Training Opportunities Scheme)

For those made redundant or taking early retirement, it is well worth checking your eligibility to take one of the 500 different courses available under the government's TOPS scheme. Tax free allowances are payable to trainees, and the scheme embraces training in clerical, commercial, craft, technician and management fields. You can apply to attend a course in shorthand typing, business administration, electronics, welding, catering and how to set computer controlled machinery.

For those committed to setting up their own businesses, special courses are run under the TOPS New Enterprise Programme. Enquiries may be made at your local Jobcentre.

London Enterprise Agency (LEntA)

This agency, set up by nine large companies, wishes to help small firms. LEntA have launched a training scheme for would-be entrepreneurs, act as counsellors, and are prepared to introduce small businesses to potential backers. In the London boroughs and outside London as well there is now a rapidly growing number of local enterprise agencies that supply services similar to those of LEntA. They are listed in a very useful BBC publication, *The Small Business Guide* by Colin Barrow.

Conclusions

Now, is all this advice you have had thrust at you worth it if you look at it in the terms of cost benefit analysis? It is surprising how many people are unaware of life expectancy figures. An average man of 60 can expect to live for another 18 years and the average woman can expect to live and draw the state pension for 22 years. So an investment in pre-retirement planning should give you a bonus in the years which lie ahead. Such preparation will enable you and your partner to enter this new phase of life with confidence. You will have planned your finances, have a safe suitable house, no bulging waistline, and you will be itching to have time at last to take up all the new activities you have arranged. *Choice* magazine, the only journal for retirement planning, can keep you up to date on matters relevant to the retired person.

The self-employed man who cannot spare the time to attend a local pre-retirement course may be interested in taking a correspondence course in the subject. This is on offer from the International Correspondence Schools under the title 'Enjoy Your Retirement'.

With the right attitude, retirement can be the most satisfying and fulfilling period of a person's life — the one period in life when the individual has complete freedom of choice to do what he wants to do, at the pace he decides. It is for you to decide in which direction you go.

Good luck!

Editor's Note: Fred Kemp was Chairman of the Council of Europe Working Party on Preparation for Retirement. Together with Bernard Buttle he is co-author of *Focus on Retirement* (1979) Kogan Page. The same authors have also written, in a lighter vein, *Looking Ahead: A Guide to Retirement*

Macdonald & Evans. Both books can be obtained from the Pre-Retirement Association, 19 Undine Street, Tooting, London SW17 8PP.

Together with Bernard Buttle and Derek Kemp he has also written *Coping with Redundancy* (1981) which contains a chapter on self-employment. The book is available in hardback from Kogan Page, 120 Pentonville Road, London N1 or as a Hamlyn Paperback from W H Smith.

Part 2:
Businesses Requiring Capital

2.1: Starting Your Business

Introduction

To buy and stock a shop, or start and run a hotel or restaurant, a building firm or a farm, is a sizeable investment — in your time, energy and, above all, money. True, if you buy premises for any type of business and the venture fails, you can cut your losses by selling the premises. You may avoid significant losses, provided you have bought at a *realistic* price, but losses there will be: on stock, on any refurbishing you carried out, and on the opportunity cost of your time and capital. So, do not rush into anything: consider the size of the investment and the possibility of failure and, conversely, recognise the personal sacrifices you must make to achieve success.

Buying a business

All investments in business ventures are a risk, but they should not be too much of a risk. Do not over-commit yourself, and aim to finance your business as far as possible from your own resources. Of course, self-financing is often not feasible and you will probably depend on finance from a clearing bank, merchant bank, insurance company or building society. In practice, clearing banks are by far the most usual source of finance for small businesses. Merchant banks and finance houses lend larger amounts, usually at slightly higher rates of interest. Merchant banks have increased their role as providers of 'venture' and 'development' capital considerably in recent years. However, they will usually be looking for companies with turnovers of £¼ million or more, and may require an equity stake in the company (ie part-ownership of the company) in return for finance. (See the table in Chapter 1.3 for information on merchant banks.) Insurance companies are important sources of *personal* finance, but are less willing to lend money to commercial ventures, as assurance policies rarely cover the size of the loan required by the aspiring businessman. And building societies are rarely prepared to give mortgages to commercial ventures.

It is usually to the high street bank that a small businessman will turn (though, with expert financial advice, good use can be made of the other sources of finance). Banks (and individual bank managers) sometimes vary in their willingness to lend to new enterprises and expanding businesses. Ask friends, people in other businesses and an accountant for advice on which bank(s) to approach. Your relationship with the bank manager is vital — both to the likelihood of your initial application for finance succeeding, and to the working of your business venture. If you have a longstanding relationship with a particular bank (and branch manager) as a *personal* customer, it may well be worth applying to that bank for *business* finance. A good record as a personal customer will go some way towards convincing the bank of your likely financial integrity as a business customer.

A more important consideration, however, is that the application you make to the bank should be clear and well thought through, and your cash flow estimates and business plans realistic and well-structured. You must be clear about how much you need, for what purposes, for how long, etc. The onus is on you to prove your case. The following list covers points the bank manager will expect you to have thought through; make notes on each point and be ready and *able* to cover each point objectively and fluently.

- ☐ What type of venture is it? Where will it be located?
- ☐ What is your experience of the trade, and how did you become involved in this particular project?
- ☐ What is the structure of your organisation, and who owns it? Is it a limited company or a partnership, or are you a sole trader?
- ☐ What business objectives have you set yourself: profitability or expansion, diversification or specialisation, etc?
- ☐ How will you market your work: advertising, representation, etc?
- ☐ What are your overheads: property, capital equipment, staff, running costs, etc?
- ☐ How will you price your work?
- ☐ What is the value of your assets?
- ☐ Can you estimate the amount of money you need, and the length of the period before you achieve profitability? Be realistic and thorough on this, as on all points.

You must be able to sell yourself and the project — a good test of *your* belief in the workability of the scheme.

A good relationship with your bank is invaluable. As well as a bank loan or overdraft agreement, your bank will offer a range of other loans for short-term purposes, such as the acquisition of property and the funding of expansion.

Chapter 1.3 gives a more detailed treatment of the subject of raising capital, but some points have been reiterated here because this section is aimed at people who will be making a large investment in property and capital equipment. Subsequent chapters deal with major business areas in which property held on lease — or freehold is central. Certain principles apply to all these areas:

- ☐ Pay a realistic price for whatever you purchase.
- ☐ Make all agreements you sign legally binding and use a solicitor to protect your investment.
- ☐ Do not underestimate the size of the investment that will be required.
- ☐ Do not over-commit yourself financially, and retain some funds or assets in case things go badly wrong.
- ☐ Consult an accountant before borrowing money from any source and make certain you know the provisions of all financial agreements.
- ☐ Have a watertight proposal to make to any potential lender.
- ☐ Use *bona fide* sources of finance.
- ☐ Your relationship with a lender must be based on mutual *trust* as well as mutual *interest*.
- ☐ Be realistic about your credit needs: buying the business is only the prelude to refurbishing and stocking it, insuring and perhaps fireproofing the premises, purchasing capital equipment and paying current expenses at a time when you are struggling to build a reputation and establish a business structure and clientele.
- ☐ Remember that you often have to give personal guarantees and/or provide security on a business loan: thus default on the latter could lead to possession by your creditor(s) of personal goods.
- ☐ Know when (and how) to pull out if things go badly: where to sell stock, how to sell the premises, how to terminate long-term loans, etc.
- ☐ If things go well, know when (and how) to expand and diversify: do not over-extend your resources; ensure that your staff can cope with greater pressures.

2.2: Farming and Market Gardening

The 'back to the land' movement has been quite fashionable in recent years, with all kinds of people giving up their jobs and homes in cities to live on smallholdings (communal or otherwise) where they try to be completely self-sufficient. Others, more commercially minded, may take up market gardening, which gives them a pleasant life in the country while they sell the fruits of their labours to others. Some more conventional souls may simply decide to buy a farm and rear cattle, grow corn or keep pigs or poultry.

In all cases, the romantic glow soon disappears. There are two essentials for any of these occupations, neither of them romantic: capital and the capacity for hard work. Take advice from professional bodies such as the Ministry of Agriculture's Advisory Service or the local county office of the National Farmers' Union. The local authority is responsible for agricultural education and you should make inquiries about courses that might be available in your area. The soaring costs of fuel and animal feedstuffs have already put many market gardeners and farmers out of business, so it is obviously essential to go into the finances of the operation very thoroughly before making a decision.

It is also essential to have the complete support of your family. This can be a very hard life, getting up early in all weathers to feed animals, breaking your back hoeing and weeding, and you have to be extremely keen and enthusiastic to take it on. If your nearest and dearest is not equally enthusiastic, forget it, for you are going to need their active help, since labour is both expensive and hard to come by.

Farming

The old joke that there are only three ways to get into farming — matrimony, patrimony and parsimony — applies even more strongly today. Unless you stand to inherit a farm, you are going to need an awful lot of money: agricultural land at the moment averages over £1,800 an acre and good quality land regularly sells at £2,400 plus an acre. The acreage you require will depend on the type of farming and the quality of the land. It could vary from 100 acres for dairy farming to, say, 300 acres for arable farming. And it does not stop there. You are then going to need working capital to buy cows, sheep, tractors, combines, etc. Even to start in a modest way could need £40,000 to £50,000, not including running costs.

You may be lucky enough to possess that kind of money, or at least have access to it; if not, you are going to need a bank loan, and here you are going to discover the other essential qualification for a farmer nowadays — technical know-how. Farming has become a technological occupation, requiring all kinds of special skills and knowledge. Unless you can convince a bank that you have this know-how (and some business experience) you are unlikely to get your money. Long-term loans for the purchase of land are available from the Agricultural Mortgage Corporation Ltd, but here again, properly prepared budgets and a realistic and comprehensive proposal will be required if the application is to be successful.

Farming is now a highly risky occupation giving only a 3 to 4 per cent return on the land. The failure rate is very high, and to take it up with little or no experience almost guarantees failure. Unless you know about fertilisers, pesticides, animal husbandry and farm machinery, you are likely to make some expensive mistakes, and remember that two bad years could wipe you out financially. The farmers who are most successful are those who start young, probably in a family owned business. By the time they take over, they have acquired the necessary experience, usually backed up these days with a course at one of the agricultural colleges. You should not contemplate farming without some practical experience, or a degree or diploma from an agricultural college, or preferably both.

A cheaper way in is to try to become a tenant farmer. You do not have the enormous expense of buying the land, but once in you are protected for life and can run things to suit yourself (except for mismanagement of course). The snag is that tenancies are in tremendous demand, and there are often as many as 100 applicants for one farm. You can also try intensive farming, where you again save on the cost of land, though remember that here your working capital requirements are going to be higher. Battery hens or other animals require a lot

191

of outlay in the form of equipment and feedstuffs, while market gardeners will find themselves spending a fortune on heating greenhouses. Soaring costs in fact have meant that intensive farming is not as profitable as it was, and many people have gone out of business. The trend in farming at the moment is in fact towards bigger, not smaller, units, because it is the only way to make a decent living.

Another idea which is very popular at the moment with the 'get-away-from-it-all-brigade' is to buy a smallholding and try to be entirely self-sufficient, perhaps even setting up a commune. It is an attractive idea, and the initial cost need not be great, but be warned: this is subsistence farming and you will find yourself working as hard as the American pioneers did. Also, even on a commune you may need a tractor and, for that, you are going to need money. You really need to be dedicated or rich (preferably both).

If the foregoing has not deterred you, get some professional advice, either from ADAS (the Agricultural Development Advisory Service of the Ministry of Agriculture) or from your local agricultural college or institute. There are also various farm management consultants and land agency firms who will (for a fee) give advice on what to do.

Even running a smallholding will demand considerable capital and expertise, as well as determination and immense hard work. Pat Burke, who runs one such smallholding, says: 'You must start with sufficient capital to carry you through the first year since you will almost certainly make nothing at all until your second year. All the self-employed work long hours but running a smallholding involves particularly long hours — weekends don't exist.'

Market gardening

Unless you take over an established business, the main problems for the would-be market gardener are acquiring the necessary land and a greenhouse. You may be lucky enough to own a suitable piece of land already, or a garden big enough (two to three acres) to be worked commercially, otherwise you may have to pay anything up to £2800 an acre. A greenhouse is the other big expense. It is a vital piece of equipment, enabling you to grow tomatoes, bedding plants, pot plants for the winter months and seedlings for early vegetables. You can do without one, but you must then make enough money in the spring and summer to make up for the lean winter months when you have virtually nothing to offer except a few winter vegetables. You also have to make provision for the cost of heating a greenhouse: recent price increases in fuel have sent the cost sky-high, so you must make sure that every inch of space is working for you, if your profits are not going literally to disappear in smoke. Even the cheapest second-hand greenhouse is likely to cost at least £1,600, while a new one costs five to six times as much.

If you are not a trained horticulturalist, it is a good idea to employ someone who is, or who has at least had practical experience of running a big garden and greenhouse. One full-time helper is probably all you will be able to afford in the early years. Seasonal help picking tomatoes, strawberries, beans, etc, costs about £1.80 an hour, and is often difficult to find. You (and your family) must be prepared to work long hours and turn your hand to anything.

For general information, particularly on the economics of growing produce, contact the National Farmers' Union which has a very good horticultural section. Another excellent source of information on what crops to grow, soil tests, etc, is the Agricultural Development Advisory Service of the Ministry of Agriculture.

One basic decision to be made, once you have decided on your crops, is how you are going to market your produce. If you are on a busy main road you may decide to rely heavily on local advertising and passing trade from tourists, etc, sending the surplus to the local market, or even taking a stall in the local market yourself. You can also send your produce to one of the big central markets, but you then have to pay a fee to the auctioneer, as well as transport costs.

2.3: Retailing

Buying a shop

No book can answer all the questions or anticipate all the problems that buying a shop or starting a retail business entails, but it can warn you of the main reasons for failure:

- [ ] Paying an unrealistic price for the business.
- [ ] Lack of experience in the trade you enter.
- [ ] Cash flow problems caused by underestimating current costs.
- [ ] Failure to recognise the level of competition to the type of goods you sell or the service you offer (are you setting up a general food store next to a round-the-clock supermarket?).
- [ ] Choice of a bad location: away from the shopping centre, in a commercial area with little weekend trade, etc.

The character of areas and shopping precincts changes rapidly. The 'centre' of your town is perhaps moving, through lack of space, to an open-plan area with a multi-storey car park and a wide range of shopping units. Long-established shops in the 'older' part of town are often unable to survive, so be wary of being offered this type of business. There are wide variations in the desirability and potential profitability of even apparently similar retail businesses.

Ask where the business you have seen advertised is. Is it well-positioned or far from the centre of trading activity? What is its reputation? Be sceptical of the seller's claims to a fund of 'goodwill' from long-standing customers. There is no guarantee that they exist and, if they do, that they will be as loyal to you. How much stock have you been offered as part of the purchase price? Does the shop need redecoration? What terms are you being offered: freehold or leasehold? What is the nature of the competition to your enterprise?

Such questions do not allow simple answers. These vary according to the type of business you intend to conduct. For example, a more specialised shop (selling, say, good quality hi-fi or photographic equipment at competitive prices) does not need to be as central as a grocer's, butcher's or general goods store. Customers will hear about it and seek it out and, having been satisfied once, will return for accessories, improved equipment and advice.

Think, too, about general location and the composition of the local population: is it predominantly young or old, middle class or working class, close to sports facilities or not, and so on. Is there a seasonal trade that you might capture? Are there shops nearby that may attract certain types of people, whose custom you might aim to tap? Would you have to work special hours to fit in with the habits of your potential customers (by for example, staying open until 7 or 7.30 pm in suburban residential areas)? Would those habits affect your trade adversely at certain times (low 'traffic' at weekends in business areas, for instance)?

In short, you must consider a whole range of locational factors before choosing to buy an established business or deciding *where* to start a new shop. Four rules:

- ☐ Talk to people who know the trade and the locality.
- ☐ Take the advice of an accountant and solicitor who will, respectively, assess the financial worth of the purchase and the legal commitments you will enter into.
- ☐ Do not buy the first shop offered to you unless *everyone* thinks it is an unmissable opportunity (and, even then, think again!).
- ☐ Always assume the seller is asking too much.

This is not sophisticated business thinking; it is plain commonsense. George Thorpe, a food retailer, stresses the need for forward planning. He says: 'Even if you have to borrow money, do not be under capitalised. Keep your shelves full and well stocked since this will attract customers . . . Apart from fruit and veg you will have to have five to seven times your weekly takings tied up in stock.'

You and your business

On a more personal level, can you and your family bear the strain of managing a shop: the hours of work, the tedium of filling in tax forms and keeping books; the problems of receiving early morning deliveries; the physical work that might be involved in taking and storing deliveries; the pressure of having always to be polite to the customers? (You might not wish to follow the dictum that the customer is always right, but would you survive? Small businesses depend on customers returning and on word-of-mouth promotion.)

Working hours are long, but made tolerable by a commitment to *your* business. You will grow to dislike VAT returns and difficult customers, and you will encounter a host of petty day-to-day administrative difficulties, but if you are serious about the move in the first place, you should survive these. But ask yourself: is my immediate family as dedicated to the project as I am? What is a challenge to you may be a burden to them. So, be as sensitive to their needs as you are to your own.

Buying an established business

Shops for sale are sometimes advertised in the local and national press and in some trade journals,* or you can consult a firm of business valuers and transfer agents. It is a good idea to write down the specific requirements that you are looking for: this will not only help you to brief your agent and any other advisers such as your accountant and bank manager, but will also help you clarify your ideas.

Shops are generally rented on a leasehold basis, and you should aim for a property with as long a lease as possible. In paying for the shop you will be buying the premises, fixtures and fittings, existing stock and 'goodwill'. How this price is arrived at depends on a number of factors, which you must analyse carefully before you commit yourself. *Stock* is generally valued for business sale purposes at current market cost price, and an independent valuation of the stock is desirable. *Fixtures and fittings* should also be independently valued, and an inventory of these should be made and attached to the contract of sale. *'Goodwill'* is a nebulous concept to which an exact value cannot be attached. Obviously, the more the shop relies on regular, established customers, the higher the value of the goodwill; conversely, the more it relies on casual, passing trade, the lower the goodwill value. The price of a shop will also to a large extent depend on the potential of the local area. You will need to make a careful assessment of factors such as:

1. Competition. Do not make the mistake of thinking that

---

* A full list of these is contained in *British Rate & Data* (BRAD), a monthly listing of all commercial periodical publications and newspapers which should be available in any reasonable business reference library.

the absence of a nearby competitor *necessarily* guarantees success. A shop that has done reasonably well in the face of nearby competition is a safer bet than a shop with a similar record which has had a virtual monopoly of local trade. There is always a danger that if there is no competition, someone else may move in after you. Another common mistake is to see only shops of the same trade as competition. Indirectly, all other traders in the area are competition, since all are competing for a share of the consumers' spending power.

2. Nearness to railway stations, bus stops, etc: this may substantially increase the flow of passing trade. A map may help to clarify the exact potential of the location.

3. Any future local development plans – check with the local authority.

It is important that you and your accountant study the books thoroughly. In particular, examine the trend of the profit and loss account over the past few years to determine whether the business is improving. Another important point to note is whether the previous trader has been paying himself a salary, or whether this has to be deducted from the net profit figure. A really excellent guide to what is involved in buying a shop is another Daily Telegraph/Kogan Page guide which is actually called *Buying a Shop* by A St J Price. The chapter on negotiating with a vendor is particularly clear and useful.

We spoke to the owner of a general goods shop who makes these points strongly: 'Location, potential competition and overheads are the three key points to watch. If you're buying an existing store scrutinise the accounts minutely. Is it possible to run it with one less member of staff for example? Are home deliveries being made – these can be very, very expensive? Don't try to compete on prices with the big boys – you'll lose! Stock lots of lines and if needs be sell say sugar at a loss knowing you've got a good margin on shampoo. There's no guarantee that goodwill will pass over to you on completion of the sale – your face might not fit and there's little allegiance nowadays from customers.'

Starting from scratch

You may want to take over premises which have previously been used for other purposes, in which case you should look closely at the previous owner's reasons for closing down and determine to what extent the same factors will affect you, even though you are engaged in a different trade. If you are going to use them for another type of business, you must get planning permission first. Or you may want to rent newly built premises, in which case you will probably have to pay a premium. The premium is based on the potential of the area, but try to get an *exact* idea of what that potential is: the number of new flats being built nearby, for example. In general, the premium should be lower than the goodwill price you would pay for a going concern, since it only indicates potential, not a record of success.

Legal obligations

The most important Acts* affecting shops are:

- ☐ Contracts of Employment Act
- ☐ Offices, Shops and Railway Premises Act
- ☐ Shops Act
- ☐ Trade Descriptions Act
- ☐ Weights and Measures Act
- ☐ Sale of Goods Acts
- ☐ Local Authority By-laws
- ☐ Consumer Credit Act
- ☐ Redundancy Payment Act
- ☐ Payment of Wages Act
- ☐ Employment Protection Act
- ☐ Sex Discrimination Act
- ☐ Health and Safety at Work Act.
- ☐ Unfair Contracts Act
- ☐ Prices Act
- ☐ Supply of Goods and Services Act.

These fall into three categories. First, employment legislation (see Chapter 1.10). Check the ages of your employees; ensure that they are taxed and that you pay your share of their National Insurance contribution; cover them regarding pensions and superannuation; know where they stand in relation to the Employment Protection Act (if they work more than 16 hours a week and more than 52 weeks (or, in a small firm, 104 weeks) continuously, they will be covered by its provisions and eligible

* Other Acts, such as the Pet Animals Act, affect specific types of shops.

to claim against wrongful dismissal, etc). Similarly, if they work full-time and have been employed for more than 104 weeks they are eligible for redundancy payments if you make them redundant.

Second, safety, security and planning. You should insure your premises and stock, and cover yourself against liability, including liability for defective goods (potential liability will vary widely depending on the goods you sell and the services you offer). In the case of a food shop, you must satisfy a health inspector, and other types of premises will have to be passed fit by a fire officer. Check these and local planning laws before you start trading. The quickest way to find out which of these laws apply to you is to contact your local Shops Act inspector. He will also provide details of by-laws on opening hours, Sunday trading, pavement displays, etc.

Third, fair trading. Know and follow the provisions of the Consumer Credit Act and the Trade Descriptions Act. There are strict rules on how you display prices, on recommended prices and 'special' offers, on the giving of guarantees, on the rates of hire purchase you can offer and the other types of credit you make available, and so on. Again, cover yourself against expensive litigation by going through existing legislation with a solicitor, looking at standard practice in businesses similar to your own, and taking advice from the local Weights and Measures Inspector.

Finally, be aware of your standing under the Sale of Goods Act. When you sell something the merchandise you sell should be in good condition and fit for its stated purpose. If it is not your customer is entitled to a suitable replacement or a refund. When you provide a service, under contract law it should be up to the required standard; if it is not the customer can claim compensation. A new Sale of Goods and Services Act passed in 1983 brings the sale of goods and the provision of services into line and makes all retailers responsible for the product or service they provide.

Keeping accounts

A great deal of bookwork will be inevitable: keeping count of stock levels and daily sales (for personal use and for VAT purposes); an elementary statistical breakdown of what is selling; keeping tabs on credit customers, orders, returned goods, etc. Your accountant and bank manager will wish to see comprehensive and up-to-date accounts to check your progress. See Chapter 1.5 for an introduction to simple accounting, but be warned: for anything more than day-to-day bookkeeping it is worth using a qualified accountant.

Leasing

Leases are written in legal jargon and for that reason the vendor is sometimes apt to sign without really understanding what the lease says. This is a great mistake, and if you cannot follow the wording or are unclear about anything, you should ask your solicitor to explain it to you. Look out particularly for restrictive covenants that prevent you from transferring the lease to a third party or from carrying on certain trades and professions at those premises.

Security

Never leave cash lying about. If there is a lot of money in the till, take out a round sum in notes and leave a chit in the till to remind yourself where it is. Watch out for shoplifters, and ensure against them as far as possible by not leaving small, valuable items in easily accessible positions. Do not leave customers or visitors unattended. Remember that you must be insured right from the start, even before you have opened up for business. The Home Office produces a pamphlet on theft by staff, which is a danger which must not be overlooked. Consult your local crime protection officer who will advise you on ways to combat both dangers.

Stock

It is sensible to buy your stock from a wholesaler, or cash and carry or from a manufacturer's agent, since you will generally need frequent deliveries of small quantities of goods. Have as few sources of supply as possible, to cut down your workload. There are a few exceptions to this. In the case of cigarettes, for example, it is better to deal directly with the manufacturer.

Make sure you know at all times what your stock levels are, and devise a system whereby you know when to re-order, before stocks run too low. The stock should be cleaned and dusted regularly and any stock that remains unsold over a long period should be discarded. Stock-taking should be carried out regularly, depending on the type of business in which you are engaged.

Layout and display

Cleanliness and hygiene are, of course, absolute musts. Layout, too, will be important. Make the interior of the shop as attractive as you can: displays, however small, should have a focal point, and should be changed frequently. Allow space for your customers to move and, if necessary, push prams, and make sure that they have access to all the goods on your shelves. Think, also, about your window displays: manufacturers will often supply signs and special display items which may improve the look of your shop.

Case studies

It would be impossible to cover the whole range of shops: general and specialist, selling goods and offering services, urban and rural, central and suburban, business and consumer orientated, and so on. A few case studies are included here only for illustration, and a note added on sub post offices which are a rather special case. But no one *type* of shop or method of operation will necessarily work. Find something that suits you, and let what you do and the style you adopt reflect your personality.

Antique shops

This is a prime example of an area where you must be experienced: you must have a thorough knowledge of antiques, of the business and of other dealers. Whether you are starting off from scratch or buying an established business, you will need funds to buy stock. If you buy a going concern, you may find that the stock consists of all the duds and non-sellers of the previous owners, and you will have to get rid of it all and start again.

You will learn the technique of buying things at auctions: always go to the preview first and mark on your catalogue the items you are interested in and the price you are prepared to pay. Beware of being 'trotted' — other dealers running up the bidding and then dropping out at the end leaving you to pay an unrealistic price. Country auctions are usually widely advertised in local papers and you will soon get to know local dealers and their specialities. You must then build up a body of reliable clients, who will form the backbone of your business. These may include other dealers and foreign buyers.

You are most likely to make a success if you specialise, and learn as much as you can about your speciality, whether it is pictures, brass and copper, china or furniture. Use *The Lyle Official Antiques Review* if at all in doubt about the auction value of any item.

One main drawback is the hours you will be expected to keep — this is *not* a 9 to 5 job! Evenings will probably be spent entering up sales, pricing new acquisitions, etc, and then foreign dealers have a nasty habit of travelling overnight and arriving on the doorstep at 8 am ready to do business.

Robert O'Connor, an antique dealer, gives would-be dealers four pieces of advice: 'Buying is the key to success — you can't ring up a wholesaler and order twelve dozen. Selling is not so difficult as long as it's the right piece and the right price. You have to know and love your subject and not be motivated by profit. Work hard at developing lines of supply and specialise in an area that particularly interests you. Go to sale rooms, visit other dealers, study, read and handle the items and your instincts will develop.'

Bookshops

The location of a bookshop is all-important when deciding what sort of books to stock: children's books, textbooks, hobbies, gardening, etc. If you live on the tourist route it might be worthwhile stocking a lot of local history, while in another area it would be a good idea to find out what the local evening classes are.

You need to be devoted to your work, since you are going to work long hours, dealing with all sorts of queries from the public and some days you may be lucky to sell one cheap paperback, despite having had an infinitely varied range of browsers in your shop. Though libraries usually buy through special suppliers some may buy from local bookshops, and, in any case, it is worth making contact with the local librarian who will be in touch with local tastes and needs. School books are mainly bought centrally nowadays, but if there is a college in your area it is well worth finding out what textbooks are required and stocking a selection. You could even put a small ad in your window to that effect and perhaps develop a second-hand and exchange system with students.

The antiquarian book trade is extremely specialised and you really need to be an expert in the subject before you can hope to make any money in this area. People do make a lot of money, but they have to be prepared to invest thousands. They also need the patience to acquire the specialised knowledge needed.

Newsagents and tobacconists

Extremely hard work and long hours are involved in running this type of shop, and it is not a particularly profitable area. You will probably need to organise a daily delivery service for newspapers, which will involve getting up very early, marking newspapers, paying delivery agents, keeping books of customers' credit, etc. You will have to deal with a large number of suppliers, whose representatives will call regularly. You will have all the headaches of VAT and the constant small price rises which particularly affect cigarettes and confectionery. Moreover, you will have to keep the shop open for as many hours as possible – most newsagents close only on Good Friday, Christmas Day and Boxing Day, the only days when newspapers are not printed. If a member of your family is available to work in the shop, the extra help will be invaluable, and you can avoid the problems which taking on staff might entail.

Ironmonger's/DIY shop

The principles for this type of retail outlet differ from those which apply to a newsagent's in several important respects: trade will often be more specialised, so location is likely to be less important; stock will often be expensive and heavy initial capitalisation may be necessary, and, because some items will be bulky and a wide range of stock must be held, relatively large premises will be required.

Russ Morgan, who runs a DIY shop, also emphasises the degree of expertise you need to have: 'You must know the tools you stock and the jobs they're capable of doing so that you can advise your customers correctly. You are not merely selling products you are also a key source of advice and if your advice is good and your products are right then people will return again and again.' He is also aware of the high cost and the importance of stock control. 'Get your stock level right. Too little and word gets around that you can never get anything there. Too much and the cost of keeping your stock on your shelves eats into profits. If you are taking £500 a week then your stock should be about £4000. But do remember if someone buys a very expensive plane to reorder immediately − if you don't someone is bound to come in next week asking for it and you won't be able to help him.'

Travel agency

Anyone can buy a shop and set up a business as a travel agent − you do not need any special licence or authorisation. On the other hand, if you want to become an authorised agent for British Rail, or any of the major airline companies, or for any of the big shipping companies, there is rather more involved. Before you can earn commission on the sale of tickets from these various bodies, you have to satisfy them that you are a reputable company; and their requirements can be fairly stringent.

Two essential requirements if you are setting up on your own are contacts inside the business and sufficient capital. Most people will acquire the necessary experience *and* the contacts by working in an agency for a year or two until they have learned the ropes. At the same time they will probably work part-time for the examination of the Association of British Travel Agents.

Most reputable agents belong to the Association of British Travel Agents, who also have to be satisfied that you are a reputable firm. If you are a limited company, they require you to have an issued share capital of £5000 and also to put up another £5000 as a bond for your bank or insurance company. To gain approval of IATA (International Air Transport Association) and British Rail (who do all their own, very thorough, investigations) you have to prove that you are a reputable firm with sufficient financial backing, that you are generating sufficient business to warrant selling their tickets (the financial requirements vary according to the locality), that your staff are sufficiently trained and knowledgeable, that your premises are of a sufficiently high standard and promote the right image. Then, and only then, will you be able to advertise that you are an authorised agent.

It will take at least one or two years to work up the necessary volume of business. In the meantime, most people concentrate on hotel bookings and package tours. You can deal in air and rail tickets, but only through another friendly agency, and of course *you* do not then earn the commission (it is illegal).

Choosing the right area is obviously important — centre of town, busy suburb, prosperous market town, for example. There is a great deal of competition and you will survive and prosper only if you provide a friendly and *reliable* service which is also competitively priced. Remember, too, that the most lucrative business is done with firms: you should cultivate every contact you can find in the hope of becoming *the* company agency for nearby business firms.

Sub post offices

As a sub post master you are effectively a 'franchisee' of the Post Office. You offer its services and sell its products at prices which it dictates and for which you receive payment. The postal services you provide will often be only part of the overall service, and the Post Office will not usually restrict other sales. But it will be an important part of the business, attracting a steady stream of customers who, once inside the shop, may be tempted to buy other things.

A sub post mastership is not *automatically* transferred from seller to buyer and the change has to be ratified by the Post Office. You should realise this when purchasing any business that includes postal services.

Owing to the decline in the number of rural and sub post offices and the demand for such businesses, competition is fierce and it is becoming increasingly difficult to obtain a sub post-mastership.

2.4: Franchising

Martin Mendelsohn

Introduction

The contribution that follows has been written by Martin Mendelsohn, a solicitor who is also the author of *The Guide to Franchising* (Pergamon Press). It should be read in the context of the spread of franchising and its growing popularity as a way of starting a business: about 100 franchises are evaluated and described in a recent book, *Taking up a Franchise* by Golzen, Barrow and Severn, published by Kogan Page.

The best known and oldest established UK franchises are Wimpy Bars and they illustrate the basic principles of what is known as the business format franchise. It is a form of business in which the franchisor — that is the party who owns the rights to the franchise — lays down a blueprint for conducting that business. It covers principally the content and nature of the goods or service being offered, the performance standards and price, and the design of premises, stationery or whatever else is directly associated with its presentation to the public. The idea is that the blueprint represents a tried and tested formula for operating the franchise profitably. Its very uniformity is a recipe for product recognition which is far greater than the franchisee — the person operating the franchise — could achieve working on his or her own. It is said that this is one of the main reasons why the success rate of business format franchises is far higher than that for new and totally independent businesses.

For the right to operate the franchise, for access to the blueprint and its built-in formula for success and for a range of other forms of help and advice, especially during the start-up period, the franchisee pays the franchisor an initial fee and a royalty. Martin Mendelsohn here provides a guide to the factors an intending franchisee should consider. Fuller accounts are given in the two books referred to above.

What the franchisor offers

One method by which it is possible to start in business and reduce the risks inherent in such a venture is to take up a business format franchise.

The business format franchise is a stage in the development of agency, distributorship, licences, and know-how type of manufacturing and marketing transactions. Instead of being limited to one aspect of business activity there has developed the concept of licensing an entire package comprising all the elements necessary to establish a previously untrained person in a business to be run on a predetermined basis. These elements comprise:

☐ The entire business concept
☐ A process of initiation and training in all aspects of the running of the business according to that concept
☐ A continuing process of assistance and guidance.

The entire business concept

This involves the development by the franchisor of a successful way of carrying on a business in all its aspects. The franchisor will develop what may be described as a 'blueprint' for conducting the business. The blueprint should:

1. Eliminate so far as possible the risks inherent in opening a new business, for example, the product range should be thoroughly market tested in pilot operations run by the franchisor.
2. Enable a person who has never before owned or operated a business to open up in business on his own account, not only with a pre-established format but with the backing of an organisation (ie the franchisor) that would not otherwise be available to him.
3. Set out in detail exactly how the business should be run.

Process of initiation and training

The franchisee must be trained in the business methods that are necessary to operate the business according to the blueprint. This may involve training in the use of specialised equipment, marketing methods, preparation of produce and application of processes. The franchisee should be trained so that he is

relatively expert in those spheres that are necessary for the operation of that particular business.

Continuing process of assistance and guidance

The franchisor will in many cases provide the following range of services on a continuing basis depending of course upon the particular type of business:

☐ Regular visits from and access to a 'trouble-shooter' to assist in correcting or preventing deviations from the blueprint which may cause trading difficulties for the franchisee.

☐ Liaison between the franchisor, the franchisee and all other franchisees for exchanges of ideas and experiences.

☐ Product or concept innovation including investigation of marketability and compatibility with the existing business.

☐ Retraining facilities and training facilities, for the franchisee's staff.

☐ Market research.

☐ National and local advertising and promotion.

☐ Bulk purchasing opportunities.

☐ Management and accounting advice and services.

☐ Publication of a journal.

☐ Research into methods.

It will be seen that the business format franchise is a comprehensive and continuing relationship in which the initial concept is always being developed. The resources available for such development are those contributed to by the franchisor and all franchisees and are therefore much more considerable than any one individual could reasonably afford.

It will be noted that reference has been made to the *business format franchise*. The expression *franchise* is now popularly used to describe all those transactions in which one person licenses another rights to do something. For example, petrol filling stations, car dealerships, the use of a sportsman's or entertainer's name are commonly called franchises. It is important that you recognise what sort of franchise you are dealing with so that it is clear what can really be expected.

The word franchising can be used as a vehicle for abuse and indeed it already has been. It is the sort of transaction that readily lends itself to fraudulent practices. Invariably the transaction falls into two stages, the first is the provision of

POTENTIAL FRANCHISEE?

OUR COMPANY PROVIDES A FULL RANGE OF SERVICES TO ENABLE FRANCHISEES TO REALISE THEIR ASPIRATIONS.

For Franchisees we offer an unequalled opportunity to review and compare the features of a wide range of franchises in your particular area. We offer personal counselling to assist the prospective franchisee in selecting the proper franchise for his or her needs. Special finance arrangements can also be made to assist in acquiring the particular franchise selected.

To: Franchise Development Services Limited
Castle House, 21 Davey Place, Norwich NR2 1PJ
Tel: Norwich (0603) 20301 or 667024/5

Gentlemen, please forward further details of your services as indicated:

Services to Franchisee ○   Services to Franchisors ○

Name ....

Position..

Company ....

Address ....

....

....

Telephone ....

pre-opening services, the second the continuing relationship thereafter. If therefore the franchisor charges too much at stage one and is not there to provide stage two the fraud is obvious. A fraud could be committed by franchising an untried and undeveloped concept resulting in a franchisee being charged fees for a right to conduct a business which in reality does not exist.

Pyramid selling

The most serious frauds which have been perpetrated upon the unsuspecting were described as pyramid selling or multi-level marketing schemes. These schemes are presented as foolproof and very tempting methods of making easy money and are often marketed by presenting successful 'franchisees' who speak of their great financial success. These schemes involve the sale of distributorships to purchasers who may divide and subdivide them and sell them on to those whom they recruit as sub-distributors. Expansion of these enterprises takes place on the chain letter principle.

The ostensible object is to build up a sales force which will sell the company's products or services from door to door. In fact, selling the goods or services is difficult; they are usually expensive and areas are often saturated with other distributors. Selling distributorships is much more lucrative and becomes effectively the company's business.

These schemes were quickly recognised by the government as containing elements which are dishonest and, accordingly, the Fair Trading Act 1973 contains provisions which prohibit pyramid-type schemes. The Act also contains provisions which permit the making of regulations:

☐ To control or prohibit the issue, circulation or distribution of documents which contain invitations to persons to participate in a scheme.
☐ Prohibiting the promoter of a scheme from performing functions which are vital to the operation of such a scheme, such as supplying goods or receiving payment for goods.

It is important to be able to recognise involvement with a pyramid-type scheme. And, obviously, before signing any contract or parting with money you should take proper professional advice. Be suspicious if you are offered or told that there will be a reward (ie payment, supply of cheaper products or any other disguised benefit) for doing something totally unrelated to the sale of the basic product or service with which the scheme is involved. For example, you may be offered a percentage payment of any sum paid to the promoter of the scheme for recruiting another participant, or for persuading such participant to purchase a higher position in the scheme. Other rewards could include a profit or commission on sales, or the provision of services or training to other participants in the scheme, or a commission on sales effected by other participants in the scheme.

Advantages and disadvantages of franchising

Advantages to the franchisee

1. The franchisee's lack of basic or specialised knowledge is overcome by the training programme of the franchisor.
2. The franchisee has the incentive of owning his own business despite the background of assistance from the franchisor. He is an independent businessman within the framework of the franchise agreement and can by his own hard work and effort maximise the value of his investment.
3. The franchisee's business opens with the benefit of a name already well established in the mind and eye of the public.
4. The franchisee invariably requires less capital than is required in setting up independently by reason of the assistance given by the franchisor. However, many franchised businesses are organised in a highly sophisticated way and a franchisee may well have a larger investment to make than he would if he were to open for business without the franchise umbrella. On the other hand, a more modest investment may jeopardise the success of the business.
5. The franchisee should (where appropriate) receive assistance in:
   □ site selection
   □ preparation of plans for remodelling the premises, including the obtaining of any necessary town planning or by-law consents
   □ obtaining finance for the acquisition of the franchised business
   □ the training of his staff
   □ purchase of equipment
   □ selection and purchase of stock
   □ getting the business open and running smoothly.
6. The franchisee receives the benefit on a national scale (if

appropriate) of the franchisor's advertising and promotional activities.

7. The franchisee receives the benefit of the bulk purchasing and negotiating capacity of the franchisor on behalf of all the franchisees.

8. The franchisee has at his fingertips the specialised and highly skilled knowledge and experience of the franchisor's Head Office organisation in all aspects of his business while continuing in a self-employed capacity.

9. The franchisee's business risk is reduced. However, no franchisee should consider that because he is coming under the umbrella of the franchisor he is not going to be exposed to any risk at all. Any business undertaking involves risk and a franchised business is no exception. To be sucussful, the franchisee will have to work hard, perhaps harder than ever before. The franchisor will never be able to promise great rewards for little effort. The blueprint for carrying on business successfully and profitably can rarely be the blueprint for carrying on business successfully without working.

10. The franchisee has the services of 'trouble-shooters' provided by the franchisor to assist him with the many problems that may arise from time to time in the course of business.

11. The franchisee has the benefit of the use of the franchisor's patents, trade marks, trade secrets and any secret process or formulae.

12. The franchisee has the benefit of the franchisor's continuous research and development programmes designed to improve the business and keep it up to date.

13. The franchisor obtains the maximum amount of market information and experience which is circularised for the benefit of all the franchisees. This should give him access to information which would not otherwise be available to him.

14. There are also usually some territorial guarantees to ensure that no competitive franchisee is set up in a competing business within a defined area around the franchisee's business address. This can give rise to some legal difficulties under the Restrictive Trade Practices Act and must therefore be handled with care.

Disadvantages to the franchisee

1. Inevitably the relationship between the franchisor and franchisee will involve the imposition of controls. These controls will regulate the quality of the service or goods to be

provided or sold by the franchisee. It has been mentioned previously that the franchisee will own his own business. He will, but he must accept that for the advantages enjoyed by him, by virtue of his association with the franchisor and all the other franchisees, control of quality and standards is essential. Each bad franchisee has an adverse effect not only on his own business, but indirectly on the whole franchised chain of business and all other franchisees. The franchisor will therefore demand that standards are maintained so that the maximum benefit is derived by the franchisee and indirectly by the whole franchised chain from the operation of the franchisee's business. This is not to say that the franchisee will not be able to make any contribution or to impose his own personality on his business. Most franchisors do encourage their franchisees to make their contribution to the development of the business of the franchise chain and hold seminars and get-togethers to assist in the process.

2. The franchisee will have to pay the franchisor for the services provided and for the use of the blueprint, ie franchise fees.

3. The difficulty of assessing the quality of the franchisor. This factor must be weighed very carefully by the franchisee for it can affect the franchisee in two ways. First, the franchisor's offer of a package may well not amount to what it appears to be on the surface. Second, the franchisor may be unable to maintain the continuing services which the franchisee may need in order to sustain his efforts.

4. The franchise contract will contain some restrictions against the assignment of the franchised business. This is a clear inhibition on the franchisee's ability to deal with his own business but, as with most of the restrictions, there is a reason for it. The reason is that the franchisor will have already been most meticulous in his choice of the franchisee as his original franchisee for the particular outlet. Why then should he be any less meticulous in his approval of a replacement? Naturally he will wish to be satisfied that any successor of the franchisee is equally suitable for that purpose. In practice there is normally very little difficulty in the achievement of successful assignments of franchised businesses.

5. The franchisee may find himself becoming too dependent upon the franchisor. This can affect him in a number of ways; for example, he may not achieve the motivation that is necessary for him to work and build his business to take full advantage of the foundations that the blueprint provides.

6. The franchisor's policies may affect the franchisee's profit- ability.
7. The franchisor may make mistakes of policy; he may make decisions relating to innovations in the business which are unsuccessful and operate to the detriment of the franchisee.
8. The good name of the franchised business or its brand image may become less reputable for reasons beyond the franchisee's control.

How to decide

In order to judge these advantages and disadvantages and the way in which they are likely to concern a prospective franchisee there should be a detailed examination of the franchisor and his scheme. However, one must not lose sight of the fact that in deciding whether or not to go into a franchise one is also deciding to go into business on one's own account, albeit a particular type of business structured in a particular type of way. It is necessary, regardless of the fact that it is a franchised business which is contemplated, to indulge in the same sort of self-assessment in which one should indulge when deciding to embark on any business venture. If one has a particular franchise in mind the self-assessment exercise is less academic but one should be asking some, if not all, of the following questions:

- ☐ Am I qualified physically and temperamentally for self-employment?
- ☐ Do I possess sufficient financial resources to enable me to start a business and survive while it is struggling to become established?
- ☐ What are my natural aptitudes and skills? Do I do my best with mental or physical tasks? Do I mix well with people?
- ☐ Do I have the ability to work hard?
- ☐ How will my family be affected by my decision? Do they wholeheartedly support my proposed venture?

Having submitted oneself to this exercise in introspection, one then has to consider three other specific areas in relation to a franchise scheme.

1. The product or service which is given.
2. The franchisor: who is he and how does he rate?
3. The operational details.

We shall examine each in turn.

The product or service which is being offered

A number of questions arise for consideration.

1. Is the product or service new? Has it been thoroughly proved in practice to be successful? Does it have staying power?
2. Is the product or service in a business area which is in decline?
3. How highly competitive is the market for the particular product or service?
4. How competitive is the price for the product or service? Can this competitiveness be maintained?
5. What is the source of supply of any products? How certain is it that the source will be available for the future? Are alternatives available?
6. Are the products or services based upon any trade mark or patented equipment and the protection thereby afforded?
7. Is there an adequate back-up in terms of guarantees and service facilities if relevant?
8. Could the supplier easily bypass the franchisor and you, and set up his own competitive franchise?
9. What is the reputation of the product and supplier?

The franchisor

The following questions should be put to a franchisor to enable one to assess him, his financial involvement and the quality of his personnel.

1. How long have you been franchising?
2. Did you run your own pilot schemes before franchising?
3. If not, why not?
4. Whether you did or not, what is the extent of your own cash investment in the business?
5. How many franchised businesses are you running at the moment?.
6. What are the addresses of these businesses?
7. May I please interview any number of these franchisees? May I choose whom I interview?
8. How many outlets do you yourselves run as at the present time?
9. What does your head office organisation consist of?
10. Can you demonstrate your capacity to provide the necessary follow-up services?

11. May I take up your bank references?
12. Are there any other referees whom I may approach?
13. How many business failures have been experienced by your franchisees?
14. On what basis do you choose your franchisees — how selective are you?
15. What is the business background of the directors and executives of the franchisor company?
16. Have you or any of your directors or executives ever experienced any business failures? If so, please provide details.
17. Has any of your directors or executives ever: been bankrupt; entered into an arrangement with his creditors; been convicted of any criminal offence; been involved as a shareholder or executive in any company which while he was a director or executive or shortly after he ceased to be a director or executive went into liquidation? If so, please provide details.
18. Have you or any of your directors or executives been involved in any material litigation with franchisees? If so, please provide details.

The operational details

1. What is the initial cost of your franchise? What does this price include? What capital costs will be incurred in addition to this price, and what for?
2. How much working capital do I need?
3. What are the costs incurred in the business likely to be, broken down into *gross* profit and *net* profit?
4. May I see actual accounts which confirm or fail to confirm your projections?
5. What financing arrangements can you make and what terms for repayment will there be? What rate of interest will be required and will the finance company want security?
6. Is the business seasonal?
7. When is the best time to open up?
8. What fees do you charge?
9. Do you take any commission on supplies of goods or materials to a franchisee?
10. Will I be obliged to maintain a minimum fee or a minimum

purchase of goods? What happens if I fail to meet this commitment?
11. What advertising and promotional support do you provide?
12. Do I have to contribute to it, if so, how much?
13. What initial services do you offer?
14. Do you train me? Who pays for my training? Where do I go for training?
15. What continuing services do you provide after the business has commenced?

CONTRACTS

1. May I have a copy of your franchise contracts?
2. Does this contract permit me to sell my business? What restrictions are there affecting my rights to sell the business?
3. For how long is the franchise granted?
4. What do I get at the end of that period? Do I get automatic renewal?
5. What will happen if I do not like the business? Upon what basis can I terminate the contract?

220

OTHER ASPECTS

1. Who will be my link with you after I have opened for business? Can I meet some of your staff?
2. What point of sale and promotional literature do you supply and what do I have to pay for it?
3. What will the opening hours of business be?
4. Will I own the equipment necessary to operate the business when I have cleared the finance company?
5. How soon will I have to spend money on replacing equipment?
6. Will you find me a site or do I have to find it?
7. What systems do you have for keeping franchisees in touch with you and each other? Do you publish a newsletter? Do you hold seminars?
8. What help will I receive in local advertising and promotion?
9. What exclusive rights do I get?
10. How will I cope with my bookkeeping?
11. What can I sell and what can I not sell?
12. Do you provide instruction and operational manuals?
13. What would happen if you misjudged the site and it did not produce the anticipated figures but resulted in a loss?
14. What would happen if I ran into operational problems I was not able to solve? What help would I get?
15. How can I be sure you will do what you promise?

The British Franchise Association (BFA)

The formation of the British Franchise Association in 1977 introduced a new element. Membership is open only to those whose franchise scheme has been operating successfully for a period of time. The franchisor is investigated before admission to membership and must accept and observe a strict code of ethical behaviour. The BFA has a disciplinary procedure which can be invoked against a member who acts contrary to the code of ethics or otherwise engages in questionable practices. New franchisors do not qualify for membership until they have been in operation for a time, though this is not to say that non-members automatically run unethical operations or should necessarily be avoided. A list of current members of the BFA is available from the Secretary (address on page 224).

AN UNIQUE OPPORTUNITY TO JOIN THE LARGEST PRIVATE AMBULANCE SERVICE IN THE UK.

Sovereign Services operate throughout the UK with vehicles based in most counties. The vehicles are fully equipped and the operators are trained to carry out this specialised transportation service in conjunction with two ambulance aircraft.

The type of transportation includes ambulant and semi ambulant patients, hospital and nursing home transfers, admissions and discharges, plus repatriation both at home and abroad.

The vehicles supplied are Mercedes and each operator is allocated an area in which he is based. The area is allocated with the intention that there is sufficient potential for development and an increase in the number of vehicles an operator may control.

Operators are introduced to the possible sources of business and are expected to develop these introductions.

The operational base of the company is at Gatwick airport, where a 24-hour coverage is maintained.

The cost of the franchise is £12,500 plus VAT.

For further information please contact the managing director, Sovereign Services South East, 39 Osbourne Road, Eastbourne, East Sussex. An appointment for interview will be arranged.

Conclusion

The advantages and disadvantages listed above, as well as the replies to the questions, must be weighed up and considered before making the decision on whether or not to enter into a franchised business venture. One must decide whether the advantages with the training and support they provide are worth having in return for the surrender of some independence to the degree of outside control which is inherent in the franchise transaction. The prospective franchisee must decide whether the particular franchisor is the right person with whom to do business; he must also decide whether he is personally and temperamentally suitable for this type of relationship.

Having weighed up all the factors and taken proper professional advice, he may also consider the advice of his bank manager or businessman whose judgement he respects; he should certainly discuss the matter with his immediate family, though he has to make his final decision. If he is not able to take this decision with confidence, after having heard all that his advisers have to say, he should consider whether he is indeed capable of running his own business.

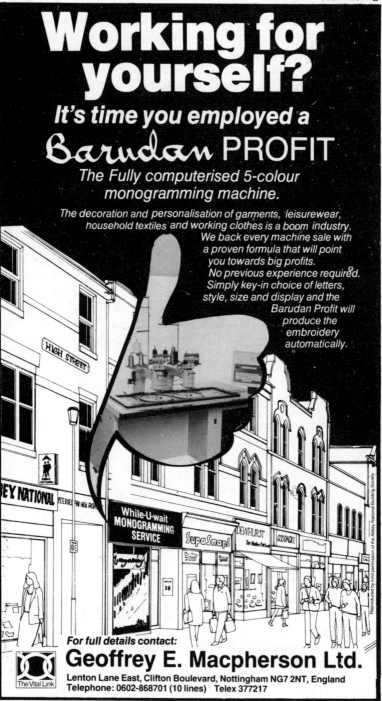

The two main books published in the UK on franchising are referred to in the introduction to this article. There is also a very brief, free pamphlet published by the Small Firms Centre, *Obtaining a Franchise*, but this is in limited supply. There is a magazine, *Franchise World*, published quarterly, obtainable from Franchise World, 37 Nottingham Road, London SW17. This magazine contains articles about franchising in general and about specific franchise opportunities as well as a mass of franchise news. *Franchise World* has also published two booklets: *How to Evaluate a Franchise* and *How to Franchise Your Business*.

There are those who describe themselves as franchise consultants but many of these represent franchisors and are selling franchises. They may be more interested in selling a franchise than in offering objective and unbiased advice.

The British Franchise Association of Grove House, 628 London Road, Colnbrook, Slough, Berks SL3 8QH may be approached, and is always willing to give advice and provide information sources. The Association also has a very active programme of seminars on the subject of franchising which may provide the answer to the questions which are in one's mind.

Checklist

Musts

1. Weigh advantages and disadvantages.
2. Assess oneself.
3. Assess the business.
4. Assess the franchisor.
5. Assess the franchise package.
6. Speak to existing franchisees.
7. Consider advice of others who are qualified to give it.
8. Make up your own mind.

Beware

1. Heavy initial franchise fees.
2. Pyramid-type schemes.
3. Franchisors whose ongoing fee income is too low to support services.
4. Contracts which do not match promises.
5. The hard sell.

6. A franchise consultant who is offering a franchise for sale and purporting to offer objective advice.
7. Get rich quick offers.
8. Franchisors who have not invested in pilot operations.

2.5: Hotels, Catering and Entertainment

Hotels, pubs, clubs and the range of independently owned eating places from simple corner shop cafes to long-established, expensive restaurants constitute a vast business. There are over 30,000 hotels and large guest houses and a vast number of pubs and clubs. And catering is, in employment terms, one of the biggest industries in the UK. The range of opportunities and business options is so wide that we can barely scratch the surface, but an outline of each area will be given and some general conclusions drawn.

The business

What is true of running a shop, that you need unstinting energy and commitment, is even truer in this field. Your hours will be long and irregular. You are likely to have to work 365 days a year. You may have to deal with dissatisfied and difficult customers. There is a mountain of paperwork to monitor and national and local regulations to understand and abide by. Your family, which is in any case likely to be directly involved in the running of your hotel, restaurant or cafe, should be as committed to succeeding as you are.

Offsetting these disadvantages, these areas, particularly owning a restaurant or hotel on which you can stamp your personality and deal very closely with your customers, have many attractions. Indeed, perhaps too many: new restaurants open with great frequency but often quickly collapse because of poor planning, bad management, lack of finance, or a simple lack of realism about the scope for *that* type of restaurant in *that* locality.

Location

As in retailing, location is crucial. Decide what sort of operation you wish to conduct and then look for the premises. If you want to start a hotel or guest house, look for an expanding inland tourist spot or popular seaside resort. In the latter think about the problems of surviving the winter, with only limited and erratic custom. Ask yourself what type of visitor the place attracts and who might be attracted by price reductions out of season (pensioners or the disabled perhaps). Understand the character of the area in which your business will be sited, and have some idea *whose* needs you will cater for. This applies as much to services as to manufacturing firms, and is crucial when you decide how to market that service.

Getting planning permission

This is more difficult than you might think. Local authorities will want details not only of what you intend to do with the premises, but of structural changes you intend to make; of the effect the development will have on other properties; of the safety factors involved; of the parking facilities available for your customers, and so on. You will have to submit detailed plans, and will probably need to consult a lawyer and a surveyor. Even then your application may not succeed, and you will have bought a good deal of expensive legal advice with no return. Remember that restaurants and cinemas may be noisy, keep long hours and attract a large number of patrons — local authorities are naturally anxious to regulate these developments, and your application may therefore be lengthy and will need to be well-planned and properly researched.

Restaurants

New restaurants open every week, particularly in the London area. But almost as many close, and only the gifted and the adaptable survive. Establishing a restaurant is extremely expensive, particularly when you have to convert premises (as is usually the case). A good idea is not sufficient; you also need diligence and above all, *money*. In a period of tight money and high interest rates financial backing for enterprises as doubtful as restaurants is in short supply.

There are basically two kinds of people who open a restaurant — the gifted amateur or professional cook, and the 'ideas man' who knows how to fulfil a taste and buys premises and finds the staff to meet that need (many of the 'in places' in London are now more rated for decor, music and clientele than for their cuisine). The main problem for the amateur or professional is

227

likely to be how to maintain standards without wasting an enormous amount of food and losing money. One answer is to have a *small* choice of dishes which are changed regularly. He will have to spend quite a lot of time finding the best sources locally for fresh meat, fish and vegetables since his reputation depends on it. The restaurateur who has a speciality (such as steaks) and sticks to it will find life a lot simpler.

Where your restaurant is located is obviously essential. If it is in the centre of town, well and good. If not, you must set about advertising, make sure your friends spread the word around, find an eye-catching decor and try to get yourself written up in the local paper. If you are sufficiently confident, you could try writing to the restaurant critics on some of the big magazines (such as *Harpers & Queen*) or newspapers.

If your restaurant is quite small, you will probably find it more economical in the long run to be as mechanised as possible with chip machines, dishwashers, freezers, etc, rather than hiring a lot of expensive, possibly unreliable, staff. Costing can be quite difficult, with the rising price of food, but beware of undercharging. There is a temptation to court trade with low prices, but you will soon find it impossible to keep up standards. Moreover, do not undercharge when you first open simply to attract customers; when your prices rise they will see through your scheme and look elsewhere. Charge the going rate: decent food, pleasant surroundings, efficient and friendly service and a reasonable location should guarantee some degree of success.

It is a good idea, too, to realise your limitations and not try to be grander than you are — if you are basically steak and chips there is no point in trying to produce cordon bleu menus: you will soon be found out!

We spoke to a restaurateur who points to seven problem areas:

1. Wastage.
2. Overheads — heating and lighting cost £50 per week for a 30-seat restaurant!
3. Payment of VAT.
4. Establishing good and appropriate decor.
5. The need to change the menu — don't let you or your customers get bored with it.
6. Maintaining your profit margins.
7. Coping with fluctuations in demand — no customers one night, 50 the next!

Cafes, snack bars, etc

The large restaurant has very different problems to the small, unpretentious cafe. The former provides particular foods with (one hopes) a distinctive touch, and will seek to build up a clientele. It may encounter problems in employing staff, dealing with alcohol licensing, regulations on opening hours, fire precautions, and so on. Moreover, it may be vulnerable to economic downturns and changing consumer tastes. By contrast, the cafe offers a simple service to the local workforce and others at a reasonable price. Fads of taste and the vagaries of economics count for little.

Owning a cafe is more closely allied to general retailing than to being a restaurateur. True, you must be able to prepare a reasonably wide range of good food cheaply, quickly, efficiently and hygienically. But this should not be beyond the capabilities of the average person.

Re-read the retailing section: location will be important and your business must be located in heavy 'traffic' areas. Recognise that each day will have peaks and troughs — a rush at 12 to 2 pm perhaps? Can you cope and, if you can, will you then be overstaffed for the rest of the day?

Your business must be covered by health and safety regulations and must be passed by a food inspector and a fire officer. Regulations on bookkeeping and VAT returns apply to you with equal force as to any other retail business.

The hotel business

You must choose your hotel or guest house with great care. It is a big investment to make, so be sure to examine the following points:

The area

What is the competition like? Are there any plans for redevelopment locally which might involve one of the big hotel groups? Is it on a main road or tourist route, or is it hidden in the back streets or down a country lane? Does the area as a whole seem to be coming up in the world, or going down?

The customers

Ideally, you want to attract a variety of clientele, so that you are fairly busy all year round. Seaside hotels are full up for most of the summer, but virtually deserted in the winter: are you going to make enough profit to cover those lean winter months? Other hotels in industrial or commercial areas will find that they are full of businessmen during the week, but that the weekends are very quiet. The most successful hotels are those which have a good mix of commercial, holiday, conference and banqueting business. Study the accounts if you can and see what the pattern of business is.

The fabric

What state is your hotel in? You must find out how much renovating or decorating needs to be done and how much this is going to cost. What are the maintenance costs likely to be?

The law

There are a number of laws that the hotelier is subject to, particularly health and safety legislation. Insure your property and protect yourself against liability; make sure you meet the necessary safety levels for fireproofing and hygiene or your insurance may be worthless. Another important set of regulations, if you are opening a new hotel, covers licensing. There are various guides to the licensing laws, but if you have to apply for a new licence, it is wise to do it through a solicitor.

Also very important is the Fire Precautions Act. Every hotel, if it sleeps more than six people, must have a fire certificate from the local fire authority. When buying a going concern, find out if it has a fire certificate, or if an application for one has been made (if not, the hotel is being run illegally). If the fire authority has already inspected the building, check on the cost of any alterations required to bring the premises into line with the Fire Precautions Act of 1971.

Staff

Good staff are obviously essential for the smooth and efficient running of a hotel, but they are very difficult to come by. This is an industry with a very high staff turnover, especially among unskilled staff, and you must expect to spend a lot of time interviewing, supervising and training. Everyone in the business agrees that it pays to take your time (however inconvenient) and select staff very carefully, rather than always employing the first person you see because you are busy.

Goodwill

Does the hotel you are considering buying have a good reputation? Will regular visitors return even though the hotel has changed owner?

Past performance and potential

How has it operated in the past: could you improve upon it? What is the sleeping capacity? Could it be increased without reducing standards? Can seasonal fluctuations be reduced by good marketing? How great are staff expenses and other overheads as a proportion of turnover? What is the hotel's net profit as a percentage of turnover?

Pubs

The following section refers to brewery tenants, not to pub managers (who are not self-employed) or to the owners of free houses, which are now so few and far between as to make the possibility of finding a vacant one very unlikely.

Tenants rent their pubs from the brewery company, paying an agreed sum to the outgoing tenant for fittings, equipment and stock. They agree to buy their beer from the brewery, and generally cannot buy stock (even of items other than liquor) from any other source without the brewery's permission. They keep their own profits and are responsible for their own losses, the brewery receiving only the rent on the premises and the guaranteed outlet for its product.

There are more applications from prospective tenants than there are tenancies available, so the breweries are able to 'pick and choose' to some extent. The qualities they look for in a prospective tenant are:

1. Sufficient capital resources to purchase fittings, equipment, and stock in hand, to cover immediate running expenses, and to provide a sufficient reserve to cover the tenant in the event of a temporary reduction in trade.
2. Married tenants are preferred. Running a pub is very much a family affair, and your spouse's experience and attitude can be a decisive factor.

3. Good health, since running a pub involves hard physical work and long hours.
4. Some managerial experience, in any trade, would count in the applicant's favour, though it is not strictly necessary. Similarly, experience or training in the liquor trade would be useful, and though not a mandatory requirement it would be useful from your point of view to have experienced the trade in various capacities first.

We spoke to one publican who offered this advice: 'Watch the optics, the fiddles and the free drinks to friends. Watch that the brewers don't send you lines you don't want. Don't commit yourself to loans and brewers' discounts — there'll be conditions in the fine print you won't like. The Weights and Measures boys will be calling often to check your measures and make sure you have price notices and age warnings up.'

Tenancy agreements

Most breweries have a standard form of agreement to be signed by the tenant. The procedure for taking over the fittings, furniture and equipment is the only area in which there may be a substantial difference between breweries: some require that the new tenant buys these items from the outgoing tenant, whilst in other cases they remain the property of the brewery, and the tenant lodges a deposit, returnable when he gives up the tenancy. Other items covered in the tenancy agreement include rent (usually paid quarterly), the term of the tenancy, responsibility for repairs, a requirement that the tenant take out employer's and public liability insurance, the terms on which the stock is purchased, the brewery company's right of access to the premises, requirements connected with transfer of the licence, and terms on which the tenancy can be terminated.

Licences

The tenant usually takes over premises that are already licensed, so he has to negotiate the transfer of the licence from the outgoing tenant to himself. It is advisable to be represented by a solicitor in your application for transfer of the licence.

Training

If you are accepted by a brewery for a tenancy, and neither you nor your wife have any experience of the trade, it is likely that both of you will be asked to attend a short residential course, run by the brewery company and lasting from one to two weeks. While you are waiting for a suitable tenancy, or applying to different breweries, it is advisable, if you have no experience, to work part-time in a pub. This will give you some experience, and will help you to decide whether you are really suited to what is in fact a very arduous job.

Other opportunities

It is possible to run clubs, cinemas, theatres and so on independently. Indeed, the attractions for the music lover or cinema buff are considerable as it seems to be possible to mix business with pleasure. But base any decision on *business* sense, not on a romantic notion of making your leisure interests pay. Can the town support another cinema, particularly if you intend to show nothing but *avant garde* and experimental films? (Whether you want to show more obscure films or not, if the major companies have tied up the distribution of the money-spinning movies you may have no option!)

You will face the same problems as the hotelier and restaurateur in choosing the right location, employing staff, perhaps getting restrictions on opening hours lifted, obtaining a licence to serve alcohol, meeting fire regulations.* (Some of these problems can be circumvented if you make your institution a private club, admitting members only at some sort of fee, though future legislation may close this loophole.) And do not forget the less well-known legislation on health, hygiene, noise abatement, etc, which may involve you in short-term inconvenience or, worse, long-term and expensive rounds of litigation.

Which business?

Whatever type of service you provide will need sound financial backing, commercial acumen, the ability to offer something distinctive and market it accordingly, and patience in choosing the right opening. Fix on a 'target' population: advertise in newspapers and periodicals which they are likely to read, and

---

* This could be extremely expensive if alterations to a club or cinema have to be made to comply with regulations. Consider this when you buy a property which you hope to convert, and check that an established business has a fire certificate.

2.6: Construction, Building and Maintenance Services

Builders, carpenters, plumbers and electricians are in constant demand. Established firms charge high labour rates, and people qualified in these trades can obtain a steady income by taking on extra work at reasonable rates. Alternatively, if you are more ambitious, you may start a building or redecoration company. You will need some capital, the necessary equipment, some means of transport, and a rudimentary administrative system — to take commissions for work, send invoices, check payments, keep tabs on costs, etc.

You may also need a tax exemption certificate, which customers (such as the local authorities) will require to ensure that you are a Schedule D taxpayer. If you work solely for private householders, small shops, etc, you will not need this certificate. But, if you work for a main contractor, local authority or government department, you will have 30 per cent of all bills (except the cost of materials and VAT) automatically deducted by them, unless you have this certificate.

The Inland Revenue publishes a guide on how to apply for and use these certificates. If you are refused a certificate, and without one you will find work difficult to get, you can appeal within 28 days to the local general commissioners.

Training

The orthodox training for these trades is by entering into apprenticeship after leaving school, but it is now also possible for older people to learn these skills at government training centres (details from your local employment office). Courses for manual trades last six months, after which there is a year's probationary period with an employer. Trainees are paid an allowance whilst taking the six-month course.

Much of the work available in private households consists either of very small jobs, such as putting up shelves or wall-papering, or conversion work, for which you must take into account building regulations and you or the house owner should get planning permission if applicable. You will find that the wider the range of skills you can offer, the more you will be in demand, since one job might involve both carpentry and decorating for example.

It is advisable to work with a partner, since you will often need help with lifting, measurement, etc. You also will find that it is invaluable to have contacts who specialise in other, related trades, since you will often find that you cannot complete a job without the help of, say, an electrician. Contacts will also help you to find work since they will get in touch with you to finish jobs that they themselves cannot complete.

The building regulations

Major structural changes must conform with national and local building regulations. If in doubt, consult your local authority (ask for the District Surveyor or Building Inspector).

Planning permission needs to be granted for external extensions exceeding 1300 cubic feet. If the building you are working on is listed as being of historic interest there may be regulations against changing its external appearance — again check with the local authority. These problems concern the person who commissioned the work more than you, but it is as well to guard yourself against liability.

How to get work

As explained above, contacts in related trades are invaluable. You might also obtain subcontracted work from small building firms. Landlords and property agents are useful people to cultivate, as they often provide a great deal of maintenance and conversion work. You may also wish to advertise in the local press. But beware of making claims which you cannot support: do not, for example, say that you are a master builder if you hold no such certificate.

Sources of information

1. The Department of the Environment publishes a leaflet called *How To Find Out: Getting the Best from Building Information Services,* listing 80 important information

sources for the construction industry. They also publish a large number of advisory leaflets on subjects such as *Emulsion Paints, Frost Precautions in Household Water Supply, Sands for Plasters, Mortars and Renderings,* etc. These are available from HMSO bookshops or from *Building Centres* and other booksellers.

2. There are 13 *Building Centres* in different regional locations. The address of the London branch is 26, Store Street, London WC1. The other branches are at Belfast, Birmingham, Bristol, Cambridge, Coventry, Dublin, Glasgow, Liverpool, Manchester, Nottingham, Southampton, and Stoke on Trent.

3. The Building Research Establishment is the largest and most comprehensive source of technical advice available to the construction industry. It operates from three centres --Watford, Birmingham and Glasgow.

Painting, decorating, plumbing and electrical work

These are areas which attract numerous 'cowboys', offering little or no expertise and a generally poor service. Fortunately, because continued custom depends so much on word of mouth, the rogues tend to fall by the wayside and only those offering a professional service survive. If you are experienced in one of these areas, try it for a while on a part-time basis and, if you have a steady stream of jobs and apparently satisfied customers, enter the profession full time.

You will probably have been employed with a firm in this capacity and may at first worry about days (or weeks) without work and a long-term shortage of orders. But you must learn to live with the downturns, and price your work for jobs accordingly. These services are always in demand, and if you do a competent job at a competitive price you will survive. Word of mouth will win you most orders but, if you can cope with additional work, go out and look for it: put ads in the windows of local shops, in local newspapers and in the Yellow Pages.

We spoke to a painter and decorator who offered this advice: 'It's silly to start with no work in hand so make sure you have sufficient work before you take the plunge. By "sufficient" I don't mean bits and pieces but solid full time jobs. Recommendation is better than advertising and do a good job for a fair price.'

237

2.7: Transport

Light removals

If you can afford to invest in a reasonable, fairly large second-hand van, you can do light removals. This service is in great demand, particularly in the larger cities. All that you need is a van, a telephone, a few advertisements in local shop windows, recommendations from friends, and you are in business! This sort of work can easily be done on a part-time basis, as people moving flats are likely to want to move at weekends or in the evenings. If you want to work full-time, though, it might be worth setting up a partnership with two or three other van owners, with a central office and a full-time receptionist to answer the telephone and arrange bookings. People wanting to hire a van for a couple of hours are likely to ring another firm if you are not in or cannot come at a particular time, but if you have a receptionist to allocate the work, three of you are each likely to get more work than any one of you could handle independently. A small van can also be used to handle small deliveries for private firms, distributing magazines, for example.

You should charge from the time you leave home until the time you arrive back (ie you include the time it takes you to get to and return from a particular job).

Heavy goods transport

This is a very different proposition to light removals. You will require a heavy goods vehicle (HGV) licence, which is obtained only by passing a rigorous driving test, and an operator's ('O') licence, which is only issued if you have both obtained a certificate of professional competence and can prove that you can finance a haulage operation.* The outlay needed to establish a haulage firm is considerable: buying or hiring vehicles, servicing them, buying parts, employing drivers. It is difficult just to

---

* You should, for example, have sound financial backing and satisfactory premises from which to operate.

operate locally: you need to be able to transport goods throughout the country, at reasonable rates, in competition with long-established and heavily-capitalised haulage operators. Do not be deterred by these problems, but be aware of them, particularly if you have to prove how workable your scheme is to a bank manager or some other source of finance.

Part 3:
Directory of Low Investment, Part-time Opportunities for the Self-employed

3.1: Part-time Work

No one knows how many people are engaged in part-time work in addition to another source of income, though a recent survey quoted in the *Observer* put the figure vaguely somewhere between 200,000 and 400,000. If you take the traditional view of what part-time work means — helping out in someone's shop, doing the odd bit of typing or repair work, or generally earning a few extra pounds in the evenings or at weekends — that may seem like an unimportant matter, but it is not a view shared by the Inland Revenue. They suspect that a significant part of the black economy, through which some £4 billion a year is being lost to the Exchequer, flourishes through part-time work. They also suspect that it is growing in extent and importance and they are probably right on both counts.

It is likely, however, that people who fail to declare their income from part-time work are more concerned to withhold their activities from the DHSS than from the Inland Revenue. One of several anomalies in the way the problem of unemployment is dealt with is that the moment you have any earned income, no matter how small, you cease to be eligible for unemployment benefit. There is a strong incentive, therefore, if you do something that brings in a few pounds a week while you are unemployed, not to declare it. Very likely the sums lost to the Exchequer in this way are quite small and one could even take the view that such black economy work takes some of the financial and psychological sting out of unemployment.

The 1983 Budget recognised the fact that income from a new business is usually less than the dole. If you are unemployed for more than 13 weeks, have a viable business idea and are prepared to put £1000 of your own money into a business, you can get a grant of £40 a week for 52 weeks from the DHSS.

Tax advantages of part-time employment

If you are a married man with another source of income, not declaring your earnings from part-time work might be a very unwise move — apart from being illegal. In the first place it is usually unlikely that you would have to pay tax on it at all because of the single person's earned income allowance of £1785. This is often referred to as the 'wife's' earned income allowance because the man of the house is generally the breadwinner, though that does not necessarily follow these days. What it means, though, is that the first £1785 of everyone's earnings is free of tax; so if you can arrange for your wife to earn that amount of money from your source of extra income, you will not pay any tax on it — assuming she does not already have a job. Remember it is the profit that is taxed, not the total earnings. If you cannot get that figure close to £1785 by setting off against gross earnings all the allowances described in Chapter 1.11, then you are either doing so well as to make it worth considering turning your spare-time occupation into a full-time activity, or you should get an accountant, or you should change the accountant you have. However, you do have to prove, to the satisfaction of the tax inspector, that your wife really is working in the business — taking messages, typing invoices, doing a bit of book-keeping, or whatever. Holding the fort by looking after the kids and doing the cooking so that you can get on with it does not count.

All this is reinforced by the fact that even if you do not pay on them, there are definite advantages in earnings that are taxed under Schedule D. You will be able to claim allowances on rates and services (gas, electricity and water) for the use of part of your house, plus a proportion of your bill for the telephone, stamps and stationery — whatever, in fact, can be shown to be reasonably related to the nature of the activity you are carrying on. Small is beautiful, provided you declare it.

Planning and other permissions; insurance

Strictly speaking, if you carry on a business from home you have to apply for planning permission as indicated in Chapter 1.2. In practice, very few people bother when it comes to part-time work, though if what you are intending to do creates a noise, a nuisance or a smell (and some crafts and home repair activities do some or all of these things even when carried on in quite a small way) you should inform the local authority of your intentions. Complaints from neighbours not only cause embarrassment, but can result in your being required to find proper premises, the cost of which may invalidate your whole idea. Applying for planning permission will highlight such potential problems and forewarned is forearmed. By the same token, if planning permission has been granted, you will be able to face most complaints with equanimity.

If you are doing anything with food — making pâtés for your local delicatessen, for instance — you should inform the environmental health inspector. Here again, very few people bother and in fact the health officials are more concerned with commercial kitchens than domestic ones, which are generally cleaner; on the other hand you could be liable for prosecution if it turns out, for instance, that the cause of someone being made ill by your pâté was a breach of the health regulations.

One important precaution you should not neglect if you are planning to work from home, whatever that work is, is to tell your insurance company. This is because your normal house and contents policy covers domestic use only and if you change the circumstances without telling the insurers they could fail to pay you in the event of a claim — and would probably do so if the loss was caused by the undeclared activity. Additional insurance cover will not normally cost you much, which is often more than could be said for any loss that occurs.

Assessing the market

From the point of view of anyone contemplating full-time self-employment, the principal advantage of part-time work is not really that it is a source of extra income, however valuable an incidental that may be, but that it serves as a trial run for the real thing. Opinions may differ as to what the prime factors here are in order of priority, but few would disagree that the most important thing is to assess whether there is a market for the goods or services you are proposing to offer at a price that will bring you a worthwhile profit. Working part time at something will give you an idea whether the demand for it and the competition will enable you to do that.

For instance, if working 12 hours a week, evenings and weekends, produces a gross £60 a week — £2880 a year allowing for four weeks' holiday — and your present income is, say, £12,000, there is a marginal case for considering full-time self-employment. By working 48 hours a week you could, on that evidence, gross about £11,500 in a 48-week year. Of course, it would depend on what your costs were, but some of the fixed ones — tools, for instance — would not change if you expanded your activities. If there was evidence for a very strong demand you might even consider raising your prices, especially if the experience you have gained about the market indicates that you are appreciably cheaper than the competition. Alternatively you might discover that by making one or two modifications you could either charge more than the competition or create a stronger demand for your original concept. It is much easier to make these adaptations to market conditions while still operating at a modest level and with a main income from another source.

Objectives

Whether the person in a £12,000 a year secure job throws their hand in for £11,500-worth of insecurity depends not only on financial factors but on personal objectives. Here again, working part time before making the commitment to full-time self-employment will help you shape your thinking about what those objectives are and what they are worth to you. If independence is the over-riding factor you might feel that even a sizeable financial sacrifice is worth making. On the other hand, if money is the main objective and you are secure in your main job, then clearly, in the instance we have given, you are much better off earning an extra £2800 a year from your part-time job, plus £12,000 a year from your main one than giving up the latter altogether — unless you could see a way of doing better than £2800 pro rated over a 48-hour week.

Another objective that could be tried out is whether you can work with an intended partner. Some very successful businesses are run by people who have little in common except a respect for each other's abilities, but it is usually very difficult to test such qualities unless you have actually worked closely with someone. Trying out a partnership arrangement on a part-time basis is a good way of doing this.

Assessing yourself

There is also the question of assessing your own suitability because there is a big gap between pipe dreams of independence and the reality, even when it comes to working full time at something you have previously enjoyed doing as a hobby. Apart from the fact that what is fun as a hobby can sometimes be quite another proposition done hour after hour and day after day, there is often a huge difference between amateur and professional standards. For instance, it may take you all day to turn out a widget — that mythical, all-purpose British unit of manufacture — whereas a professional can do it in a couple of hours. That is fine when you are doing it more or less for fun, but fatal if you are trying to earn a living, unless you are confident you can get to professional standards fairly quickly.

Whether you can actually do so usually depends on how good you are at working for very long hours, initially for not much money and spending a great deal of what used to be your spare time on administration: keeping records, writing letters and preparing quotes. You will not know your capacities in this respect until you try, but at least working part time will give you an inkling.

It will also give you some indication of your family's attitudes to your work. If you are working part time on top of a full-time job, you are probably reasonably close to putting in the sort of hours that are needed to make a success of self-employment at least for an initial — and usually prolonged — period of time. In other words, your family will not see a great deal of you unless they are able and willing to pitch in as well. They may view this prospect with equanimity; on the other hand, workaholism can be as great a source of family tension as alcoholism. When working part time, it is quite easy to cut down the hours you are putting in, or even to stop altogether. If your living depends on it, the case is altered completely.

Financial commitment

One of the advantages of part-time work is that you are keeping your overheads, or fixed costs, low. You can work from home instead of renting premises or offices. You can hire equipment instead of buying it. You may even be able to use facilities available at your place of work — photocopying, for instance — though to what extent this is a wise move depends on the attitude of your employer. Some take it as a sign of initiative, provided it does not interfere with your regular job. Others hate it, in which case you will have to be very careful how you go about it, and at least account for everything you use. The point is, though, that for part-time work you will not have to 'tool up' expensively and, indeed, you should avoid irreversible financial commitments as much as possible. Do not, for instance, buy a van until you are sure you are going to get profitable use out of it, or unless you want one anyway. Do not, to take another case, buy a knitting machine — hire it and see whether you really can make knitting pay.

The principle can be extended to any given activity. Earlier in this book we have stated that you should never buy anything unless you have to and until you have established an ongoing need for it. That was in reference to full-time activities. It is even more the case with part-time work, because by definition the number of hours you have in which to amortise the cost — to make a profit and get your money back — are far fewer.

Types of part-time work

Extension of full-time employment

In the previous section we have referred to the situation where someone is carrying on into evenings and weekends private work normally done for an employer in the day time: typical examples might be repair and building work, some forms of design and teaching extended into exam coaching. The great advantage of this type of work is that it can give you a direct access to the market. Everybody who walks through the door at your place of employment is a potential private customer, whereas in other forms of part-time work, finding the market is an important but difficult part of the total concept. Furthermore, private part-time clients can later be turned into sources of work on a larger scale, either directly or as leads to other work. Even suppliers can be useful people to get to know, both in terms of establishing your credibility when it comes to asking for credit and in the matter of sorting out good and reliable suppliers from the many other varieties.

The principal disadvantage of this type of work is that it can lead to a conflict of interests. The temptation to steer work your way rather than towards your employer can be very strong. It need not be anything as blatant as buttonholing your employer's customers at the door. There are subtler ways of bending the rules. The best way to avoid such temptations is to develop your own clients and contacts as soon as possible.

Turning a hobby into a source of income

This is usually the most satisfying form of part-time work

because people generally perform best at what they most enjoy doing. Furthermore, many people, especially the over-30s, find that they have gone or been pushed into careers that do not reflect their real interests or skills; or that they have simply developed new ones that they find more satisfying than what they do for a living. Practising crafts of various kinds is a case in point.

The trap here is the one that we have referred to earlier — that there is a world of difference between doing something for fun and working at it full time. Professional craftsmen have years of experience which enable them to turn out work quickly and economically. They also know the market: who buys what, at which price, what sells and what does not. In the case of photography, to take another instance, the good amateur turned professional is competing in a field where contacts are all-important and where high standards of work depend not only on individual skill, but on having the latest equipment.

Learning a new skill

Sometimes people learn a new skill, perhaps at an evening class, which is capable of being turned to commercial use — particularly these days when the range of services available from shops and manufacturers has become increasingly scarce and expensive. Popular examples are picture framing and upholstery.

There are also non-manual skills which can be turned to good account, like selling; quite a number of people, especially women, are engaged in party plan or catalogue selling. The problem there, however, is that it is difficult to go into a higher, full-time gear to make a living from that type of work, because commissions are fixed percentages and, in the case of catalogue selling, quite small ones.

Reviving an unused skill

This is also very popular especially with women thinking of returning to work. The most frequently cited example is typing, but as it happens this one neatly illustrates the importance of observing the laws of supply and demand in choosing even a part-time source of income. Because there are many women available for such work, the rates are not particularly good. The only way you can lift yourself into a higher bracket is by identifying a service which few other typists offer and for which there is also a demand: in a university town, for instance, there might be a call for someone who can type theses quickly and accurately. An exporter, to take another example, might have a demand for someone who can type accurately in another language.

The same supply-and-demand principle also applies to translating. There are many graduates around who can translate from one of the main European languages into English, but rather fewer who can do the more difficult, reverse kind of translation: from English into idiomatic French, German or Spanish. Even rarer, and therefore more marketable, is fluency in another language *plus* a qualification in a specialist subject, like law or science.

Using an existing asset as a source of income: accommodation

By far the biggest asset that most people own is their house and when there is a need for more money, or as members of the family grow up or move away, that asset can be a source of income: rooms can be let, the house can be subdivided into flats or even — ultimately — the whole place can be turned into a guest house. The advantage of these courses of action is that little skill or training is required to turn them into money making activities. The disadvantage is that they are full of legal pitfalls which deter a great many people. The common option is to circumvent the law by moving into a cash only, black economy relationship with tenants, but by that token you also lose much legal protection that would be available if there was a dispute. By getting a tenancy agreement drawn up, you can protect yourself to a large degree, especially if you are also the kind of student of human nature who can spot a potential troublemaker before he or she crosses your threshold.

The best kind of asset to have is a country house grand enough to attract paying sightseers rather than tenants. But in that case you would have an army of legal and financial advisers at your elbow and perhaps would not be reading a book like this!

Letting rooms

In recent years, and especially since the 1980 Housing Act, there have been many horror stories about the difficulty of getting rid of unwanted tenants, even, on occasion, where they have been well behind with the rent. For this reason it is very unwise to let rooms without having an agreement drawn up by a solicitor; even the Citizens' Advice Bureau staffed, in general, by people whose natural sympathies lie with the tenant, recommend this. It is usually unwise, incidentally, to have a room letting agreement which runs much longer than on a month-to-month basis, because except in extreme circumstances, the courts are likely to take the view that an agreement will have to run its full course before being terminated.

The other piece of legislation to beware of is the Rent Act of 1977 which gives the tenant the right to go to a tribunal and ask for a 'reasonable' rent to be applied if he or she thinks you are asking too much. A register of reasonable rents is kept at your local authority's Rent Assessment Panel office, if you want to check what these are, but you will often find that these do not allow for subtle shades of amenity — the social difference between nearby streets, for instance.

The best way to get good tenants is to select then. — not by race or sex, which is illegal if done openly — but by asking for references from their previous landlord.

3.2: Crafts and Domestic Skills

Cooking

With restaurant prices as they are, taking people out for a meal — even on an expense account — can be an alarming prospect. It is quite easy, for instance, to run up a bill well in excess of £100 for wining and dining four people. You can do the same thing infinitely more cheaply at home, but not everyone has the skill, the inclination, or the time to do it and this is where the private caterer comes into the picture. Even firms trying to cut down on lavish entertainment are tending to invite customers to lunch or dinner in private dining rooms rather than taking them out to what is often an indifferent, though expensive meal.

If you are a good cook and interested in applying your skills in order to earn money, it is worth putting the word around to firms in your area. You can do it indirectly by letting it be known you are available through friends or quality food shops who sometimes get asked to recommend cooks; directly by letters to the chief executive of local firms, or by advertising.

Generally speaking, you do not have to be up to cordon bleu standards. The average businessman is reported to prefer good, orthodox well-cooked food to anything exotic. You present your customers with a range of possible dishes from a menu — which is in fact your repertoire — and then let them order in advance the meal they want you to cook.

They may have a kitchen on the premises, in which case you will have to make sure that the equipment, crockery and cutlery are adequate. Otherwise you will have to cook the meal at home and bring the necessary adjuncts with you, or buy them. If you have to cook at home, you will either have to stick to cold buffets or make sure that suitable facilities are available for warming up the dishes on the spot. In other words, a gift for efficient administration and organisation is almost as important as cooking skills.

This also extends to doing your costings. If you cook at home, you will have to take account of the use of gas and electricity; indeed the agreement you make with your customers should specify clearly who pays for what. Do you buy the food on their account or do you buy it and put it on the bill? What happens to food that is left over? And who does the washing up or indeed serving at table?

The simplest way to keep matters straight is to charge an hourly rate to include shopping time, preparation of food and cleaning up afterwards. It is generally reckoned that you should aim to clear £20 from the average meal prepared for six people.

The trend towards home cooking and baking also opens up opportunities to supply the growing number of wine bars and speciality food shops. They are often interested in buying from private individuals who can make pies, pâtés and other forms of cooked food. Looking at what they have on offer will give you an indication of demand and going rates. The prices shown will reflect a mark-up of 30 to 40 per cent of the price at which they are bought.

Dressmaking

There are various types of dressmaking that can be done at home: outwork for the garment trade; running up made-to-measure clothes; repairs and alterations; and specialised work such as leather work, embroidery or crochet, which can be sold to boutiques or through mail order. 'Outwork' is repetitive and the pay is low: it is not recommended. Making clothes for friends and for customers brought in by advertisements and recommendations is much more interesting, though even here the rewards may not be high. The easiest type of work is when the customer presents you with a commercially produced pattern and fabric for it, so all you have to do is cut it out and sew it together. Making your own patterns, on the other hand, requires a fair amount of skill as translating a flat piece of paper into a three-dimensional garment is quite a complicated business. If you *do* know how to make your own patterns, then the customer can present you with a rough sketch, or even just a description, and you work from there.

If the customer does not present you with the fabric for the garment she may give you vague instructions and then be unhappy with your interpretation of them. A compromise could be for you to go shopping with her, to ensure that the chosen fabric is suitable and that sufficient quantities are bought. Thread, zips and trimmings can be bought at the same time. Alternatively, you could build up your own stock, by buying remnants and reduced lines, and offer the customer a choice from these.

It is important to have a fitting as soon as the garment is in one piece, and a second fitting may be needed to check on details such as the hang of a sleeve or to make sure that the collar lies flat.

Alterations (zips, hems, etc) form quite a high proportion of the work of many home dressmakers. These jobs can be fiddly and time-consuming, but it is not possible to charge much for this type of work, so if you advertise your services you may find it worth your while to emphasise the fact that you do not do alterations.

Embroidered, leather or crochet garments and knitwear can be sold to boutiques or by mail order (most women's magazines carry small ads for clothes). You must make sure that you have sufficient stock to cover any bulk orders you may receive. You also need a talent for sensing fashion trends almost before they happen, as it will take several months before your garments appear in the shops.

You really need an electric sewing machine: a swing-needle one will enable you to do zigzag stitches, useful for buttonholes, neatening off raw edges and simple embroidery. A zip foot for the machine is also desirable. Other pieces of equipment you will need are pins, shears, needles, thread (keep two or three reels of black and white in stock, and buy other colours when you need them), french chalk, a buttonhole cutter, a tape measure and a steam iron.

Jewellery

The designing and making of jewellery is a highly competitive business. Before investing in expensive materials and equipment, you must prove to yourself that you have some flair for design and are suitably skilful with your hands. Starting off with lapidary work is a good way of finding out if you have the necessary artistic ability, and, most important, if anyone wants to buy your designs. From there, the best plan is to take an art college or City and Guilds course in jewellery, and sell the results while you develop some expertise. The great advantage of doing this is that you can use college equipment while you gradually build up your own collection of tools.

The most successful students find that they have no

difficulty in selling their work while they are still at college. Start by showing off your handiwork to friends, if your work is good enough your reputation will spread by word of mouth and you will soon find the orders coming in. From there you can progress to taking samples of your work round the various jewellers and department stores in the hope of getting orders. You can also hire a stall in a street market on Saturdays and see how successful you are.

The initial outlay on tools can be quite small, especially if you are able to use college equipment as well. Eventually, of course, you will need your own equipment and this can be expensive so you would be wise to save some of your initial profits towards buying equipment. Materials are also expensive, and it is important to get the pricing right, if you are going to make a reasonable profit. Here your best plan is simply to show samples to a well-established jeweller. He will soon tell you how much he would charge, since he obviously does not want to be undercut by a newcomer.

Lapidary work

Lapidary is the art of working in gemstones or pebbles and it forms an excellent introduction to the art of making jewellery, since the basic materials are not so expensive as in jewellery proper.

Learning the techniques of lapidary work is quite simple: there are many books on the subject, as well as clubs and societies. *Gems* is a monthly magazine which lists suppliers, as well as clubs and organisations. Most books will also give you a list of the tools and equipment required. The main item of equipment for lapidary work at home is a tumbler, which is used for grinding and polishing the stones (obtained from craft shops) which are then set in silver, copper, steel etc to make rings, pendants or brooches.

You will have to be patient; it can take up to 12 weeks to polish a consignment of stones. But you should then have no trouble selling your pieces via local shops, stalls in the local market, department stores, even coffee mornings. Do not undersell your work, look round the shops and see what comparable pieces fetch before offering your work to a shop.

Making loose covers and curtains

To make a living sewing, you must be an experienced and fast worker. Loose covers in particular involve far more work than the inexperienced would ever imagine, so do not gaily undertake to re-cover someone's sofa over the weekend. There are plenty of good handicraft books that give step-by-step directions, and provided you follow them accurately you should not have any problems, even as a beginner. The most important point with loose covers is to know how to measure up accurately, and this is essential when dealing with expensive fabrics.

You will need a sewing machine with a piping foot, enough room to lay the material out properly for cutting and measuring, a really good pair of dressmaking scissors, and a good deal of patience.

You will soon find work by advertising in the local papers, and by word of mouth, once you have done a few jobs. To find out what to charge, ring up one of the big department stores that offer this service and ask them for a quote: make sure your quoted price is then a few pounds cheaper and you will have no trouble finding more work.

Beware of taking on too much and so failing to deliver the goods in time. Take on one job at a time, until you know exactly how long it takes you to do a pair of curtains, or a chair cover, etc. Otherwise, you will end up with a lot of irate clients and a bad reputation for being unreliable.

Picture framing

Some local authorities run evening courses in picture framing. It is also possible to learn the craft by working in a gallery, though usually galleries are rather a 'closed shop'. Basically, as with all crafts, it is best to experiment as much as possible before you undertake commercial work. You need a good work table and some large shelves on which to store your work. Basic tools are a mitre saw for the corners; clamps, to hold the corners together while they are being glued; accurate rulers and a set square; hammer and nails, and a vice and mount cutter are useful, though not strictly necessary.

You will also need mouldings, a backing board, which can be either card or hardboard, and glass. Your local glass merchant will cut glass to the right size for you: this is easier than doing it yourself.

Suppliers are often unwilling to supply materials in small quantities, but if you look around, you should be able to find some small firms who are willing to do so. If you are keen on jumble sales, you will find that you can often pick up old picture frames for next to nothing, and these can be revamped.

For making the actual frames, great care and accuracy is needed in order to get the mitred edges to fit exactly. Step-by-step instructions for making different types of frames are given in *Framing* by Eamon Toscano. Compare prices by asking galleries and picture-framing shops for quotations.

Pottery

It is possible to 'teach yourself' by reading and experiment-ation, but if you want to take a course many local authorities run evening classes in pottery (they are popular so book as early as you can).

Unless you are going in for pottery in a small way, you will need plenty of space for working and storage. It is a good idea to convert your garage, or an outside shed, into a work room since it then won't matter if you make a mess. Your work room should ideally be equipped with a decent-sized sink, a solid work-surface, preferably with a plain wooden top, plenty of shelves, a damp cupboard (which can be a wooden cupboard lined with plastic sheeting or with slabs of plaster which are periodically soaked in water), and a waterproof container for storing clay. Other basic requirements are the kiln (if you are eventually planning on a high turnover of work, you will need to buy the largest kiln you can afford); the potter's wheel (though this is not absolutely necessary for a beginner, since you can do mould, slab and coil pottery without one); an assortment of bowls, buckets, basins, sieves, etc; and a set of small tools — cutting wire, a knife, scrapers, 'bats' (squares of hardboard used for carrying and drying pottery), sponges, brushes and modelling tools.

You may prefer to use your own local clay, in which case you will have to devote time to its preparation; or you can buy it ready-prepared from a potter's merchant or pottery supply house. Local brickworks will often supply clay cheaply, though it may need some extra preparation. It is usually supplied by the hundredweight, and smaller amounts are proportionately more expensive. It is important that it should be kept in a cool, damp place.

You can buy ready-made glazes, though it is possible to mix your own. You will also need sand, slow-setting potter's plaster grog, oxides, slips (englobes) and wax. A detailed list of suppliers is given in *Simple Pottery* by Kenneth Drake, an excellent book which is recommended for the beginner.

If you visit craft shops with samples of your work, you will find that some will take pots on a sale or return basis, whilst others will buy a small quantity of your work outright and order more if it sells. Alternatively, you may want to sell your work direct to the customer, in which case you could start off by hiring a market stall, with the eventual aim of owning your own shop.

Upholstery

This is an area where it really pays not to price yourself out of the market. The real dyed-in-the-wool professional is so expensive that many people cannot afford the prices. If you have served a long apprenticeship you are of course entitled to charge the top rate; but if you are planning to work as you learn, set your sights a bit lower financially and you will find far more work. You can either buy junk furniture to do up yourself, or advertise to do up other people's furniture. Until you have had some experience, it is probably best not to invest too much money in buying furniture, unless you have lots of storage room and no immediate need for the cash.

You can start out via evening classes, or inquire at your local public library. There are plenty of good books on the subject, and you should soon be able to tackle bedroom or dining room chairs, footstools, etc, without any trouble, but do not attempt buttoning, springs, chaise longues, etc until you have had a bit more experience.

There is a tremendous demand for reasonably priced upholsterers, so you should not have much trouble finding work. Advertise in your local paper or even in the national press, once your work is good enough to tackle big pieces. It is also worth visiting a few antique shops, since they often have upholstery jobs to be done.

The right tools are very important and not too expensive. You will need a webbing stretcher, tack hammer, set of upholstery needles and a regulator. You can buy the tools and materials from specialist suppliers, which are listed in the Yellow Pages.

Trevor Constable, a furniture restorer, mentioned some of the pitfalls to beware: 'You can't go for work like a bull at a gate. Antique dealers will promise you lots but little will materialise. If you've got the skill word will get around and work will come in. Don't put all your eggs in one basket. Get a range of customers and don't rely on one source for more than say a third of your total work. If you are totally committed to one source and it dries up . . . you're out of business.'

3.3: Driving

Apart from orthodox taxi firms, which employ full-time drivers 'plying for hire' (ie to a large extent picking up fares on a casual basis in the street), there are also cab hire firms who supply cars with drivers on demand, in response to a telephone call or some other kind of prior arrangement. These firms do not maintain a vehicle fleet of their own but employ outside people, generally part-timers, who drive their own cars, picking up the cab hire firm's clients. The cab hire firm thus acts in somewhat the same way as an employment agency; they supply the leads for drivers on their books.

To get this type of work you should have a clean driving licence and you must take out a special 'hire and reward' insurance. Remuneration varies from place to place and from firm to firm, but like ordinary taxi fares it is based on the mileage, the time the job takes and the hour at which it is carried out. The cab hire firm lays down the rates and a percentage of the fare has to be paid to them on each job, though there are some firms that make a flat weekly charge to drivers on their books.

Work is obtained initially by phoning in to base, which is obviously chancy. However, once you have established your status as a regular, many cab hire firms will offer to lease to you or otherwise supply you with a two-way radio and this is a much more reliable way of keeping up the flow of jobs.

Cab driving involves working long hours in order to make an adequate income, and remember that you must allow for petrol, depreciation and insurance. However, the casual nature of cab driving makes this a suitable occupation for those who are filling in time between salaried work.

Cab hire firms are to be found in Yellow Pages. Alternatively, your local garage may be able to advise you of good firms who are looking for drivers with their own cars.

In London, all cab drivers must be qualified with the Metropolitan Police Vehicle Carriage Centre and must have passed the so-called 'knowledge'. This is an arduous process, requiring considerable driving skill and an intimate knowledge of routes throughout London. Even if you pass successfully, getting your own cab will be difficult and self-employment proper may have to be preceded by a period spent driving for one of the many London cab companies, who provide and service the cab and take a substantial cut of the total 'take'.

3.4: Entertainment

Disc jockeying

Most people start doing DJ work because they enjoy entertaining people and listening to music. Essential requirements for the DJ are a lively, outgoing personality, a good knowledge of pop music (some DJs specialise in one particular type of music) and as large a selection of records as possible. Disc jockeys are engaged by clubs, pubs, etc, either on a regular basis or for one-off sessions. They are generally expected to bring their own records, but equipment may be provided.

The minimum equipment needed to run a mobile disco is a pair of turntables, an amplifier of about 50 watts, more if you think you will play at outdoor gigs or bigger venues, at least two 20-watt speakers, and some form of transport, preferably a van rather than a car. Shop around and find out what discounts are available through the Disc Jockey Federation. Above all, sound quality must be high and no amount of 'extras' will compensate for poor sound.

For the more ambitious, and those with more money to invest, a magnetic cartridge, which improves the quality of the sound, is recommended, and this involves the use of a pre-amplifier and a mixer. You will probably want to use more than two speakers, and a more high-powered amplifier. You may want to invest in stereo equipment, although you will find that this can create problems caused by the many different kinds of rooms in which you will want to use the equipment. Beyond basic equipment, you will decide to provide 'extras' such as a light show, a microphone for the DJ, a strobe, all of which can push your costs up considerably.

If you are going to operate a mobile discotheque as part of a public performance, which is defined as one which takes place 'outside the domestic or home life of the participants', it is necessary to obtain a licence from Phonographic Performance Ltd, 14-22 Ganton Street, London W1. A licence is needed for *any* kind of public performance: even a performance at a firm's dinner dance, for example, would need to be covered. The fees for a licence are on a sliding scale, depending on the amount of time and size of audience for which it is granted.

Playing a record involves two copyrights: that of the record company, which is covered by the licence from Phonographic Performance, and that of the music publisher and composer, which is covered by the Performing Right Society Ltd, 29 Berners Street, London W1. Most public halls are covered by a licence from the Performing Right Society, but you should check up on this before operating in a public place.

There are a large number of mobile discotheques operating, particularly in London and the Home Counties, so you will find that competition is keen. Demand tends to fluctuate seasonally, with November and December being the best months for bookings.

Advertising in local papers and magazines and the distribution of printed leaflets or business cards are recommended ways of getting bookings.

Pay is variable, according to the type of function and equipment used. Mobile discotheques charge between £40 and £60 a night for private parties, more for weddings and public functions. You must 'cost' your time to a certain extent: if you are playing at a private party, for example, it is likely that you will have to carry on well after midnight, and you should allow for this.

3.5: Media and Communications

Indexing

Publishers have a constant need for indexers whom they can trust to work quickly, efficiently and thoroughly. Indexing requires the ability to understand the arguments and principal themes of a book and organise the material by key words, often to a brief given by the author or publisher.

Various professional qualifications are obtainable in indexing, and the Society of Indexers operates a scheme of registered indexers for those with experience. Indexing is a skilled task and the hourly rate for a qualified indexer about £4. As in many other areas, freelance indexers will tend to develop relationships with particular publishers, perhaps even with individual editors, especially if the indexer concentrates on a specific subject area.

Market research interviewing

Market research interviewing mainly involves either visiting people in their own homes to ask them their views about commercial products (or possibly about social issues) or stopping people in the street to ask them a series of questions about a particular subject.

Basic requirements for the job are patience, perseverance, and the ability to relate to a wide variety of different types of people. You must be available to work some evenings and weekends, and possibly to spend the occasional night away from home. A car is not absolutely necessary, although it does help; and you must be on the telephone.

A short training course is provided by the large, reputable market research companies. It is fairly easy to be accepted for a training course, as interviewers are generally in short supply, but is is important to show that you are going to be available for work on a long-term basis, as the company sees your training as an investment.

We are looking for small businesses looking for money.

In a time of recession, you may well be thinking the prospects of obtaining a business loan are wilting fast. Nothing could be further from the truth.

Because we at NatWest are convinced that financial assistance for the many up-and-coming businesses in this country is exactly what our economy needs. That's why we pay out some £35 million in Business Development Loans each and every month to over 3,000 customers.

And why we're looking to talk to more small businesses in need of finance for sound and promising business ventures.

NatWest Business Development Loans range from £2,000 to £250,000 and can be granted for periods between 1 and 20 years. The rates of interest are highly competitive.

Rates are fixed in advance, and repayments are worked out in equal monthly instalments.

So everything's planned in advance and cash flow's kept well under control.

Now we've made our postion clear, all that may stand between you and a flourishing business is a phone call to the Manager at a NatWest branch near you.

Fixed sum • Fixed interest • Fixed repayments • Fixed term now up to 20 years…for easier cash flow.

 **NatWest** *Ready to do business.*

Most interviewers put their names down with several market research companies. They can expect a steady flow of work, particularly in London, though probably less in the rest of the country.

Opportunities exist for promotion from interviewing to supervisory and managerial posts, but after promotion one would no longer be working on a freelance basis. Other types of freelance work, besides interviewing, are sometimes available from market research firms: clerical work, for example, or the coding of questionnaires.

If you are interested in working as a market research interviewer, write to the Market Research Society who will supply on request a list of research companies employing interviewers. Or you can contact one of the bigger, more reputable market research agencies such as the British Market Research Bureau Ltd or Research Bureau Ltd.

Pay rates are about £12 to £15 for a six-hour day, plus expenses. Pay can be higher for experienced interviewers.

There are also a surprisingly large number of small market research companies, one- or two-man bands who compete with the larger market research organisations. They have often left the latter to set up on their own, perhaps specialising in a particular area and using the contacts drawn from their previous commissions.

Teaching and tutoring

If you have a degree, teacher's diploma or some other qualification, it is worth thinking about private coaching, especially if you have children of your own and perhaps find it difficult to work normal school hours. Try advertising in your local paper or, better still, in the personal columns of *The Times, Daily Telegraph* or *Times Educational Supplement*. State the subjects and the level to which you are prepared to teach. Demand will depend a lot on the area in which you live: you might do better in the 'smarter' areas where parents tend to worry more about their children's chances of winning scholarships, achieving university entrance, etc. There is a particular demand for tutors in mathematics and science subjects. As well as normal school subjects, there is also a demand for people who can teach the piano and other musical instruments or give extra coaching in various languages. The average rate for private tuition is £5 to £10 an hour, depending on your personal qualifications and the level to which you are teaching.

You can register with a local or national educational agency such as Truman & Knightley or Gabbitas-Thring. It is also worth contacting your local education authority, which may have received an inquiry from parents or students. They might also put you on their books as someone who can do supply teaching in an emergency, which is also paid by the hour.

Translating/interpreting

The growing emphasis on exports and on our links with the continent means that this is an expanding field. It is also a highly competitive one, though, and you need to have quite a lot to offer to make a successful living. Most translators work in French and German, for example, so it helps if you are an expert in one of the more unusual languages: there is a great demand at the moment for specialists in Chinese, Japanese and Arabic.

As well as having a language qualification, either a degree or college diploma (such as the Institute of Linguists qualification), you should also have some other skill or professional qualification to offer. Few firms employ translators for their knowledge of the language alone. They want people who can deal with business correspondence, translate engineering and computer manuals, medical textbooks, technical leaflets, advertising brochures for all kinds of products etc. It always pays to cultivate a special subject and become known as the expert in that field.

To get started try writing to all the translating agencies in the Yellow Pages. Business firms tend to put their work through these agencies, so unless you already have good contacts with a few firms, it is a good idea to get on to the books of an agency. If you fancy literary translating, the best idea again is simply to write round to the agencies and to publishing firms noted for their foreign literature back lists.

Rates of pay vary considerably, depending on the quality of your work, the degree of difficulty and the quality sought by the employer. Chinese and Japanese translators are the best paid, and European language translators the worst, with Arabic and Russian specialists somewhere in the middle. If you work for a company direct, without going through an agency, you can charge more. You *can* take on work for private individuals

267

— letters, etc, but it is unlikely to be worthwhile financially, since you can't charge so much.

Translation work requires a complete knowledge of at least one language other than your own, a broad education and a wide range of interests. You will also need a well-stocked personal reference library: translating is a highly skilled technical task which will need back-up from all manner of dictionaries and reference works.

Similarly, work as an interpreter requires rapid intelligence, great stamina and complete fluency in two (and probably more) languages. These qualities are especially needed for conference work — very few people are good enough, and there are only about 50 conference interpreters in the country, but you can also find work at exhibitions, business meetings, as couriers for travel agencies and guides for the London Tourist Board or the British Tourist Authority.

Writing

Freelance writing is a profession to which many are called but comparatively few are published and from the outset it should be said that, unless one is working or has worked on the staff of a newspaper or magazine of some standing, by which a network of professional contacts has been built up, it is a very difficult field for the total newcomer to break into. The best policy then is initially to consider freelance writing as a means of earning extra money over and above that earned from a regular job which will provide the safety net of a dependable income. If the job is in a related field, such as public relations, advertising or book publishing, so much the better from the point of view of giving the potential writer constant practice at the basics of word craft as well as the opportunity to make new and helpful personal contacts. For the purpose of this section it is assumed that the would-be freelance writer is considering producing articles and short fiction for newspapers or magazines, since first novels, always a favourite with new writers, are notoriously hard to place and, as the recent pressure for Public Lending Right shows, even well-established novelists find the financial returns on their work almost impossible to live on.

The basic requirements of the journalist's craft and the key to success in placing articles are:

1. The choice of a subject to write about.
2. Ensuring that the subject is presented in such a way that

it can be readily assimilated into the publication to which you submit it.

The choice of a subject to write about is a more subtle and demanding undertaking than simply avoiding the submission of cookery articles to political weeklies. Such publications as *The Writers' and Artists' Year Book* list the basic spheres of interest of hundreds of periodicals and newspapers, but after such listings have been scanned for initial guidance, the freelance writer should then study with care several issues of the publication to which he would like to submit material. He should then aim to research and write up a subject which will fall within the sphere of interest of the publication, but which is unlikely to be covered by the full-time or regular part-time contributors to the publication. Similarly, it is best to avoid initially articles which involve a political or serious economic stance, since these are subjects for which even well-established staff are chosen carefully.

The aim, then, is to select a subject which is original and about which one may even have special knowledge in the hope that it will land on an editor's desk as a delightful addition to his page rather than a dubious repetition. Sometimes this oblique approach to freelance subject selection can turn into a more permanent proposition if one happens to stumble across a subject which a magazine or newspaper feels it is worth ultimately retaining a correspondent for. A classic example of this is beer, a subject for which at least one national newspaper now retains a correspondent in the manner of the already well-established wine or food correspondent.

In the case of writing short fiction a major market is the supply of romantic short stories to women's magazines. Here, although the choice of subject is in principle already determined the detailed development of the subject needs to be very accurately tailored to a specific magazine.

Many fiction editors on women's magazines receive a steady supply of short stories from literary agents, but it is virtually useless for the new freelance writer to attempt to place work by these means. The vast majority of literary agents will not agree to place short fiction, or indeed any short pieces, for writers who are not already on their books either as novelists or full-length non-fiction writers.

Presentation

Having thought out a suitable subject, equal care should be expended on the literary style of the potential piece. Here again, range of vocabulary, approach and length, not only of the piece but of paragraphs, can only be judged by a careful study of the publication to which the piece will be submitted. Major points to observe in the presentation of work may be summarised as follows:

1. Work should be typed, using one and a half or double spacing on one side of a sheet of paper only. Always retain a carbon copy.
2. Always read your typescript carefully before submitting it and make any corrections, which should be very minor, as clearly as possible.
3. Never submit a manuscript without a covering letter, but keep the letter brief. A covering letter should give the gist of your piece in no more than a sentence or two and draw to the editor's attention any recent or particularly prestigious published work which will help him to get a fuller picture of you.
4. Before writing a covering letter, telephone the publication to obtain the name of the person to whom you should submit the work. This is particularly useful when submitting material to newspapers which tend to be very departmentalised.
5. If your article has any particularly topical connections which give it a limited 'shelf-life' say so in your covering letter and then telephone after several days for a decision. Many articles, rejected by one publication, can quite often be quickly but sensitively revamped and successfully placed with a rival magazine.
6. When submitting articles to illustrated magazines it is often useful to team up with a freelance photographer, if, and only if, your article directly benefits from illustrations.
7. Never submit uncaptioned photographs and present captions typed on a separate sheet. Remember that two apposite and technically excellent photographs are better than half a dozen fuzzy snap-shots.
8. If your article is rejected accept the editor's decision cheerfully and courteously and never attempt to get him to change his mind by arguing. Rejecting scores of

unsolicited articles by telephone is one of the least pleasant editorial jobs and whether you agree with them or not, editors know what they want. Nor should you expect editors to constructively criticise your work, after all they are running publications, not a school of journalism.

Finally, two rules:

1. Never turn a job down, however small and anonymous that job may be and always get commissioned work in on time.
2. Spare no effort when checking that your facts are right. The beginner who acquires a reputation for inaccurate reporting or slip-shod research may as well give up. If a paper or magazine accepts your article, but holds it over for several months, remember to keep abreast of any new developments in the interim: accuracy applies not only to the time or writing, but more important, to the time of publication.

One full-time writer we approached gave this advice: 'Discipline, discipline, discipline! These are the three key words for any budding writer to remember. Get up early and keep at it. If you're stuck for words get something down regardless — you can always change it later. Work hard at your contacts, the people who will buy or recommend buyers for your work. It's no good writing the finest short story or the best technical description of a new widget if you can't then sell your piece.'

3.6: Office Skills

Home typing and secretarial work

This kind of work is well suited to those who wish to work from home. Little capital investment is needed; obviously one's own typewriter is necessary, but a second-hand, electric typewriter can be hired for around £50 per month, or bought for about £250 upwards (depending on the model – less if you buy privately through *Exchange & Mart* or similar publications). A good electric typewriter is usually required, since good-quality copy may encourage customers to use you in the future. Remember, too, that the prices of electronic models, with self-correcting facilities, built-in memories and small VDUs, are now falling fast, and such a model might be a good investment. No one is going to make a fortune doing typing at home, but the skilled typist may be able to make more money at home than in the average secretarial job, provided she can find sufficient work to do. There are certain pitfalls to be avoided, such as envolope typing, which is notoriously underpaid, but on the whole this is an area in which it is possible to make a reasonable amount of money, and which has the advantage of being flexible enough to fit in with domestic commitments.

We talked to a secretary working at home who gave three pieces of advice to other competent typists/secretaries thinking of working independently: 'Aim your services at the person who does not have sufficient work to employ a secretary (eg local small businesses) or the person with the one off major job (eg the PhD student with a 500-page thesis). Price your regular work by the hour and for one-off jobs quote an overall fee. Be wary of offering to let your clients quote your phone number as a place that messages can be left. You'll be woken up during the night and if you pop out to the shops a desperately urgent call will go unanswered.'

How to find work

Classified advertisements are one source: authors sometimes advertise for people to type their manuscripts, for example. However, you will probably do better to insert your own classified advertisements in selected newspapers or put a note on the local university notice board, offering to type manuscripts, theses, etc. Another good place to advertise is the trade press, particularly if you have experience of doing secretarial work in a specialised area. Local advertising in shop windows, local newspapers and magazines might also be effective, as people requiring your services would have the advantage of knowing that you were close at hand.

It is perhaps better, though, to contact potential employers directly. People such as local clergymen, doctors and architects, and various clubs, associations, and even some businessmen often require part-time secretarial services, which can easily be provided from home. For this kind of work, it helps if you can do audio-typing, as you can then collect tapes and take them home, rather than having to take shorthand dictation.

Rates of pay

Pay for home typing is around £3.50 to £5.00 per hour, or more if you are particularly skilled, if you are typing mathematical formulae or if you are working to a tight brief. Thesis and manuscript typing is sometimes paid according to the number of words typed, with a fixed charge per 1000 words, though this is not a sensible arrangement if the quality of the copy from which you have to work varies considerably. For letter typing an hourly charge is usually preferable. Remember to keep an accurate record of the number of hours worked, and include the time that you have to spend collecting and delivering work.

Running your own typing agency

The employment agency field no longer offers the kind of opportunities it once did, as many large firms have moved into the area. However, there is one type of agency, admittedly limited in scope, which is a reasonable proposition for the independent operator. This is the small envelope typing and direct mail agency. You contact firms which do a lot of their business by sending circulars out to people, offering to handle their whole distribution, typing envelopes or labels,

273

inserting circulars into envelopes and postage. The administrative work for this kind of business can easily be handled by one person (from their own home if convenient) and the actual mechanical work of envelope typing and stuffing can be farmed out to outworkers.

Typesetting

If you are a *very* good typist, one of the most interesting and worthwhile possibilities for freelance work would be typesetting. A high degree of skill is needed, and a fairly large investment (particularly for a photosetting machine) but this area offers far greater potential for high earnings and job involvement than straightforward typing.

The job involves preparation of typed matter which will eventually be printed photographically. Most magazines, advertisements and books are now produced in this way rather than by traditional letterpress printing.

The best way to get involved in this area would be to gain some initial experience by working for a small typesetting firm, before setting up on your own. It may also be important to join one of the unions involved in printing (the National Graphical Association is the largest), since many printers will not accept work from non-union typesetters. Check this out thoroughly before setting up your own typesetting operation.

Rates for jobs vary considerably — according to the type of job, the deadline to be met, the quality of your machine, your accuracy, etc. It is best to quote per page rates, and you will need considerable experience to be able to assess and 'price' whole manuscripts! Work can be obtained from publishing firms, design consultants, advertising agents, etc.

3.7: Playgroups

Playgroup leaders

Playgroups cater for pre-school age children, and are usually run on a fairly informal basis, either by one woman in her own home (possibly with the help of a friend or neighbour) or, for larger groups, by several people using a public hall or similar premises.

No formal training is needed. The criteria for playgroup leaders are laid down by each local social services department. Many local authorities now organise courses for playgroup supervisors, and the National Extension College (32 Trumpington Street, Cambridge CB2 1SQ) runs a correspondence course.

If you are planning to run a playgroup in your own home, you must be prepared to invest a certain amount of money in sturdy, sound equipment (climbing frame, sandpit, painting equipment, constructional toys, etc). You will need insurance, and you will have to make sure that your home meets the required safety standards, so the Fire Officer will have to inspect your premises. You will also need planning permission, and you are legally obliged to register your playgroup with the local Department of Social Services. It is able to reject planning permission and prohibit that group being organised if it feels that the applicant is not suitable to hold the position.

Most of these requirements also apply to larger, hall-based groups, though you will probably not need to apply for planning permission, since most halls have permission for a variety of community activities which would include playgroups. Larger groups are often run by a committee consisting of the supervisor, at least one parent, the local health visitor, a secretary and chairman. Staff requirements for a large group (of, say, 25 children) would include a supervisor, one or two paid assistants, and helpers working on a rota basis.

Fees can be calculated by adding together total costs (wages, rent, insurance, a fund for equipment, day-to-day expenses such as postage, repaires, etc) and dividing the total by the number of children that will be attending. If you find that the resulting fees are too high for local mothers to afford, the playgroup can be subsidised by fund-raising activities such as fetes and bazaars. It will help you to cover your costs if you charge fees in advance, and it is also a good idea to charge an 'absentee' fee of half the normal rate for children who are unable to attend for short periods. For further information, contact the Pre-School Playgroups Association (PPA). They have offices in London (Alford House, Aveline Street, SE1), Glasgow (16 Sandyford Place) and Belfast (6 Lower Crescent).

3.8: Selling

Dealing in antiques

If you know what you are doing — and it must be stressed that this is a big 'if' — you can make money out of buying and selling antiques, either to dealers, on a market stall, or at one of the increasing number of 'antique fairs' that are organised in various kinds of public buildings.

Standard antiques are easily recognised and their values are well known through the existence of various price guides. You are unlikely to get a bargain there, though you may pick up the odd underpriced item. A more promising avenue is to specialise, preferably in an area that is not well charted and where you can use your knowledge and taste to beat the odds: clothes are a case in point. However, if you have an expert knowledge, even of some well-known area like pottery, you can pick up bargains in the sense that you might be able to get a piece that is marked at normal antique shop prices but that you know to be worth far more.

Mail order selling

Many people, particularly women, earn money acting as agents for mail order companies. Anyone over 18 can apply to become an agent, based at home and offering the company's goods as advertised in catalogues which are produced once or twice a year. They receive a commission of 10 or 12½ per cent on sales they make, in return for which they collect and record payments from customers and send regular payments to the mail order company. There may be additional problems of receiving and distributing goods, returning faulty products, dealing with bad debts, etc. These may be considerable if the agent tries to build up a large number of clients, drawn from a wide circle. Many do not do so, preferring to use the catalogues as a source of goods, purchased on credit terms, for friends and family. Few people earn a decent income as an agent, and some who do experience administrative and other difficulties.

Market stall selling

Although street vending proper tends to be dominated by full-time market sales people with their own barrows and storage lock-ups, there are quite a few vacant sites up and down the country where much more informal market trading goes on. Some of these belong to local authorities, others to private landlords. They have fixed stalls, which are let at weekends on a first come, first served basis. There are limitations on what you can sell — some places, for instance, will not let you sell fresh food or produce because of environmental health regulations — but otherwise the field is wide open. Existing stallholders will usually tell you about the conditions and where to apply for a stall. They can usually be rented on a daily basis at between £8 and £12.

Party plan selling

A more elaborate, but also better paid form of selling is party plan selling, of which the oldest and best known example is the Tupperware party. The agent in this case recruits hosts or hostesses to give a tea or coffee and biscuits party at which guests are invited to inspect and, hopefully, order the goods brought in for display by the agent. He or she picks up the orders, then delivers the goods to the hostess who is responsible for getting them to the customers and who herself gets a gift for her trouble. The agent's role, in other words, is as much to recruit hosts as to sell the goods. This is a much more demanding form of selling than a mail order agency and is correspondingly better rewarded — commissions run as high as 30 per cent, with bonuses over and above that.

Selling produce

Anyone who has a big enough garden or allotment can make money selling produce: flowers, fruit, vegetables, herbs, honey, home-made jams and chutneys and eggs.* If you live on or near a main road the easiest way to sell things is simply to put up a stall or barrow at your gate, or else a notice directing people to your house. If you live right off the beaten track you might find it easier to sell to your village store or to one of the 'farm shops'

* Before you start apply for planning permission and ask a lawyer or the local Citizens' Advice Bureau whether your action would contravene sales legislation or EEC regulations on the sale of farm produce.

that are to be found now in many villages. In the summer you can make a lot of money from passing trade — tourists and city dwellers on the lookout for country produce.

Two worthwhile investments, when you have made enough money, are a deep freeze and a greenhouse. With a deep freeze, you can freeze surplus fruit and vegetables to sell in the winter, or for people to transfer to their own freezers. This enables you to make a bit more money in the lean winter months. With a greenhouse, you can grow some of the more exotic vegetables such as green peppers and aubergines, potted plants, especially for the Christmas trade, and offer bedding plants such as tomatoes for sale to other gardeners.

How much should you charge? A quick scout round the local shops will tell you what the going rate is for the more usual fruit and vegetables. You should of course charge more than shop prices for home-made jams, jellies and chutneys.

Part 4:
Freelance Work

4.1: Introduction

There are obviously overlaps between working part time and working as a freelance. A person contributing regular articles to journals and newspapers could be doing so part time and still be described as a freelance. In general, though, a freelance is regarded as someone who is self-employed full time, providing a service to a range of different principals as the demand occurs, or as he or she can persuade them to buy the service that is being offered.

Some occupations have a very high freelance content because of the unpredictability of the flow of work. The prime example is the world of films and television. Over a third of the 23,000 members of ACTT (Association of Cinematograph, Television and Allied Technicians), the principal trade union in this sphere, are freelances, employed by a variety of different companies for anything from a day to six months, according to the duration of a particular project. Performing artists, too, tend almost exclusively to be freelances, even though they may have spells when they are attached to a particular orchestra or a repertory company.

In the media and even in certain parts of industry, the tendency to put work out to freelances and other suppliers of ad hoc labour is growing rapidly. When trading conditions are uncertain, employers are reluctant to commit themselves to taking on people full time. It makes more sense to bring them in as and when they are needed or to commission them — even to the point of sub-contracting whole jobs to them.

There are also many tasks in many firms which need to be done but where the in-house demand is neither large nor constant enough to justify the employment of a full-time member of staff. It is people in such occupations, which can range from manual jobs like that of the firm's carpenter to services like public relations, who often find themselves at risk when times get hard. Yet, operating as freelances for their own firm, plus other clients, they often have a highly profitable new lease of working life.

How freelances find work

The circumstances just described bring out a number of points about freelance work. It is often very difficult, for instance, simply to decide to 'go freelance' as many redundant executives have found to their cost when they wanted to set up as consultants. You have to have contacts, reliable sources of work and a known track record in your chosen area. Many freelances report, in fact, that their first client was their previous employer or someone whom they got to know through their former workplace.

Even so, freelance work is patchy and unpredictable. The elements of self-marketing and constant self-motivation are vital. Freelance management consultants, for instance, reckon to spend at least 40 per cent of their time hunting for work: identifying opportunities from reports in the business, trade or professional press and following them up with letters, phone calls or proposals. The same pattern can be seen in other freelance occupations: photographers and entertainers check in with their agents, writers prepare material 'on spec' for book and magazine publishers. It is a fairly insecure life until you get established and clients start ringing you, rather than the other way round. Indeed, many freelances are of the opinion that to make a success of it, you need at least one reliable source of regular work — someone who brings you in for one day a week, for instance.

Characteristics of freelance work

The reason why a lot of practising freelances recommend getting this kind of underlay is not purely financial. There are also psychological factors involved, especially for those who have previously worked alongside others. Freelancing is a lonely way to earn a living. With some kinds of job — writing for instance — you can spend weeks on end without seeing anyone.

It is also unpredictable. There can be long periods, particularly when you first start, when little or no work comes in and your bank balance sinks as low as your spirits. As a self-employed person, you cannot even claim unemployment benefit either, even though no work is coming through. On the contrary you still have to pay your National Insurance stamp.

Periods of inactivity may be broken up by spells when the workload is almost too much. Very few freelances ever turn work away, though. Once you lose a potential customer — even though you may not need him at that juncture — he is very difficult to get back when circumstances change. If, however, you can't do the job because it coincides with something else, it is essential to say so rather than to make promises that cannot be kept. This applies to delivery dates as well.

Costing and pricing

Broadly, the rules set out in Chapter 1.8 apply, but there are additional factors to consider. As we have said, you often have to spend a considerable amount of time just looking for work; it varies, obviously according to your status and occupation. On the other hand, whether you can reflect this fact in full in your scale of charges depends on our old friends, supply and demand. As against that you have the advantage, in the case of many types of freelance work, that you are working from home. Usually your equipment costs are low too, though that would not be true of photography. The employer, in engaging you, should consider that it is generally reckoned that the cost of having a person on the staff full time is twice their annual salary, taking into account NI contributions, holidays, pensions and so forth.

Income tax and freelance work

Freelances are normally taxed under Schedule D. However, as we have pointed out at the end of Chapter 1.11, the Inland Revenue are challenging Schedule D status where a substantial amount of work is done for one particular employer, as that in effect constitutes a master and servant relationship. This is a particular danger when people work through an agency and are paid by the agency, not by the client.

4.2: Management Consultancy

Anybody can call themselves a management consultant, though there is a professional organisation, the Institute of Management Consultants, membership of which is reserved for people who have actually practised in a recognised consultancy firm. Such people should find it relatively easier to get freelance assignments and there is in fact a body called the Richmond Group which consists of some 80 to 100 independent management consultants — mostly people who have worked for bigger firms and then set up on their own. Though based in London's World Trade Centre, they embrace a nationwide network of freelance consultants, all of whom, they stress, must have the MIMC qualification.

What happens if you are not qualified? Many redundant managers think that setting up as a consultant is the answer to unemployment, but unless you have very specific expertise to offer and are known in your industry, this is by no means easy. The best way to start is by getting an assignment from your own firm. It is always easier to get more work if you can point to a task you are already doing or which you have completed. Former business contacts are also a possible source of work, but you have to come up with a specific proposal to have any chance of success with your approach: a suggestion for action in some area where you know they have a problem and you have the expertise to solve it. It is generally considered that the going rate for freelance consultancy is around £20 an hour.

4.3: Media and Communications

Art and design

There are numerous opportunities for freelances in this area if you have talent, creativity, the ability to meet deadlines and a range of contacts in the business. You may be a book designer, illustrator, clothes designer, cartoonist, or furniture or three-dimensional designer. The message is the same: if you are good and people who have used you have liked your work, you will be given a steady stream of work, for which you will be well paid.

You will probably have a design qualification, and you should specialise, but your chosen specialism does not have to be the area in which you qualified. Many designers and illustrators supplement their income by taking on freelance work, and graduate to full self-employment later.

If you are successful as a freelance designer, you should invest in a good, well-lit, well-ventilated studio in which to work. And if demand for your services is very great, think about expansion: is there someone whose work is good who could be taken on as a business partner, perhaps, and could you delegate administrative chores to someone?

Editorial work

For proof-reading and copy editing, experience in a publishing house is a prerequisite. People tend to feel that proof-reading, in particular, only requires a good command of spelling and an eye for detail, but in fact it really requires some knowledge of the way a book is actually put together, and an eye for the kinds of mistakes that an inexperienced person would not necessarily pick up. No inexperienced person would be able to obtain freelance editorial work from any publishing firm. However, if you have worked in publishing, you may be able to obtain freelance work through personal contacts. Forget the idea of advertising your services: it will almost certainly not work.

Editorial work is particularly suited to freelancing: most of it can be done more quickly and thoroughly in the quiet of one's own home than in the distracting hubbub of an office atmosphere. It also has the advantage of being time-consuming; once you have obtained a particular piece of work, you will usually find that it guarantees you one to two weeks' employment, and so you do not get into the situation in which some freelances find themselves, of having to spend much of your time collecting and delivering work.

Film-making

This is a notoriously competitive area; for every success, there are 99 (perhaps 999) failures. You will need experience of a range of techniques, including video and slide presentation, and you should work quickly and creatively, fulfilling commissions on time and to the specified budget. Only the fortunate few will *choose* which films to make; the rest will have to be satisfied with industrial, training and promotional films and perhaps commercials. But, remember, these often require great skill and imagination, will provide good experience and may lead to more ambitious and more personally fulfilling projects later.

Freelance journalism

Freelance journalism sounds like an attractive occupation, but it is an extremely difficult one to break into unless you have previously worked as a journalist and have the necessary contacts. Certainly, general journalism can be written off as a dead loss. Freelances writing about politics, literature, humour, sport etc do make a great deal of money once they are established, but the number that fall into this category is probably less than two or three dozen in all. The only place where an outsider has a chance is in specialisms, particularly in technical subjects where few professional journalists feel at home. There is, for instance, a great need for freelances in various aspects of information technology and computers.

If you are interested in freelance journalism in spheres like this — and have the necessary background knowledge — read the main journals to see what sort of topics they cover and how long their articles tend to be. If you see any gaps that you think would be interesting, write to the editor with your suggestions and state your qualifications and background. Going rates at the moment are between £60 and £100 per thousand words.

Photography

As in other fields, in freelance photography you are more likely to succeed by organisation, reliability and perseverance than by sheer talent alone. If you are submitting samples of your work to magazines, journals and newspapers you must expect to have a large proportion of your work rejected; but on the small proportion that *is* accepted you can gradually build up your reputation with your clients.

Don't be misled by camera fanatics — it is important, of course, to have good, reliable equipment, but you don't necessarily need the most expensive, up-to-date gadgets and accessories to be a successful professional photographer. Far better to have sound, reliable equipment which you are happy with and you *know* that you can take good pictures with, and to take great care with the presentation of your work.

How to get work

Freelance photography covers such a wide area that it is difficult to cover all the possible avenues of entry to the profession. One fact stands out: there are a great many competent photographers, and so to be successful your pictures will have to have some special quality that makes them stand out, not necessarily in terms of technical proficiency but in terms of ideas. If you are trying to break into the women's magazine field, for example, it is no good taking along a portfolio of photographs which are almost exactly the same as the ones the magazine uses already; they know photographers who can produce these, and you must give them a very good reason for using you, as opposed to people they already know and trust.

Most of the larger magazines commission work, for which the photographer is paid on a fee basis. Standard practice for obtaining commissioned work is the submission of a portfolio, backed up by one or more personal visits, and it is likely that your personality and ideas will carry more weight with the art editor than your technical expertise, though of course you must be technically competent. Again, it may be worth specialising: in landscape photography, fashion, sport, or a similar area with a readily definable range of potential users of your material.

Submitting work 'on spec'

It is possible to make a living by submitting selections of prints to magazines 'on spec', particularly if you concentrate on small, specialised publications and local magazines and newspapers.

Presentation of your work is very important. Prints should be of the highest quality possible, and should be carefully packed to avoid damage by the Post Office. Your work should be clearly labelled, and it is a good idea to have a referencing number to each photograph, to avoid confusion.

You should offer 'single reproduction rights': this means that the print can be resold at a later date, and you retain the copyright.

Wedding photographs, passports, portraits

This area is one of the most attractive to people who want to make extra money from photography on a part-time basis, possibly graduating to full-time freelance work when they have established themselves. Work can be obtained through local advertising and personal contacts, and your local camera club should be able to give help and suggestions.

Payment

Rates of pay vary tremendously, since the work itself is so varied. Fees for commissioned work for the high-circulation magazines can be substantial, but most of this work goes to established photographers.

It is important to remember when dealing with magazines that payment may be delayed by as much as six months, and if you try to push for early payment you may make yourself very unpopular. It is unlikely, in any event, that you will be paid before publication. If you are going to be a full-time freelance photographer therefore, you shouldn't under-capitalise yourself, as it may be a year or so before you really begin to make enough money to live on.

PR and advertising consultancy

This is an expanding area with good opportunities for the self-employed person who has worked in promotion and marketing and now wants to work independently. But there are problems: how do you compete with large agencies with massive resources? The answer is that, for the most part, you do not: you offer consultancy (often to the agency rather than to the firm) on specific projects, in areas in which you have expertise. You can then allow your enterprise to develop, perhaps employing staff, developing and diversifying your services and challenging the larger organisations. In the short term, cultivate contacts, specialise in a single area, show very personal attention to clients and be satisfied with a steady flow of small projects.

We spoke to a public relations consultant who gave this advice to people thinking of going it alone: 'You have to do two things simultaneously — first the work in hand and second the constant search for new clients. Doing the former will obviously help with the latter, but don't get so tied up in your current work that you neglect to look ahead. If you start getting fairly regular work from a client then suggest you move from billing on a job by job basis to an annual contract; this will help your cash flow enormously and such a contract is also of very high value when talking to your bank manager or building society.' One caveat: many firms include a clause in your contract which stops you working with a client for a given period if you leave that company. This reflects the closeness of customers and particular individuals within their agencies. So, check the small print of your contract before trying to bring your three closest contacts among your old company's clients into your newly formed outfit.

Research

The term 'research' covers a broad area. Many researchers for television and radio, for various companies, for advertising agencies and marketing organisations — are not freelance. Some people do part-time market research (for which a telephone and car and an outgoing personality are necessary). Others work in individual research projects, for which particular academic and professional qualifications may be necessary. In general, a researcher should have had varied experience, have the capacity to work independently and quickly and to understand a library cataloguing system, be able to write reasonably well and to type. Opportunities to work may be erratic, and a range of very different projects may be taken on. There will probably be less opportunity to build relationships with particular clients, and assignments will often be one-off jobs. Rates of pay will also vary considerably.

4.4: Repairs and Servicing of Vehicles

Every car owner believes himself to be a mechanic, but to be able to work on a wide range of cars and deal with many different types of problem requires considerable expertise. So, do not set up a car workshop if you do not have the necessary training and experience. Moreover, you will require a good deal of capital — to acquire large premises, and the range of materials and fittings needed to undertake the work. Competition is also severe — there are many large, established garages with a team of mechanics. Can you provide services at competitive prices and with comparable efficiency and speed? Garage mechanics get a bad press, but this does not necessarily make the area an easy one in which to establish a new operation.

Dennis Edmonson, who specialises in car repairs and servicing, emphasises the need for expertise: 'Don't be tempted to take on work you are not sure you can complete to a high standard. Familiarise yourself with all the rules and regulations which surround the transport industry today, and don't get flustered by the bureaucrats who will constantly be on at you. Be wary of the travellers and agents who will call every week trying to con you into purchasing materials/machinery you don't really need.'

Appendices

1: Further Information

Before taking the plunge, it is absolutely essential to get all the help and advice you can, especially if you are planning to invest a lot of money in a business. Ring one of the specialist bodies listed below, go to the public library, do as much background reading as you have time for, consult your bank manager, solicitor and accountant, and talk to any friends who have succeeded in the area in which you are interested.

Small Firms Division Department of Industry
Ashdown House
127 Victoria Street
London SW1E 6RB
Tel: 01-212 8667
The Department of Industry has also established a number of regionally-based small firms centres.

The London and South Eastern Region
8-10 Bulstrode Street
London W1M 5ST
Tel: 01-487 4342
Freefone: 2444

South Western Region
5th Floor
The Pithay
Bristol BS1 2NB
Tel: 0272 294546
Freefone: 2444

Northern Region
Centro House
3 Cloth Market
Newcastle upon Tyne NE1 3EE
Tel: 0632 25353
Freefone: 2444

North West Region
320-5 Royal Exchange
Manchester M2 7AH
Tel: 061-832 5282
Freefone: 2444

Working for Yourself

1 Old Hall Street
Liverpool L3 9HJ
Tel: 051-236 5756
Freefone: 2444

Yorkshire and Humberside Region
1 Park Row
City Square
Leeds LS1 5NR
Tel: 0532 445151
Freefone: 2444

East Midlands Region
48-50 Maid Marian Way
Nottingham NG1 6GF
Tel: 0602 49791
Freefone: 2444

West Midlands Region
Ladywood House
Stephenson Street
Birmingham B2 4DT
Tel: 021-643 3344
Freefone: 2444

Eastern Region
24 Brooklands Avenue
Cambridge CB2 2BU
Tel: 0223 63312
Freefone: 2444

Northern Ireland
Local Enterprise Development Unit
Lamont House
Purdy's Lane
Mewtownbreda
Belfast BT8 4TB
Tel: 0232 691031

Northern Ireland Development Agency
Maryfield
100 Belfast Road
Hollywood
County Down
and
11 Berkeley Street
London W1
Tel: 01-629 1265

Scotland
57 Bothwell Street
Glasgow G2 6TU
Tel: 041-248 6014
Freefone: 2444

The Scottish Development Agency
(Small Business Division)
102 Telford Road
Edinburgh EN4 2NP
Tel: 031-343 1911

Wales
16 St David's House
Wood Street
Cardiff CF1 1ER
Tel: 0222 396116
Freefone: 2444

The Welsh Development Agency
(Small Business Division)
Treforest Industrial Estate
Pontypridd
Mid Glamorgan CF37 5UT
Tel: 044-385 2666

Advisory, Conciliation and Arbitration Service (ACAS)
Cleland House
Page Street
London SW1
Tel: 01-222 8020

Agricultural Cooperation and Marketing Services Ltd *(advice for farmers)*
Agricultural House
25 Knightsbridge
London SW1
Tel: 01-235 7853

Agricultural Development Advisory Service *(advice for farmers)*
Ministry of Agriculture, Fisheries and Food
Great Westminster House
Horseferry Road
London SW1
Tel: 01-216 6311

Agricultural Mortgage Corporation Ltd
Bucklersbury House
3 Queen Victoria Street
London EC4N 8DU
Tel: 01-236 5252

Alliance of Small Firms & Self Employed People
42 Vine Road
East Molesey
Surrey KT8 9LF
Tel: 01-979 2293

Association of Invoice Factors
109-13 Royal Avenue
Belfast BT1 1FF
Tel: 0232 24522

BBC External Services *(translation/interpreting work)*
Bush House
Strand
London WC2
Tel: 01-240 3456

Booksellers Association
154 Buckingham Palace Road
London SW1
Tel: 01-730 8214

British Franchise Association Ltd
Grove House
628 London Road
Colnbrook
Slough
Berkshire SL3 8QH
Tel: 02812 4909

British Institute of Management
Small Firms Information Service
Management House
Parker Street
London WC2B 5PT
Tel: 01-405 3456

British Insurance Association
Aldermary House
Queen Street
London EC4 4JD
Tel: 01-248 4477

The Building Centre *(building trades work)*
26 Store Street
London WC1E 7BT
Tel: 01-637 9001

Building Research Establishment *(building trades work)*
Bucknalls Lane
Watford WD2 7JR
or
Scottish Laboratory
Kelvin Road
Glasgow

Choice Magazine *(retirement planning)*
Bedford Chambers
Covent Garden
London WC2

Confederation of British Industry (CBI)
Smaller Firms Council
Centre Point
New Oxford Street
London WC1
Tel: 01-379 7400

Co-operative Development Agency
20 Albert Embankment
London SE1 7TJ
Tel: 01-211 3000

Council for Small Industries in Rural Areas (CoSIRA)
141 Castle Street
Salisbury
Wiltshire SP1 3TP
Tel: 0722 6255

The Design Council
28 Haymarket
London SW1 4DG
Tel: 01-839 8000

Equipment Leasing Association
18 Upper Grosvenor Street
London W1
Tel: 01-491 2783

Federation of Master Builders
33 John Street
London WC1
Tel: 01-242 7583

Finance Houses Association
18 Upper Grosvenor Street
London W1
Tel: 01-491 2783

Franchise Development Services Limited
Castle House
21 Davey Place
Norwich NR2 1PJ
Tel: 0603 20301 or 667024/5

Highlands and Islands Development Board
Bridge House
Bank Street
Inverness IV1 1QR
Tel: 0463 234171

Hotel Catering and Institutional Management Association
191 Trinity Road
London SW17
Tel: 01-767 1431

Industrial and Commercial Finance Corporation (ICFC)
91 Waterloo Road
London SE1 8XP
Tel: 01-928 7822

Institute of Directors
116 Pall Mall
London SW1
Tel: 01-839 1233

Institute of Linguists
24a Highbury Grove
London N5 2EA
Tel: 01-359 7445

Institute of Management Consultants
23-24 Cromwell Place
London SW7 2LG
Tel: 01-584 7285

Institute of Patentees and Inventors
Staple Inn Buildings South
335 High Holborn
London WC1V 7PX
Tel: 01-249 7812

Institute of Small Businesses
13 Golden Square
London W1R 4AL
Tel: 01-437 4923

Law Society
Legal Aid Department
113 Chancery Lane
London WC2A 1PL
Tel: 01-242 1222

London Chamber of Commerce
69 Cannon Street
London EC4 5AB
Tel: 01-248 4444

Market Research Society
15 Belgrave Square
London SW1X 8PF
Tel: 01-235 4709

National Farmers' Union
Agriculture House
Knightsbridge
London SW1
Tel: 01-235 5077

National Federation of Retail Newsagents
2 Bridgewell Place
London EC4
Tel: 01-353 6816

National Federation of Self-employed and Small Businesses Ltd
32 St Anne's Road West
Lytham St Annes
Lancashire
Tel: 0253 720911

and
45 Russell Square
London WC1
Tel: 01-636 3828

National Research Development Corporation
Kingsgate House
66 Victoria Street
London SW1 6SL
Tel: 01-828 3400

**The National Union of Small Shopkeepers of Great Britain
and Northern Ireland**
Westminster Buildings
Theatre Square
Nottingham NG1 6LH
Tel: 0602 45046

Office of Fair Trading
Field House
Breams Buildings
London EC4
Tel: 01-242 2858

Pre-Retirement Association
17 Undine Street
London SW17 8PP
Tel: 01-767 3225

Richmond Group
World Trade Centre
London E1 9AA
Tel: 01-488 2400

Small Business Bureau
32 Smith Square
London SW1P 3HH
Tel: 01-222 9000

Society of Indexers
25 Leyborne Park
Kew Gardens
Surrey TW9 3HB
Tel: 01-940 4771

Technical Development Capital
91 Waterloo Road
London SE1 8XP
Tel: 01-928 7822

Translators' Association
Society of Authors
84 Drayton Gardens
London SW10 9SD
Tel: 01-373 6642

2: Select Bibliography

Part 1

Be Your Own Boss: How to become Self-employed, John Blundell
(National Federation of the Self-employed)
Company Law, 5th edition, M C Oliver (Macdonald & Evans)
Croner's Reference Book for the Self-employed, ed Daphne McAra
(Croner Publication Ltd)
Daily Telegraph Guide to Income Tax, B Budibent (Collins)
Fair Deal: A Shopper's Guide, Office of Fair Trading
Focus on Retirement, Fred Kemp and Bernard Buttle (Kogan Page)
Going Solo, William Perry and Derek Jones (BBC Publications)
Guardian Guide to Running a Small Business, 3rd edition,
ed Clive Woodcock (Kogan Page)
A Guide to Franchising, Martin Mendelsohn (Pergamon Press)
The Hambro Tax Guide, A S Silke and W I Sinclair
(Macdonald & Janes, published annually)
How to Collect Money That is Owed to You, M Lewis (McGraw-Hill)
How to Read a Balance Sheet, 5th revised edition (ILO)
Law for the Small Business, 3rd edition, P Clayton (Kogan Page)
Local Initiatives — Great Britain (New Foundation for Local Initiative
Support)
Looking Ahead: A Guide to Retirement, Fred Kemp and
Bernard Buttle (Macdonald & Evans)
Management of Trade Credit, T G Hutson and J Butterworth
(Gower Press)
Managing for Results, Peter F Drucker (Pan Books)
The Money Book, Eamonn Fingleton and Tom Tickell (Penguin)
More Profit from Your Stock, 2nd edition, E A Jensen (available from
the author, 39 Withdean Crescent, Brighton)
Occupation: Self-employed, Rosemary Pettit (Wildwood House)
Raising Finance: The Guardian Guide for the Small Business,
Clive Woodcock (Kogan Page)
The Small Business Casebook, Sue Birley (MacMillan Press)
The Small Business Guide, C Barrow (BBC Publications)
Small Business Kit, National Extension College
Small Firms Centres Publications 1-20 by various authors (Small Firms
Centres)
Success in Bookkeeping for the Small Business, G Whitehead
(John Murray)
Success in Principles of Accounting, G Whitehead (John Murray)
Understand Your Accounts, A St John Price (Kogan Page)
VAT Made Easy, A St John Price (Kogan Page)

Zoning In On Enterprise: A Guide to Enterprise Zones, D Rodrigues and
P Bruinvels (Kogan Page)

A more extensive bibliography, divided by area of interest, is available
from the Small Firms Service. Many of the pamphlets produced by the
Department of Industry, the Department of Health and Social Security,
the Inland Revenue, the Department of Employment and the Department
of the Environment will also be of value.

Parts 2, 3 and 4
British Rate & Data (monthly)
Buying a Shop, E A Jensen (available from the author, 39 Withdean
Crescent, Brighton)
Buying a Shop, A St John Price (Kogan Page)
A Catering Business of Your Own, E M Turner, revised R H Johnson
(Barrie & Jenkins)
Chaffer's Handbook to Hall Marks on Gold and Silver Plate
(William Reeves)
A Guide to the Building Regulations, A J Elder (Architectural Press)
How to Earn a Second Income, G Golzen (Muller)
How to Form a Playgroup (BBC Publications)
Money and Your Retirement, E V Eves (Pre-Retirement Association)
The Other Careers — Earning a Living in the Arts and Media,
Mike Bygrave, Joan Goodman and John Fordham (Wildwood Press)
Restoring Old Junk, Michele Brown (Lutterworth Press)
Running Your Own Hotel, Arthur Neil (Barrie & Jenkins)
Setting up a Workshop (Crafts Council)
Soft Furnishing — A Practical Manual for the Home Upholsterer,
A V White (Routledge & Kegan Paul)
Taking up a Franchise, Golzen, Barrow and Severn (Kogan Page)
Technical Translator's Manual, ed J B Sykes (Aslib)
'Vogue' Guide to Knitting, Crochet and Macramé (Collins)
'Vogue' Sewing Book (Butterick Publishing Co)
Working with Gemstones, V A Firsoff (David & Charles)
Working with Languages (Institute of Linguists)
Writers' and Artists' Yearbook (A & C Black)
Writing for Television in the Seventies, M Hulke (A & C Black)
Writing for the BBC (BBC Publications)

3: Glossary of Key Business Terms

It is too often assumed that the new or recently established small businessman will be conversant with all the technical jargon used in the fields of business and management. To counter this, we have included a short glossary of key terms and a list of more detailed practical reference works you may wish to consult. We acknowledge the assistance of John Blundell in the compilation of this glossary.

account(s)
1. **annual accounts** financial records of your business prepared by your accountant for the Inland Revenue.
2. **credit account** agreement whereby a valued and trusted customer is allowed to buy goods/obtain services for which he pays later (say monthly or quarterly).
3. **current account** bank account on which the bank does not pay *interest*, and from which the customer can make immediate cash or cheque withdrawals.
4. **profit and loss account** record of profits before tax, the tax due and profits after tax. Depending on your business it will also show other factors, allowances and amounts brought forward from the last financial year and to be carried forward to the next financial year.
5. **statement of account** record sent to you by your bank or a company with which you are dealing showing all transactions over a given period and concluding with the amount due from you or to you on a certain date.
6. **trading account** record showing *gross* profit only.

Articles of Association the rules which establish how a company must be run. They are drawn up when the company is formed and represent a contract between the company and its shareholders. Standard Articles of Association are now used by most new small companies.

asset piece of property owned by a company or one of its directors; see *liquid assets.*

audit process of checking the accuracy of company financial records by a third party (auditor) which is independent of both you and your accountant. He checks your financial records, states whether in his view they are accurate and may make recommendations on the future keeping of books/*accounts* by you or your accountant.

balance sheet record of your *assets* and *liabilities* at a particular date, normally the end of the financial year.

bankruptcy situation 1. where an individual cannot meet his bills 2. where a debtor (individual or company) is declared *insolvent* and his property thereafter administered for the benefit of his proven creditors.

black economy that part of the economy which does not appear in official statistics and which thus illegally avoids tax and *National Insurance* payments.

broker person who acts as an agent for others; usually used to describe 1. a person who acts for one or more insurance companies 2. a person who buys and sells stocks for members of the public on the Stock Exchange.

budgetary control system of monitoring and controlling expenditure to keep it in line with income and company financial projections.

capital total resources (of a company, etc) including property, cash, equipment and other goods.

capital gains tax tax on the profits resulting from the sale of *capital* interests and assets.

cash book day-to-day notebook in which are recorded payments and receipts.

cash discount deduction of a given amount from the price of an article or service, usually in return for cash payment, early purchase, etc.

cash flow flow of cash required to finance a business for a given period.

cash flow chart record of all payments and receipts over a specified period which establishes the *cash flow* position of a firm.

casual an employee who does not work for you on a regular basis. He/she is normally paid *net* but can be paid *gross* by prior arrangement with the Inland Revenue. It is essential to keep a complete and accurate record of all payments made to casual *employees* including their names and addresses.

chartered accountant fully qualified account who is a member of the Institute of Chartered Accountants and qualified to *audit* public company *accounts.*

clearing bank bank which is a member of the London Bankers' Clearing House, which settles inter-bank accounts at the end of each day's trading.

commission percentage of sale price paid as a fee to an agent for arranging that sale.

company corporate body established under the Companies Act.

credit 1. period allowed for repayment of loan or payment for goods or service 2. borrowing limit imposed by bank or other creditor 3. addition to financial records made on the right-hand side of the books; cf *debit.*

Customs and Excise body responsible for the collection of customs duty, excise duty and *VAT.*

debenture legal document specifying the terms of a loan.

debit deduction recorded on the left-hand side of an account.

dividend share of profits paid by a company to its shareholders.

education visit visit by a *Customs and Excise* officer to a business soon after it has registered for *VAT* or a request to educate the trader in keeping VAT records, etc.

employee person working for you either on a regular or casual basis. Unless he is working for you temporarily he will have a contract specifying the conditions of work, level of remuneration, etc. You must in most cases deduct Class 1 *National Insurance* and Schedule E tax *(PAYE)*.

finance company corporate body which lends larger amounts and for longer periods than clearing banks.

financial year period covered by your profit and loss account; ie a company's accounting year.

fixed cost expense or *overhead* which does not vary with the level of production.

franchise the right to sell the product or service of a franchising company or to carry on a business using a name belonging to, or associated with, a franchisor.

freehold land or property owned (rather than leased or rented) by an individual, company, etc.

gilt-edged (refers to) investment where there is effectively no risk of loss or default.

goodwill *asset* consisting of the good reputation and established clientele of a retail or other business. It is difficult to determine the cash value of goodwill and its subjective nature is likely to cause difficulties if the person selling a business claims goodwill as a major factor in setting the sale price.

gratuity tip; taxable.

gross total before deductions; cf *net.*

income tax tax on an individual's income. The flat rate is currently 30 per cent and the tax is graduated so that higher income earners pay a larger percentage of their salary to the Inland Revenue. Most employees are taxed at source *(PAYE)*, but most self-employed people make annual income tax declarations and pay a lump sum to the Inland Revenue.

indirect tax tax levied on expenditure rather than income (eg *VAT*).

inflation 1. annual increase in the supply of currency 2. (more commonly) the rate at which prices are increasing (usually judged by the retail price index).

insolvency situation in which a person, company, etc, is not able to pay his/its bills. Insolvency does not constitute *bankruptcy* however, as the insolvent may have assets which can eventually be realised to pay his bills while the bankrupt is deemed not to have such assets.

inspection visit visit by the *Customs and Excise* officer to a business every three or four years to inspect the financial records for *VAT* purposes.

interest money paid (usually as a monthly or annual percentage) for the use of *capital.* Rates of interest vary according to the nature and length of a loan, prevailing economic conditions and the government's fiscal policy.

internal audit *audit* of a company's books and appraisal of company efficiency conducted by an *employee* of that company.

invoice document issued by a business to a client giving full details of a transaction or series of transactions and indicating terms of payment. If they are registered for *VAT*, there is a legal minimum of information you must provide.

liability a debt.

limited company business association in which the liability of the directors in the event of *bankruptcy* is limited to the loss of business (ie not personal) *assets;* cf *partnership.*

liquid asset asset which can be realised into cash very quickly.

liquidation legal process of closing down a *bankrupt* company and selling off its *assets* to pay debts.

liquidity extent of the cash *assets* of a company or its ability to realise other assets into cash.

loan capital finance lent to a company for a specified period at a fixed rate of *interest* and normally secured against, say, the business premises of that company. It differs from share capital in that the provider of loan capital has no 'share' of the profits or control in the running of the company.

loss leader goods/services deliberately provided at a loss in the hope that it will attract customers who will buy other goods/services from which the provider of those goods/services will profit.

market research process of identifying and assessing the market for goods and services. It attempts to break down the market into segments and identifies motives for buying a particular good, trade-offs between price and quality, likelihood of repurchase, frequency of purchase, etc.

minimum lending rate rate of interest at which the Bank of England will lend money to other banks. If affects all other interest rates which tend to other banks. It affects all other interest rates which tend to rise or fall in line with it, and is a major tool of government fiscal policy.

National Insurance state-run scheme by which all employees, employers and self-employed people pay a percentage of their earnings to the government in return for payments in periods of unemployment and/or sickness.

net total after deductions, cf *gross.*

opportunity cost the amount of money which would have been earned if you had used your time and money elsewhere. If you are spending £20,000 on buying and stocking a shop, remember that over a year, with interest rates of 16 per cent, that would have earned an additional £3200. This is the opportunity cost of using your *capital* to set up a retail business.

overdraft 1. amount owed to a bank 2. ceiling to which a business creditor can borrow, an overdraft, unlike a loan, can be recalled by the bank at any time.

overhead cost which does not vary according to the level of production; see *fixed cost.*

overtrading situation in which a company is unable to support its high level of trading activity with sufficient capital, causing *liquidity* and *cash flow* problems.

partnership business association in which the partners are formally and personally responsible for the debts they incur. Certain professions (eg lawyers and architects) must engage in this form of association (ie are not allowed to form a *limited company*).

patent exclusive privilege, protected by law, to make and sell an invention or new product for a specified period.

PAYE pay as you earn; method of collecting tax from employees at source. Employers must *debit* the necessary amount of *income tax* and *National Insurance* from their *employees'* salaries and forward it to the Inland Revenue.

registered office the office which is registered with the Registrar of the Companies.

Schedule D — cases 1 and 2 Inland Revenue Schedule which defines the tax allowances available to *self-employed persons.*

Schedule E Inland Revenue Schedule which defines the tax allowances available to employed persons.

secured creditor person whose debt is guaranteed, for example, by using his business premises as collateral in any transaction.

self-employed person one working on his own, in a freelance capacity or in his own business. He is not under the control, direction or supervision of an employer, will supply his own equipment and organises his own work, hours, etc. He pays tax under Schedule D and pays Class 2 and 4 *National Insurance.*

shop premises where goods or services are provided to the public on cash or credit terms. If your premises meet these criteria, you should understand and comply with the regulations stated in the Shop Act 1950 and the Shops and Railways Premises Act 1963.

stock finished goods, goods in the middle of production and raw materials in store which count towards the *capital* resources of a business.

tax exemption certificate photo identity card issued to builders by the Inland Revenue which allows main contractors to pay them *gross* (ie without having deducted 30 per cent of the contract price minus the cost of materials and *VAT*). Without this certificate a main contractor will deduct this sum automatically and forward it to the Inland Revenue.

trade discount percentage reduction in price offered by one trader to another in an allied area of business (eg standard 33⅓ per cent discount on the price of books given by a publisher to a bookseller).

value added tax (VAT) percentage tax imposed at all stages of production. The trader forwards (usually quarterly) to *Customs and Excise* the amount of tax he has collected and the amount he has paid out. The rate of VAT is currently 15 per cent and is levied on all businesses with a turnover (or self-employed people with an income) greater than £17,000 per annum (not excluding goods which are exempt from VAT).

variable cost cost which varies according to the level of production; cf *fixed cost, overhead.*

wholesaler person or company, between the producer and the retailer who buys in large quantities from the former and sells in smaller quantities to the latter.

working capital proportion of a company's capital which is tied up in the normal day-to-day business of the company.

OTHER REFERENCE WORKS

Company Auditing: Concepts and Practices, T A Lee (The Institute of Chartered Accountants in Scotland)
Handbook of Industrial Relations Practice, Kevin Hawkins (Kogan Page)
Handbook of Management, ed Thomas Kempner (Penguin)
How to be a Better Manager, Michael Armstrong (Kogan Page)
International Dictionary of Management, Hano Johannsen and G Terry Page (Kogan Page)
Operations Management, T E Vollmann (Addison-Wesley, USA)
Penguin Dictionary of Commerce, ed Michael Green (Penguin)

Index

Accommodation, letting 250-1
Accountants 82
Accounting terms, *see* Glossary 307
Accounting systems 89-98
    retail shops 199-200
Acid test ratio 97
Administrative costs 112
Advertising 122-4
    consultancy 291
Agricultural Development Advisory
    Service (ADAS) 192, 193
    address 299
Antique dealing 277
    shops 201-2
Appeals against tax assessment 148
Art and design work 287
Articles of Association 36
Assessments, tax 144-5, 148
Association of Certified and Corporate
    Accountants 82
Audit requirements, limited companies
    30

Balance sheet 95-6
Banks:
    advice 84-5
    loans 41-5
    overdrafts 44, 76
    start-up schemes 48
Bankruptcy:
    limited companies 29
    sole traders 27
Black economy 152
Bookshops 120-1, 202-3
British Franchise Association 221
    address 300
Budgeting 104-8
Building regulations 236
Building trades 235-7
Business expansion scheme 46-7
Business expenses 139-41
Buying a shop 196-7

Cab driving 260-1
Cafes 229

Capital 74-5
    allowances 141-2
    percentage return on 96
    raising 41-80
    share 34-6
Capital gains *and* loans 46
Capital Gains Tax (CGT) 148
Capital Goods Ledger 93
Capital Transfer Tax (CTT) 147
    and pensions 166
Cash book 90-3
Cash flow:
    budgets 42-3
    forecasting 104-8
    and sales 119-20
    VAT 76, 151
Cash management 75-8
Catering 226-34, 252-3
Certificate of Incorporation 37-8
Chambers of Commerce 87
Cinemas 233
Clearing banks, *see* Banks
Codes of conduct 163
Companies, *see* Limited companies
Companies Act 1948 36
Company directors 38
Company seal 37
Complete Traders Account Book 91
Completion dates, law 162
Computers, *see* Microcomputers
Conditions of work 135
Construction trades 235-7
Consultancy work 179-80
Contents of premises, insurance 85
Contracts:
    employment 128-30
    franchising 291-2
Cooking 252-3
Corporation Tax 146-7
Costing 109-17
    freelance work 285
Costs, manufacturing 118
Council for Small Industries in Rural
    Areas (CoSIRA) 48-9, 301
Crafts 252-9

Credit:
    accounts 100
    cards 90, 101-2
    control 99-103
    factoring 77
    references 101
Current ratio 97
Curtain making 256

Debts, collection 100-1
Decorating 237
Department of Industry 48, 49
    see also Small Firms Centres
Depreciation costs 111-2
    and taxation 141
Design work 287
Development areas 48
Direct mail promotion 124-5
Directors, limited companies 38
Direct response promotion 124-5
Disc jockeying 262-3
Disclosure, limited companies 32
Dismissal, unfair 130-2
Distribution 118-9
DIY shops 203-4
Domestic skills 252-9
Dressmaking 253-4
Driving 260-1
Driving licence insurance 86

Editorial work 287-8
Electrical work 237
Employees 128-36
    hotel 230-1
Employers' Liability Insurance 86
Employment:
    contracts of 128-30
    discrimination in 132
Entertainment work 233
    mobile 262-3
Equipment, costs 111-2
Estimates, law 162
Expenditure, evidence of 90
Expenses *and* taxation 139-42

Factoring 77
Farming 190-2
Film making 283, 288
Finance:
    costs of 111
    loans, *see* Loans
Finance Houses 49-73
Finance Houses Association 51
Financial management 75-8
Franchising 207-25
    advantages 213-4
    assistance 210-11

contracts 219-21
    disadvantages 214-6
    pyramid selling 212-3
    training 208-9
Freelance work 283-93
    charges 109
    market for 121-2
    national insurance 137-8
    taxation 152, 285
Freepost facilities 125

Goodwill 231
Government assistance 21, 48-9, 87
Guarantors, loans 45

Health 172-3
Heavy goods transport 238-9
Hire purchase 51
Hobbies: as part-time work 248-9
    in retirement 180-1
Hotels and catering 226-34

Income tax 137-46
    change in status 26-7
    freelance work 285
    see also Taxation
Indexing 264
Industrial and Commercial Finance
    Corporation (ICFC) 44
    address 301
Institute of Chartered Accountants 82
Insurance 83-7
    life and pensions 166-70
    part-time workers 244-5
    premises 85
Interpreting 267-8
Interviewing 264-5
Investment criteria 50-1
Invoices 99-103
Ironmongers 203-4
Issued share capital 34-6

Jewellery making 254-5
Joint Credit Card Companies 101, 102
Journalism, freelance 288-9

Lapidary work 255
Leases:
    law 163-4
    shops 200
Ledgers 93
Legal insurance 86
Legislation:
    business 160-4
    employment 128-36
    hotels 230
    retail trade 198-9

LEntA (London Enterprise Agency) 74,
    183
Life assurance 169
Light removals 238
Limited companies:
    accounting requirements 89
    costs of setting up 30-1
    documentation 34-8
    private 29-31
    share capital 34-5
    taxation 146-7
Liquid assets 97
    capital 104-5
Loan guarantee scheme 47
Loans:
    bank 41-5
    finance houses 49-73
    government 48-9
    private 45-7
    start-up schemes 48
London Enterprise Agency (LEntA) 74,
    183
Loose cover and curtain making 256
Losses, taxation 144

Mail order selling 277
Mailing list brokers 125
Management consultancy 284, 286
Manufacturing *and* marketing 117-19
Market gardening 192-3, 279
Marketing 117-27
Market research interviewing 264-5
Market stalls 278
Media and communications work
    264-71, 287-92
Memorandum of Association 34-6
Merchant banks 49-73
Microcomputers 153-9
    consultants 157-8
    limitations 156-7
Minute Book, limited companies 36-7

National Association of Trade Protection
    Societies 101
National Computing Centre 158
National Federation of Self-employed
    and Small Businesses 86-7
    address 302
National Insurance:
    contributions 137-8, 173
    pensions 165-6
National Research Development
    Corporation 49
    address 303
Newsagents 203
Nominal share capital 35
Northern Ireland Department of
    Commerce 21

Off-the-shelf companies 30-1
Office of Fair Trading 162
    address 303
Office skills 272-4
Overdrafts, bank 44, 97
Overheads 110

Painting and decorating 237
Partnerships:
    agreements 27-9
    in retirement 179
    sleeping partners 28
    taxation 146
Part-time work 243-51
    taxation 145-6
Party Plan selling 278
Pay As You Earn (PAYE) taxation 137,
    145, 149
Pensions 165-70
    insured 167-8
    state 165-6
    unit-linked 168-9
Personal guarantees, limited companies 29
Personal liability, partnerships 27
Petty cash books 93
Photography 289
Picture framing 256-7
Planning permission:
    home working 26, 244-5
    hotels and entertainment 227
Playgroup leading 275-6
Plumbing 237
Post offices 205
Pottery 257-8
Premises:
    costs 111
    insurance 85
Press:
    advertising 122-4
    releases 124
Pricing 113-4
Private Company 74
Private limited companies 29-31
Private loans 45-7
Produce selling 279
Professional advisers 81-8
    charges 83
    choice 82
Profit to sales ratio 97
Profits, taxable 143-4
Progress payments 76
Promotions 122-5
Public liability insurance 86
Public relations 124, 291
    consultancy 291
Pubs, tenancy 231-3
Purchases Day Book 93

Pyramid selling 212-3

Quotations:
  law 162
  preparing 114-16

Recruitment 133-5
Redundancy 132-3
Registered Offices, limited companies 33
Registrar of Companies 30, 31, 37-8
Registration of business names 31-3
Research work 291
Restaurants 227-8
Retailing:
  accounting 199-200
  law 198-9
  market for 120-1
  new ventures 197-8
  premises 194-7, 200
  and retirement 178-9
  stock 200-1
Retirement:
  finance 173-4
  self-employment in 171-83
  see also Pensions

Salaries 112-13
Sale of Goods Act, 1979 160
Sales Day Book 93
Sales:
  documentation 99-103
  large companies 119-20
  law 160-4
Scottish Development Agency 21
Secretarial work 272-3
Security, shops 200
Self-employed Account Book 91
Self-employment:
  aptitude for 22-4
  charges 109
  National Insurance 137-8
  pensions 165-70
  planning 20
  and retirement 176-8
  taxation 26-7, 152
Selling work 277-9
Service industries, marketing 120-1
Share capital:
  issued 34-6
  nominal 35
Shops, *see* Retailing
Skills, acquiring 249-50
Sleeping partners 28
Small Firms Centres 21, 49, 87
  addresses 297-9
Sole traders 26-7
  accounts 90

Solicitors 82-3
Sources of finance 52-73
Spare time work, *see* Part-time work
Staff, *see* Employees
Statements of account 100, 102
State pension scheme 165-6
Stock:
  insurance 86
  retailing 200-1
  tax relief 143
  valuation 142
Stockbrokers 74
Sub-post offices 205
Superannuation, *see* Pensions
Supply of Goods and Services Act, 1982
  162

Taxation 137-52
  appeals 148
  capital allowances 141-2
  Capital Gains Tax 148
  Capital Transfer Tax 147
  Corporation Tax 146-7
  expenses 139-42
  liabilities 98
  partnerships 146
  part-time work 243-4
  pensions 166
  personal 137-46
  profits 143-4
  Schedule D 137-45
  Schedule E 137, 145-6
  Self-employed status 152
  see also Value Added Tax
Taxi driving 260-1
Teaching 266-7
Television 283
Term Assurance 169
Tobacconists 203
Trading and Profit and Loss Accounts
  93-5
Trading associations 163
Training Opportunities Scheme (TOPS)
  182
Translating 267-8
Transport work 238-40
Travel agencies 204-5
Tutoring 266-7
Typesetting 274
Typing 272-4

Unfair Contract Terms Act, 1977 160
Unfair dismissal 130-2
Unit-linked pensions 168-9
Unlisted Securities Market 74
Upholstery work 258-9

Value Added Tax (VAT) 137, 149-51
    accounts 89, 102
    and cash flow 76, 151
    invoices 99
    quotations 113
    tribunals 86
    writing down allowances 142

Variable costs 113
Vehicle repair and servicing work 293

Welsh Development Agency 21
    address 299
Working conditions 135
Writing down allowances 141-2
Writing, freelance 268-71

Index of Advertisers

Auto-Smart, 33
Badge Man Ltd, 6
The Big Orange Ltd, 16
Copygirl Ltd, 209
CoSIRA, 39
Franchise Development Services
    Ltd, 211
Franchise World, 220
Geoffrey E. Macpherson Ltd, 223
ICC Legal Services, 31
KK Printing (UK) Ltd, 206
London Enterprise Agency, 37
Mr Slade Dry Cleaning, 219

National Federation of Self
    Employed and Small Businesses
    Ltd, 9
National Provident Institution,
    Inside front cover
National Westminster Bank plc, 5,
    265
Save and Prosper, 19
Scottish Life Assurance
    Company, 43
Sovereign Services (SE), 222
Vocational Guidance Association, 79